SIX MONTHS WITH
THREE] [ES

The
2650 miles, ... Canada.

André and Lian de Jel

Translated by: Desiree Spinhoven

FriendlyHiker.com

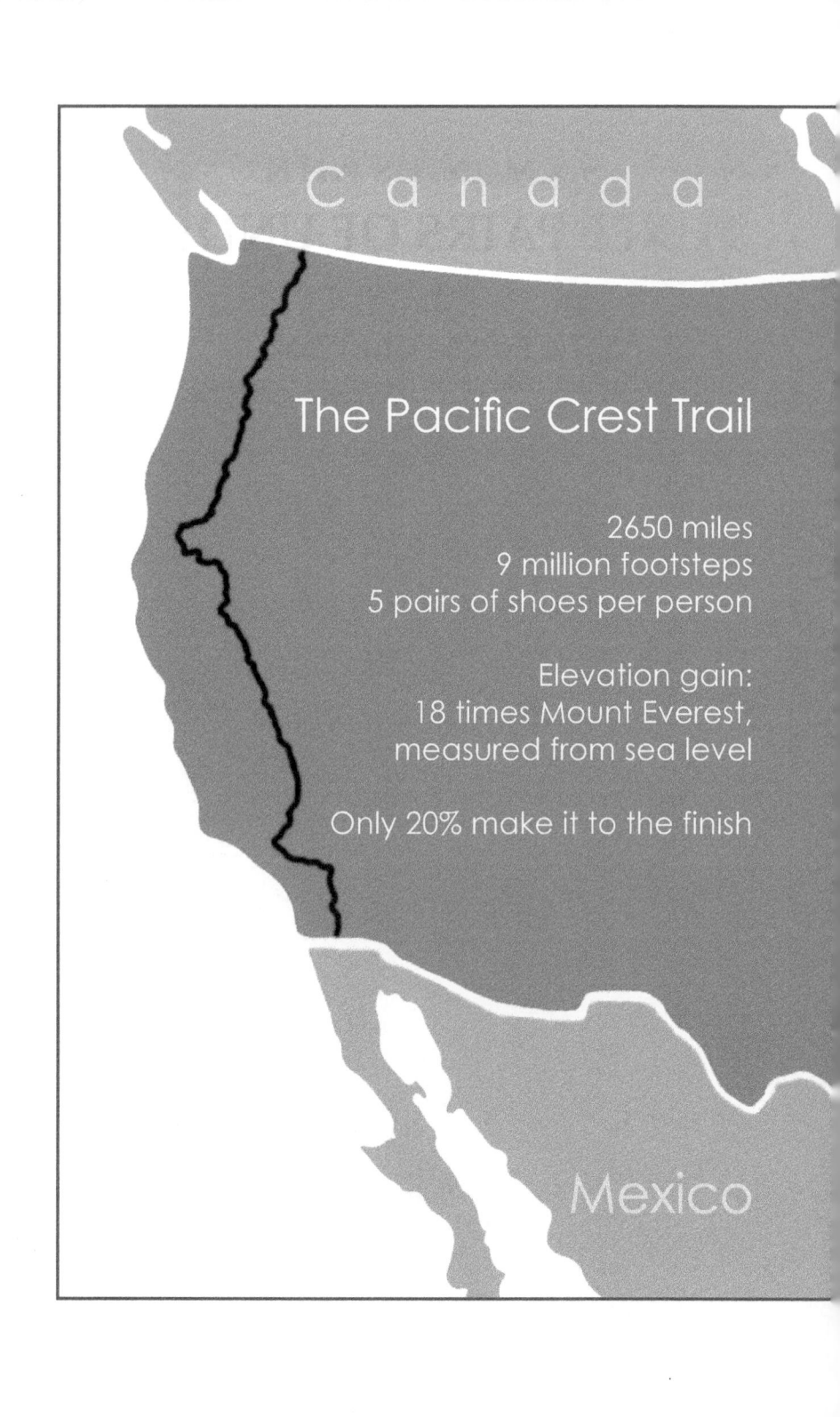

The Pacific Crest Trail

Canada

2650 miles
9 million footsteps
5 pairs of shoes per person

Elevation gain:
18 times Mount Everest,
measured from sea level

Only 20% make it to the finish

Mexico

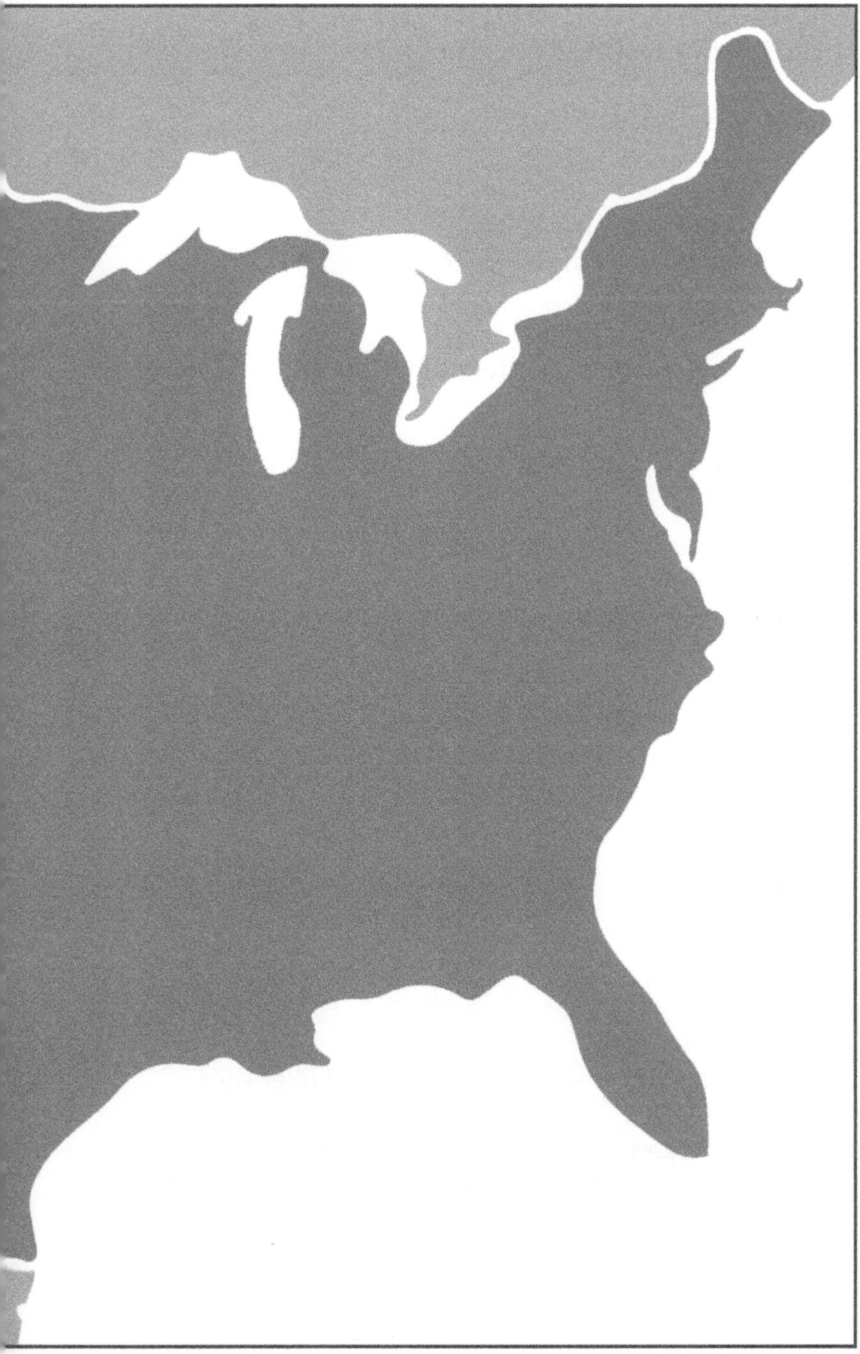

SIX MONTHS WITH THREE PAIRS OF UNDIES
The Pacific Crest Trail

ISBN: 978-94-6406-347-9

1st edition
Published: November 2020
Published by FriendlyHiker.com

Authors: André and Lian de Jel
Photographs, design & illustrations: André and Lian de Jel

Other publications:

English: Special Color Edition with photos
ISBN: 978-94-6406-350-9 Paperback
ISBN: 978-94-6406-353-0 E-book

Dutch
ISBN: 978-94-6345-560-2 Paperback
ISBN: 978-94-6345-561-9 Paperback, Special Color Edition

© 2020 Lian and André de Jel, FriendlyHiker.com

All rights reserved. No part of this publication may be reproduced, stored in a retrieval system, stored in a database and/or published in any form or by any means, electronic, mechanical, photocopying, recording or otherwise, without the prior written permission of the publisher.

About the Authors

Lian and André de Jel have been wilderness guides and mountain leaders for a large part of their lives. André started long distance hiking in 1988 with an expedition through Scandinavia where he covered 2000 miles. When Lian met André in Iceland, she immediately fell in love with him and decided to accompany him on as many adventures as she could. During the following 30 years, they had many beautiful and amazing experiences hiking, kayaking and diving all over the world. They regard their journey on the Pacific Crest Trail as one of the highlights of their lives.

Acknowledgements

We would like to thank all our family members and friends who have supported us in this endeavor from day one. Your encouraging words, especially during our journey, at our lowest moments, you have done more for us than you could ever know.

We would especially like to thank:

Tim Potter, Tim Sharp, Samantha and Donald McCarthy for their excellent help in reviewing the English version of our book. Your time and effort is highly appreciated. Your thoughts and suggestions helped us a lot in creating a high quality book.

Caithlin and Jeether Antonissen for all their help with the design of this book.

The PCTA and all the Trail Angels. Without your devotion this journey would not have been the unforgettable experience it turned out to be.

*"It is only a mountain when you're down below.
Halfway up it's just a big hill.
Before you know it, you're at the top."*

André de Jel

Nothing is impossible.

Content

Prologue 10

Part One: Desert 14
   What Are We Getting Ourselves Into... 16
   Black Out 20
   Desert Flowers 26
   Trail Magic 30
   Morning Star and CookieMonster 36
   Soaking 40
   Contrasts 45
   The Cocoon 50
   Junkies at McDonald's 53
   The Oasis 57
   On Which Snake Will Lian Step? 59
   Ghost Town 62
   Casa de Luna 66
   Mission to Mars 71
   The Vortex 76

Part Two: High Altitude 82
   Bear in the Night 84
   Mount Whitney 87
   Euphoria 91
   Hollow Inside 98
   The Ravens 95
   Rescue in the Snow 100
   Our Morning Ritual 106
   Pure Wilderness 110
   Summer in Yosemite National Park 113
   Bzzzzzzzzzzzz 118
   The Atomic Bomb 122
   Flowers, Flowers, Flowers 126

Part Three: Fire Hazard 128
   Hiker Hunger 130
   Intensive Care 133
   Have You Seen My Dealer? 137
   No Food, What Now? 139
   Thick Clouds Gather in the Sky 144
   Woohoo! Half way there! 147
   Rotting Eggs 152
   Kangaroos? Really? 157
   Unexpected Love 161
   Buns and Bears Don't Go Together 166
   Close Encounter 169
   The Pancake Challenge 173
   Mind Games 177

Part Four: Volcanoes 180
   Shooting Stars 182
   Green Islands in a Black Sea 187
   Grey Chameleons 191
   Deep Dark Thoughts 195
   Bridge of the Gods 199

Part Five: Fall 204
   Eeeeeh, Crrrrrack, Whooshhhhh, BOOM! 206
   Two Brawlers on a Mountain 209
   Rainbow Wedding 213
   Heroes 219
   Like Walking Inside a Painting 223
   Geisha Girl 226
   Extreme Weight Loss 230
   Black-Haired Monster 233
   Goodbye Sweet Angels 235
   The Home Stretch 240
   The Roller Coaster 245
   Canada 252

Epilogue 258

Prologue

In the early afternoon I see the postman driving off. "Maybe it came today?", I say to Lian. "Maybe it did. We've been waiting for so long." We've been wondering for days now when, or even if we would get an answer. Our mailbox is at the end of our driveway, by the street. I put my coat on, go outside, walk over to it and open the mailbox door. There's a letter. I pull it out and turn it over. It has a big logo on the top left corner. It's from Canada.

Impatiently, I take the letter from the envelope, open it and read. After just a few sentences my eyes light up and I feel an explosion of joy bursting inside of me. Yes, finally! The last one is in! I rush back into the house. "Uhm, Lian?", I say. She looks up from her sewing. She's repairing her backpack and immediately notices the huge grin on my face. With one hand I hide the letter behind my back and say:

"American visa for six months, check.
Pacific Crest Trail permit, check
California back country fire permit, check.
Search & Rescue PLB transmitter permit, check.

Aaaaaaaand... The special visa that allows us to enter Canada from the United States through the mountains... CHECK!! All the permits and visas have arrived!"

I pull the letter from behind my back and show it to her. The smile on her face is now at least as big as mine. She shoots up from her chair, takes the letter from my hand and starts reading. Her eyes light up. "Yesss!!! We can go!!", she says and with the letter still in her hand she hugs and kisses me.

This was the last permit we were waiting for. Preparations for the Pacific Crest Trail had required quite a bit more attention than most of the hikes we had done before. There were so may pieces to this puzzle and we needed to solve every single one. It was especially difficult, because we had no idea what the final picture would look like. What is in this puzzle? Which pieces are there? Do we know all of them? Are we maybe forgetting something without even realizing it?

With her arms still around my neck, she looks me in the eye. "Do you remember, a year and a half ago, when we decided to do this trip? We had no idea what it would all entail. My mind was bursting with questions. And now... now it's all done. It's time. We can go!" She sighs as though a weight has been lifted off her shoulders. It's not surprising. In the beginning our minds were so full of questions. It was like an unclimbable mountain.
However, as always, it's only a mountain when you're down below. Half way up it's just a big hill and before you know it you're at the top. Nothing is impossible. Keeping that in mind, we decided not to get flustered. We categorized everything expedition style. Route planning, food provisioning, the desert with its heat and lack of water, the high mountains with their snow and cold. What equipment will be useful and what can we do without? But also: what are the financial consequences? Like our mortgage, the costs we incur during the hike, taking unpaid leave from work and therefore having no income? Which possible risks are we taking and how can we eliminate or mitigate them? What if something bad happens to us? Should we revise our will? So many questions.

Now that I think of it; training was another one of those things. What is the best way to prepare your body and mind for such an ultralong hike? We have already walked over 680 training miles in the past year. The last few months we even attached weights to our ankles to simulate slopes. We thought we were doing a pretty good job.

11

But you can also train too much...

The last few weeks have been tense and confusing. I put too much strain on the muscles on the inside of my knee and now there is excess fluid in the knee cavity that's pressing on the tendons. This is the last thing we need this close to our departure. We were doing so well, and now this.
My leg is covered from top to bottom with black sports tape. I stare at it wistfully. I'm disappointed and worried. Depressed even. We've just returned from a training weekend in the German Eifel. But after about three hours of hiking, I got a stabbing pain in my knee cavity. We had to stop and go home. I couldn't walk anymore.

Lian sees the gloomy look on my face and now she looks worried, too. "How's your knee?" she asks. Pfff, Lian, I don't know. I'm not feeling anything at the moment, but I'm not putting any pressure on it now. "I have an appointment with the physical therapist tomorrow. He'll have something to say about it." She wants to talk about it some more, but I avoid the topic. After all this preparation... What if I have to quit the PCT after only one day and go home? I just don't want to think about it.

The physical therapist gives me a new hiking schedule. I have to walk at a slower pace and take a break every hour to do stretching exercises. He teaches Lian how to apply the sports tapes on my leg. Tomorrow we leave for our last major training session. Ten days of hiking on La Gomera, a dry and hot volcanic island near Tenerife, North Africa. We want to do lots of climbs and descents and get used to hiking in hot weather. In less than a month we'll be starting our PCT hike in the desert. This is also our last equipment check. Whatever we bring along now is also really going on the hike. We're excited and curious to see if it all works out.

On the kitchen scale in front of me is a small pile of black fabric. They are my new underwear and they look as thin as lace. We are literally weighing everything, in an attempt to get the total weight of our load under 17 pounds and these three pairs of underwear are 2.5 ounces lighter than the previous ones. "Do you think they'll last the whole trail?", I ask Lian. "They're sports underwear. They should, shouldn't they?", she answers. She sounds uncertain. I'm not entirely confident either. At least these undies have enough ventilation to prevent my butt from sweating.

I guess we'll see...

Part One
Desert

Kennedy Meadows
Tehachapi
Mojave Desert
Casa de Luna
Cajon pass
Los Angeles
Mt. San Jacinto
Palm Springs
Idyllwild
Stagecoach Inn
San Diego
USA
Campo
Mexico

What Are We Getting Ourselves Into...

Today is D-Day. It's April 15th and here we are in Southern California, pumped up and ready to go. Ready to begin our 2650-mile adventure straight through the United States of America. A six-month hike through wilderness and secluded nature reserves. What a challenge. Quite overwhelming actually. Especially since statistics show that only twenty percent of all the hikers that start the trail, make it all the way to the end.

Still feeling a little bit nervous, we stare at the monument. Five white poles with the Pacific Crest National Scenic Trail logo written on them. Yes, this is real. We're here. It's about to begin. With a slight sense of disbelief, we look at the barbed-wired metal wall that separates Mexico from the United States. In front of us only dry, barren, grey-brown wasteland littered with rough bushes and cacti. What a barren place! It's so dry, it's making Lian a bit nervous. Where will we ever find water? Will the two gallons of water in our backpack be enough to get us to the next well or livestock trough? What kinds of adventures will we have in the 41 national parks and wilderness areas? We have no idea. Suddenly everything's going so fast. Another hiker agrees to take a photo of us at the monument. Then we kiss, touch the border wall, and take the first steps. This is it! We have started our journey! We're actually going to do this!!

It feels strange to begin, a bit unreal. It's really not so surprising if we look back at the past few days. After the intense training on La Gomera, which went well by the way, we specifically wanted to take it easy the last week before we left. We had thought we might be able to rest, leave all the hard work behind us and just dot a few i's and cross the t's before embarking on our trip. All we wanted to do was focus on the last little things on our to-do list and relax. After all, everything had been prepared in detail, expedition style, for over a year. However, things didn't work out as we had planned, and the stress only got worse... Like the day before we left...

"Oh no! This can't be happening right now!" Lian screams. If looks could kill … She points at her backpack: there is yet another tear in the titanium welded seam. Oh no, not this again! "Now what? We leave tomorrow and I am not carrying that heavy back-up backpack! Absolutely not!" We are using superlight, somewhat experimental backpacks. They still have a few flaws here and there. This particular flaw had already been an issue during one of our training weeks. "It's late." I say. I am upset and frustrated. "I don't know if I can reach the welder who helped us fix this the last time." I anxiously pick up the phone and dial the number. It rings and rings. It feels like hours but finally he answers the phone! I explain the situation and even though his shop is closed, he agrees to help us. I get in the car, drive over to him and that same night, at 7 p.m., he repairs Lian's backpack and reinforces mine just in case. Fantastic! Gerrit, thank you so much!!!

The next morning our friends Melissa and Nils take us to the airport and after a fourteen-hour flight we arrive in San Diego. For the first two days we stay with Scout and Frodo, extremely kind PCT volunteers called Trail Angels. These are not their real names, by the way. On these kinds of long-distance trails, the other hikers give you a nickname.

Our stop in San Diego is mostly spent on grocery shopping and making resupply packages which mostly contain food, but also maps and sometimes equipment like new shoes. We're sending them to different locations in the wilderness, where we can't buy any of those things. Locations like Trail

Angels that live close to the trail or gas stations and post offices of teeny-tiny towns. "Close to the trail" is a relative concept. At times we have to take a detour from the trail for a day to retrieve our supplies, and then walk the same route back to where we left off.

At Scout and Frodo's, we are approached by a young, fit-looking woman. "Hi, my name's Happy Feet. Have you heard?! Yesterday someone had to turn back, because she'd been bitten by a rattlesnake!" This scares me. Nervously, I scratch my ear. Uhm... did we bring some kind of antidote? Not really. We ask around and the American hikers reassure us. They never bring anything for it. "If they bite you, tough luck. Usually people don't die right away, but a few species will kill you instantly. There isn't a hospital anywhere near the trail anyway, and by the time the helicopter arrives, it'll probably be too late." Alright ... Is this supposed to be comforting? We are wilderness guides, specialized in the Northern regions. Bears and such. We understand them. We have a lot of experience with them. But this is our first time hiking in the desert with snakes, poisonous spiders, and scorpions. Despite our thirty-year wilderness experience we kind of feel like beginners right now.

And off we go. Scout and Frodo were nice enough to take us to the starting point of the trail. We've taken the picture and are walking the first steps. We've got two gallons of water and food for six days in our backpacks. The base weight of our packs with all our gear is only fifteen pounds, but with all this extra food and water we are carrying almost forty. But this is what we've trained for. So, for the first day we happily strut through the landscape that is best described as a moon landscape interspersed with green grass, yellow flowers and pine trees that have cacti growing up against them. Extraordinary. It's spring and... everything is in bloom!

Very soon the uncertainty of the start is replaced by amazement with everything we see, smell, and hear. The cacti are in bloom, and everywhere we look there are butterflies enjoying the nectar. Lizards are scattering away in front of our feet. We see a tall agave with a beautiful flower bud, and the smell of fresh pines opening up in the sun fills the air. But also the clear, open night skies, where we can always see the milky way, astonish us. And the beautifully colored birds we have never seen before. Fortunately, there is an app for that, so we regularly check our nature and star guides on our phones. We are in no hurry here. We are deliberately only walking fifteen miles a day to find our rhythm and to get used to the heat. We have all the time in the world to look around and enjoy all the beauty that crosses our path. Who would have thought the desert would look so incredibly beautiful in spring?

Let's do this!

Black Out

Today I've got the biggest smile on my face. This is such a wonderful day! I am so happy. We've walked through open terrain with amazing views all day. Lots of bushes and lush vegetation. There are so many beautiful things to see! At some point we run into about twenty hikers sitting in some shrubs. We come closer and I stop at the first group. "Hello there, nice gathering." They look up. "Hey, so nice to see you. Come and join us." I don't know them, but it doesn't matter. We should take a break around now anyway. We take off our backpacks and sit down with them.
"Cookie?" The man next to me offers me a packet of cookies that he just got from someone else. "Oh yes, I love cookies!" I take one and pass the packet on to the next person. "Why are you all sitting here?" A young man with a head full of curls looks at me and answers: "Oh, the heat. It's way too hot to hike. We're waiting it out in the shade." It's really nice and friendly here. We listen to their conversations. They are very motivated, and we notice that they all have their own personal story and reason to be here.

"I've been working in the IT business for a while now. Ten-hour workdays, hardly any free time and the enormous pressure to perform and succeed made me think. I'm not sure what I want, but I hope to find out who I am at the end of this six-month trip", says the young man across from me. A few others nod in agreement. It turns out a lot of them have seen the movie 'Wild' and were inspired by it. The movie is about a young woman who, after a life full of domestic violence and drugs, decides to walk part of the PCT. She has no experience, buys equipment that's much too heavy and reaches the end of her rope at times, which actually gives her life a new incentive. Many of the people we meet here see it like this: "If it worked for her, why wouldn't it work for me?" Yes, well, why wouldn't it? It's a great source of inspiration, but some people are a bit too naïve. We hear things like: "I'll get fit on the trail" or "How hard can it be, it's just walking." Hmmm… going on an ultra-long-distance hike like this one, almost completely unprepared; I'm not so sure about that. I'm sure it will bring them a wonderful adventure, but they are bound to run into places and situations they wish they hadn't. In the movie 'Wild' those are the moments that give the main character strength. Let's hope it will do the same for them.

After an hour or so we get up. "This was really nice, but we should get going. Maybe we'll see you tonight or in the next couple of days?" André says. He picks up his backpack and swings it on his back. "Are you sure?" a young woman asks. My guess is she's no older than 22. "Yes, why? It's not that big a climb, is it?" André answers, as he fastens his hip belt. "Well, we're all staying here until that wall has cooled off. I'm from here. That's the south wall and it's been baking in the sun all day. It's not a good place to be right now. André stops what he's doing and looks at her. "It can't be that bad, can it? It's just a few hours until we reach the lake. It's not far." She shrugs. "I still think it's better if you wait for a little while." The others nod in agreement. In the meantime, I'd already gotten up as well. We look at each other and without saying anything we decide to take her advice and sit back down again.

It's around five when the first hikers start to leave the shade. We're leaving too. The path zigzags up the hill and is quite easy to walk. "Jeez… it is quite hot here," I say while turning my head towards André. He's behind me, just out of my view. There's no wind and the bare stone wall is scorching hot. The invisible infrared radiation coming from the rocks is very intense. The hikers were right: this is not a good place to be during the day. I use my umbrella to shade my head and body from the heat. André only has his hat with neck protection. We don't talk much and keep on going until suddenly something tugs on my backpack. I turn around and what I see scares me to death. It's André! He's grabbing onto my backpack with his right hand and he's white as a sheet. He stumbles forward. "I don't feel very well," he says weakly. He staggers and suddenly falls forward onto the ground. Boom! With a big thump he falls flat on his face. My goodness, what's just happened, what's going on! He's lying still on the ground. He's not moving! My heart is beating like crazy as I walk towards him... "What's wrong?! What's wrong?!" I cry anxiously. He was walking behind me; I didn't see it coming. He'll be all right, won't he?

I grab his arm. "Huh?" He looks up at me with dull eyes and he's somewhat disoriented. "Why am I on the ground?" His face is grey and it's not just the dust. It's pale, like all the blood has drained from his face. It's a strange sight in this heat. Just a few minutes ago he looked completely different. "I feel sick. Like I'm going to throw up," he says. I help him up slowly. "Wooooow! I'm dizzy. I'm blacking out." That's all he can say, and he faints again. I look around anxiously. My head is spinning. There isn't any shade anywhere. No plants or overhang, nothing at all. What the hell am I going to do? I see a big rock to our left. "André, can you hear me?" Nothing. I slap his cheek softly. He wakes up and lifts his head. "Come, I'll sit you down on that rock, so you can rest and drink some water." I pull him up and lead him there. He sits down. His elbows resting on his legs and his hands holding his head. He needs shade. Uhm, oh yes, I get his umbrella, open it, and let him hold it. His head hangs down. With my index finger I gently lift his chin up, so he can stare at the horizon. His eyes glaze over. I don't understand any of this. I'm completely fine, but he's having trouble focusing. We're not sweating any differently than earlier today. "Sweating. Yes, water!" I say half out loud. I get my water bottle and let him drink. He gulps it up quickly. "Blaaargh!" He bends over and all the water comes back out. "Take it easy. Small sips!"

Bit by bit I start to remember these symptoms: this looks like heatstroke. Strange. He's wearing airy clothing, and a hat with neck protection, and sunscreen. While he sips the water, I watch him anxiously. His body must be overheated, maybe even feverish. I can recall the articles I've read about this clearly in my mind. I have to cool him down immediately. But how? There is no shade here, no wind and the ground and rocks are very hot. I look at my water supply. I have enough to cool him down a little bit, but I can't make him a shower. I take his hat, soak it in water and put it back on. "Better?" The drops of water stream over his neck flap down his back underneath his shirt. It's lukewarm water, but he looks a bit better for it. "Yes, I feel a bit better." He says softly.
I look at my water again. "Give me your umbrella and take off your shirt. I'll soak that with water, too." Slowly, he does what I tell him. I don't have much water and we still have a few hours to go. I have to consider my personal safety. I mustn't use all the water. I'll just wet the core then. He gives me his shirt and I wet the heart and lungs area and the back. He puts it back on and holds the umbrella over his head.

I keep talking to him to make sure he stays awake and after thirty minutes, two hikers approach us, a couple. They see him sitting there, and the worried look on my face must have alarmed them. "Hey, are you alright? Can we do anything to help?" I look at them, back to André and back to them. "Yes, he's fainted in the heat; we have to get out of this oven." Their expressions change. They look concerned now. "That doesn't look so good," says the woman. It annoys me. "Yes, well that doesn't really help now, does it?" My strong reaction startles her. "Oh, I'm sorry, I didn't mean it like that." I look at her and sigh. "No, I'm sorry. I'm just tense." She nods. The man who's with her takes over. "What do you want to do? Go back or keep going? Do you have enough water?" No, we can't afford to lose any more water. It's getting late and we've already used most of it.

We discuss whether it would be wiser to walk back to the bushes or continue on the trail. Our planned camp by the lake isn't far now and back down there is shade, but no water. "We should go on. Is it OK with you if we walk with you? Just in case?" They nod. "Of course it is." André looks up. "Yes, let's keep going," he says. He's looking a bit better now. "How are you now?" He tries to get up. He succeeds. "Fuzzy, whatever, let's just go." Slowly we walk on and together we look out for André. "I think you should eat something. Get some energy." I give him a granola bar. That wasn't a good idea. It comes right back out. Eating and drinking is still difficult. His stomach can't handle it. "We're almost at the top. We'll leave this oven behind us forever," I say to cheer him up. And sure enough; after an hour we reach camp where we meet a couple of Trail Angels. They see us coming and have André sit on a chair under the canopy of their RV. They give him water and a banana. They go down all right. We talk for a bit and then I put up the tent nearby. When I finish, I go back, thank them for their help and take André to the small lake close to the camp. We get in the water to cool down. He looks a lot better now, but he's exhausted. We walk back to the tent. He crawls in, pulls the sleeping bag over his body, and falls asleep right away.

I am wide awake and still thinking about the story the Trail Angels just told us. It's stuck in my mind. She said: "Last year a man died on that same path. He sat down to rest for a bit, but encouraged his young son to go on. "Go on, I'll be right behind you," he said. His son was reluctant, but slowly kept going up the hill. He stopped every now and then to look back. However, when his father didn't catch up with him after an hour, he went back. He found his father on the same rock where he had left him. He had died."

Chills go down my spine just thinking about it. This was a close call. Day one and he almost died... I can't get the thought out of my mind. In my sleeping bag I listen to André. I hear a regular, comforting breathing. Thank God. I relax and slowly I start to feel sleepy too. I try to fight it so I can keep listening to André breathing, but I can't. Relax Lian, he's OK, he's just sleeping. With that last thought I fall into a deep, restless sleep. This first day has really put us on edge. This was nothing like training on the warm island La Gomera.

We have to be careful.

Desert Flowers

"Chrétien, one of my best friends, texts me: "Hey, André. Does it look like the game Red Dead Redemption out there?" "Hi Chrétien. Yes, it's exactly like the game. All I need now is my horse!" I reply. I neglect to tell him how much more it really is. Even though the western game does a very good job of creating this world; it doesn't allow you to smell it or feel it. Like the humming bumblebee flying by. It lands on a plant with lots of tiny, light-blue flowers. Next to it are many more bumblebees and honeybees. We take our time to look at them and smell the sweet perfume coming from the flowers. "Magnificent, isn't it?" Lian says. I nod with a smile. She is as happy as a child in a playground. Some mornings, we take all the time we need and walk very slowly so we can thoroughly enjoy everything around us.

A bit further along we discover plants with large amounts of big, white flowers. They smell amazing. "I can't figure out which plant this is," Lian says, looking through one of the nature guides on her smartphone. Like the other ones, this plant is also covered in insects. They look like crane flies. Only smaller, with a black grid-like effect on their transparent wings. "Let me see." I take the phone from her and start scrolling. "Did you find anything?", she asks after a while. I look at her and shrug my shoulders. "I'm trying, but I can't find the plant either." Too bad, but names are just labels, it's still a beautiful thing to see. I put the phone away, stand next to her and we move in a little closer. Together we marvel at the insects as they crawl across the flowers with their long legs, we watch as they bend their antennae backwards and venture headfirst into the flower. A hiker approaches in high speed, leaving behind a cloud of dust as he walks. "Hello." He greets us without looking up, his eyes focused on the screen in his hand. His finger swipes across it. "I don't understand why so many hikers wear earphones on their hike," I say to Lian. She nods. "I don't understand it either. Who listens to music or a book when there is so much beauty to see? How can you fully enjoy the peace and quiet and the beauty of the landscape?" I feel exactly the same. We've seen many people do this. I do understand why they do it. Music is emotion and it can elevate and strengthen your mood considerably. But I prefer taking in my surroundings without distractions. Lian is the same. For me it isn't just about walking from point A to point B, it's about exploring and enjoying nature as well. I wouldn't be able to do that if I was distracted all the time. I wouldn't be open to it. For me, walking while listening to music is like driving a car through a landscape. I'm there, but I'm not really there.

"It is so beautiful here. This is so different than what we're used to!" says Lian, as she takes in the surroundings. It's such a treat to see her so happy. We're in a small chasm in the shade. The wall is moist and lots of things grow on it. A small kind of leather-leaf fern catches her eye. It's small, dark green with yellow dots under the leaves. "I feel like one of the great explorers Stanley or Livingstone in Africa. In a completely alien world, discovering new treasures one after the other." I know exactly what she means and answer, "Yes, I feel the same way. I don't get why so many other hikers think the desert is the least interesting part of this trail and feel like they need to entertain themselves. This first part is amazing!" Lian lets go of the fern leaf and stands up straight. She points to the wall and then to the open desert. "Yes, look at the wonderful, interesting things we have seen in the short time we've been here."

For some reason I've always pictured the Sahara when we were preparing for this desert section at home. But this is nothing like what I imagined; we thought it would be more like a barren sea of sand with high dunes. It doesn't look at all like the wasteland of an average western movie.

We do see the rattlesnakes, lizards, hovering vultures and such, like you do in the movies. I also thought it would be really tough and boring. Something to get through in the first month. Nothing could have prepared me for the enormous sea of flowers and the wonderful plants that grow here. It is a wonderful surprise and makes the hike so much more fun. This desert is very special.

Nevertheless, the hot sun shines right through us. We are literally burning away. I grab the sunscreen from the pouch in my hip belt and put it on as I walk.
"Jeez, Lian. We can't seem to put enough sunscreen on in this sun. It's just not working. I think we might be doing this the wrong way." Her feet sink into the loose sand. She stops and looks puzzled about what I just said. "What do you mean?"
"Well, most hikers get up around eight and start hiking at nine. That's good fun and all, getting up together and chatting away, but I'm not really comfortable hiking at the hottest time of day."
She nods. "Yes, I've been thinking about that, too. By the way, we've also started carrying more water. We're now using 2.5 gallons of water a day each. I think it's because we lose so much moisture during the day in this heat." I contemplate this for a minute. "Hmmm… It's like a vicious cycle. The hotter it is, the more we sweat, the more we drink, the more we have to carry. That puts extra weight on us, which means we get tired more quickly, which makes us sweat more and drink more. Rather foolish I guess." She starts walking again. "What are you thinking?" I put my foot down and almost step on a lizard that shoots across the trail. "Well, why don't we do what the Mexicans and the Spanish do? Start early, have siesta at the hottest time of day and then get back to it. Those people know how to handle the heat." She whirls around. "That's a great idea! I say we start in the middle of the night. I've had it with this heat." She's totally on board.

Even though I overheated on the first day, the next days have proven that she is much more vulnerable to the high temperatures. "OK. How about getting up at four-thirty and setting off at five-thirty from now on?" She nods. "Yes! Let's do that. Maybe even earlier." I laugh. "I think four-thirty's early enough."

It turns out to be an excellent decision. Now, in the early morning we hike for about 10 miles without breaking much of a sweat, which means we can carry about two pounds of water less in our backpacks. It's now eleven a.m. We stop, because it's siesta time. I point to an overhanging rock with some bushes. We walk over there. There isn't much space, but it's quite cool and there's enough shade. Lian gets out the cooking gear and after a short while we're having dinner in the middle of the day, just like the Mexicans.

After dinner we sleep for an hour or two and at about five p.m. we start walking again. "It's really making a difference isn't it? It's like I'm full of energy again." Lian nods. "Yes, I agree. This is a much nicer way to hike."

In the evening we hike another 6 miles and they go by so fast; we hardly notice them. The next days we repeat this new schedule and it works like a charm. It even gives us the courage to walk an extra 3 miles a day. We're getting ahead of schedule. It's going so well!

Trail Magic

"André... how is your leg feeling?" I need some reassurance. We've been on the trail for ten days and we've already walked almost 180 miles. In all that time he hasn't said anything about it. "Yeah, it's actually OK. It's not bothering me at all anymore." He looks at his leg. Three long black tapes run up his leg in different directions. "How long are you going to leave on those tapes?" He picks at it. "Yeah, I don't know. Long, I guess. I'm afraid it'll start hurting again if I take them off. I think I'll just leave them where they are." He sounds a bit uncertain. I replaced the tapes two days ago and I'm not sure I put them on correctly. It was the first time I did that by myself. The physical therapist showed me how to do it, but still.
He's still looking at his leg. "In the beginning the muscles in my leg felt a bit tight, but that's all gone now. The hiking schedule is working, I think." Thank goodness. All the insecurities and stress from the beginning of the hike are finally fading away. The only question left is whether André's leg is going to hold out. I like this hiking schedule as well. Every hour we take a fifteen-minute break. It gives the body a chance to cool down, and André does the exercises the therapist gave him. I am happy. Slowly all the burdens are falling off my shoulders and I'm walking along the trail carefree and relieved.

"Hey, what's that thing doing there?", I say. We're in the middle of nowhere and I'm surprised to be looking at a big blue box with a white lid on it. It's lying a bit further down the trail. It's like Harry Potter conjured it out of nowhere. "Do you know what that is? Why is it here?" I ask André as I look around to see where it might have come from. There's not a soul to be seen and there are no other trails or roads for miles. "I think there's something written on the lid", he says. Curiously, we come closer.

It turns out to be a cooler. One of those boxes you use on a camping trip. Someone's taken a sharpie and written 'TRAIL MAGIC' on the lid. "What does that mean?" I look at André. "I have no idea. Well, we are on the trail... maybe something to do with magic, tricks?" He starts laughing, loudly. "Maybe someone's trying to prank us and a clown on a spring will pop out when we open the box, hahaha. A Jack-in-the-Box!" I chuckle, but I'm really quite curious to see what's in it. André grabs the lid, opens the cooler and... "Whattt!! Good food and cold drinks!", he shouts. We stare at the box in disbelief. "Who could have left that here? And why?!" I look inside the box and find a laminated note. I take it and read it out loud: "Dear PCT hikers. We thought you could use something nice and cool right about now. Please feel free to take something from the cooler and enjoy it! Kind regards, Trail Angels Mary 'Bongo Bongo' and Marc 'Footloose' Richardson." With a big smile we look at each other. We can definitely use something nice and cool! The cooler is stuffed with goodies: cookies, crisps, soda, fruit... "This is so great! How much do you think we're allowed to take?" André grabs a coke. "I don't know, but I don't think we should take more than one thing. That way the people coming up behind us will have a nice surprise waiting for them, too. I'd hate to think they'd open the lid and find it empty." I take a tangerine and start peeling it. We close the box and take a moment to sit down. It's funny. Here I am, in the middle of absolutely nowhere, eating a tangerine, which I got from people I don't even know. I did not expect this at all. I look at André. He holds his can up as if he's making a toast and says: "Thank you Trail Angels!!" I love this moment. I am truly enjoying this!

'Trail Magic', that's just another thing we knew nothing about. We had already encountered the Trail Angels phenomenon; help, a place to stay, taking you to the trail, etc. But this is something completely new to us. It's like the locals are cheering you on all the way. Amazing! In the next couple of days, we have many more moments like

31

this. And it is in fact magic, because it just seems to appear out of nowhere; like a car that pulls over and the driver enthusiastically gives you a chocolate bar. Or a weekend hiker telling you that it's his dream to one day walk the PCT, who spontaneously starts sharing his apples with you. Sometimes people park their car at a popular trial crossing. They'll have large cans of water or other stuff to share with us. It's so nice. This free-spirited help doesn't only happen in small gestures.

Sometimes they go big.

"Hey, we can dump our trash there." André points at a large dark blue industrial container. I suppose the local graffiti artist has been at work here, because the lid has been painted colorfully, with two big eyes, like a huge owl that is looking right at you. Next to the container is an old worn out sofa. Beige velvet. It makes me think of old people. Why does it make me think of that? I chuckle. Maybe because we both turned fifty this year? André wanted to hike the PCT last year, but I like the idea of celebrating our 100-year combined birthdays on this trail. Also, I wanted to avoid having to celebrate it at home… In the Netherlands, when you turn 50, there is this custom where family and friends make life-size dolls that look like really old people. They put signs next to it with phrases like: Now you're finally among the 'wise' people. As if becoming fifty makes you an old person all of a sudden. We don't see each other as old farts and we would much rather be on a trail somewhere, or do something else that's awesome.

I walk over to the container and try to lift the lid. "Can you help me, please?" We hold on to the lid and push it open. I almost lean in, to throw in our garbage bag, but then my eyes nearly fall out of their sockets. "What is this?!" André laughs. "What an amazing trip this is!" I couldn't agree more! The container is filled to the rim with food:

fruit, candy, soda, bananas, cheese crackers… all kinds of things. A huge stockpile. There are even bags of macaroni, rice, cans of fuel and small gas tanks in there. "Hahaha, it's almost like a prepper stock." I look at him, puzzled. "Huh?" He grins and takes a banana. "You know, those Americans who think the apocalypse is coming and have a nuclear bunker full of canned food and survival equipment next to their house. They're called Preppers." Never heard of it. Strange people. I grab a banana too, close the lid carefully and then we sit down on the dusty old sofa together. Fresh fruit is amazing to have on the trail. We only eat dried fruit because it weighs less. It's at moments like these that you really notice the difference. Wonderful, this Trail Magic!

It reminds us of the biggest walking event of the Netherlands, the 'International Four Days Marches of Nijmegen', where complete strangers hand out water to the hikers, and flowers at the finish. But at that event, we know we can expect it. Here, we have no idea. Every time it happens is a complete surprise!

"What time is it?" I check my sports watch. "Six o'clock." I know what he's thinking. We're losing light and we still have a tent to pitch. We're walking on a boring tarmac road, a detour around a burnt area, and I'm keen to leave it. "According to the map, the US Forest Service Public Lands area should be close. A bit more than half a mile I think." I hear André say. Indeed, not too long after that, we pass a huge house and we find a nice camping spot next to it. There's not much there, just a piece of land where you can pitch your tent. And the house, but that's private property. We put down our backpacks and I start unpacking the tent.

"Get away from me, f**cking dogs," André shouts. I turn around quickly. Two big, scary, barking dogs come running towards us! "Lian, grab something. A stick, your backpack, anything and get ready to defend yourself. Those are Rottweilers!" What is he saying? I don't really

33

like dogs and I really don't like the looks of these ones. He gets out our tiny Swiss army knife and snaps out the blade. "That's not going to do anything. Look at those jaws and teeth! Isn't there anything else you can use?!" I scream at him. "Tell me something I don't know." He looks around and picks up a rock. With his back arched, he stares down these dogs heroically. His left arm bent in front of him like a shield, the rock firmly in his hand above his head. "Stay behind me! Never step into their line of attack. Whatever you do, stay behind me!" This is not a request, it's an order. I'm scared now. "Well, what are you going to do about that?! I say as I get behind him. "We'll see about that when it happens!" He is deadly serious. The dogs are barking like crazy and they're getting closer and closer. André is completely tense and I hear him take deep breaths. In and out. His eyes squinted, fixated on the threat. He's bracing himself for an attack. Still barking like crazy they come racing towards us. Then, six feet away from us they come to a sudden halt and run around us in circles, still barking. Oh my God how is this going to end?! I can't speak. This is terrifying! Just when I think something horrible is going to happen, I hear a distant whistle. Tweeeeet! It sounds like a police whistle. The dogs stop in their tracks and turn their heads towards the house. Two men approach us on foot. I watch them and notice the left man is hiding something behind his back. I don't like this at all.

"Well, I hope they didn't scare you too much?" says the man with the rugged brown beard, he looks at André. The other man is bald and still hiding something behind his back. André doesn't look up. He's still firmly holding on to the rock with his right hand, and he's not letting the dogs out of his sight for a second. "I believe we're on US public land and we're allowed to camp here. If I'm mistaken and we're on your land, please accept our apology and we'll be on our way," André says with a low strong voice, still staring at the dogs. The bald man laughs. He moves his hands from behind his back. Two boxes and a familiar sent emerge. "No, man. Relax. Everything's fine. No problemo."

André looks up with fierce, squinted eyes and sees the men's smiling faces. One of them makes a hand gesture and the dogs sit down. André looks down again and sees them looking at their owners calm and relaxed. Their tongues hanging from their mouths. André's starting to relax now too. I don't feel completely safe and hang on to my backpack just to be sure. They notice our apprehension and the bearded man starts talking. "I'm so sorry if we scared you. But... we've brought you some pizza, and some Coca Cola, Fanta, a dr. Pepper and a Sprite!" We start laughing, still a little bit unsure about what's happening. André drops the rock and I put down my backpack. "That's very kind of you," André says with a dim voice. The bald man nods enthusiastically and says: "Yeah, we saw you coming by and thought you must be PCT hikers. We had more than enough pizza, so we thought we'd surprise you!"

Well, they succeeded in surprising us! The tension subsided quickly, and we ended up having a wonderful evening! This was also Trail Magic and it was absolutely perfect and super nice of them to do. It's so nice to see that the United States has a completely different side than the violent and self-absorbed side we see on tv. Trail Magic. This was a beautiful evening, even though it started out a bit scary.

Morning Star and CookieMonster

I'm admiring the pretty purple flowers of a cactus. It's a typical kind of cactus which has flat discs growing on top of each other. They grow together in small groups here in the dry, brown landscape. I don't know what they're called, and I don't feel like looking it up. I'm enjoying the moment. Next to the 'flat disc' cacti are the 'ball-shaped' cacti with lots of big fat yellow spines. Some grow very tall and have arms. "They look like big fat green forks. Tridents, like Poseidon's," I say to Lian. "Those are two different types of cacti. The small, ball-shaped one is called a Barrel cactus. The tall forky one is a Saguaro." I'm astonished. How does she know all this? "Uhm Lian, Melissa always calls me the walking encyclopedia. Do you want to take on that role now?" She laughs. "Oh no, I just happen to remember it from one of our trips a few years back, the one in Nevada and Utah." She looks at the cacti again and adds, "I don't think these cacti should even be growing here." She might be right. We are currently in front of the Stagecoach Inn. It's a shop with a few small cabins you can rent. The Inn looks like the backdrop of a western movie. It even has two actual periodic stagecoaches next to it. It feels like any minute, Clint Eastwood and John Wayne can come walking through the batwing doors of the saloon, wearing their cowboy hats. These cacti complete the setting beautifully.

We go in, order something to drink and sit with a group of hikers we know. They all started on the same day as we did, and we run into them every day. The conversation quickly moves to 'Trail Names'; a very typical American phenomenon. In Europe we have no such thing, but it is handy. It's hard to remember everyone's names, and so everyone gets a nickname at some point on the trail. You can't choose your own, other hikers have to give you the name. Usually it's something funny or stupid you did, or something you carry or wear.

"How about Snow White?" The young woman next to me looks back at me in terror. "I am not a princess! I work in the woods. Princesses are not tough at all." Lian responds immediately, "Oh no, no, not at all. No, we've noticed that, when you arrive, you're always in the lead, with a following of dusty bearded men on your tail." She thinks about it. "If you look at it like that, it's kind of cute. Yes, I do lead them most of the time. Hahaha. Yes, it's funny. I accept the name." I smile. It's nice to make someone happy.

I start thinking again. Danny hasn't got a name yet. What moves through the desert quickly? Suddenly I think of the Looney Tunes cartoon 'Wile E. Coyote and the Road Runner'. "Hey guys, I have an idea for a Trail Name for Danny. He hikes so fast, whenever he walks by, a big cloud of dust follows. How do you like Road Runner?" Lian looks puzzled and shakes her head. "Roadrunner? No, that's not him. How about Turbo?" Hmmm... Turbo. I don't know. I look around and think of a different cartoon and suddenly blurt out, "How about Speedy Gonzales?!" Everyone nods and the guy next to me responds instantly. "Yeah, that's cool! Hey Danny! Dan! Come here! We've got a name for you!" Danny's in the back of the store. He looks up and walks towards us. "What's up?" He bends over the table with his long, slender body. "You've just become Speedy Gonzales!" I say cheerfully. He stands up straight and looks up. "Speedy Gonzales, Speedy..." he mutters softly. "A superfast mouse. Yes, I can live with that. But just Speedy then." We laugh. "Cool. Now the rest of us," says the guy next to me.

In the meantime, it's two o'clock and it's scorching hot. "Timberrr!!" I jump from the poolside and splat! Water splashes in every direction. The Stagecoach Inn has a small pool for guests and we're allowed to use it to cool off. "The water is so nice!" I shout to Lian. She's still not sure about going in. In fact, the water is freezing. It's strange that all the little lakes we come across are lukewarm and this little pool is so cold.

37

You would think the sun would warm it up quickly. "Are you coming in?" It's easy for me to say. I'm a bit chubbier and I don't get cold easily. "I'm not sure." Doubtfully she dips her toe into the water. "Oooooo! It really is freezing." She looks me in the eyes and backs up a few steps, folding her arms around her chest in an attempt to stay warm. "No way!" The others all stand around as well. Speedy walks up to the ladder and gets in very slowly. When the water reaches his waist he stops, with his arms still in the air. "Hahaha, you look like a gibbon monkey now," I blurt out. He puts his arms down into the water, his eyes become large and he looks right at me. He sighs, lets go of the ladder and falls into the water. "Oh, wow, that's cold." He swims a few strokes and turns around towards the poolside. "It's wonderful, once you get used to the temperature." Slowly the others start joining us in the pool. Together we pass the hottest time of day like this; swimming and eating ice-cream and hamburgers.

The next day we arrive at a small bush. It's blazing hot and almost time for siesta. In front of us is a lonely sign that says "Water". Underneath it, there is an arrow that points to a small path. The sign is a little crooked, like it's thirsty too. This is an ideal place for siesta. We can cook in the shade and fill up on water. About two hours later the others join us. They started a bit later this morning. "You know, I've been thinking," Snow White says. I give her a cracker and wait for her to continue. "I think I'll name you Morning Star. And you should be CookieMonster." What? Morning Star? Where did she get that? "Please explain how you came up with those?" She sees my surprise and answers, "Well, you know, you always set off so excruciatingly early. Like this morning. Our alarm went off at five, we looked out and it was still pitch dark, and your tent was already gone. Suddenly we saw two little lights moving on the mountain, like morning stars. That's when I knew, it has to be Morning Star." I take a minute to think about it, but I don't really like it.

"Morning Star... it sounds a bit feminine. Don't you have anything a bit more manly? Like Eagle Eye? Or Early Wolf? One of those tough Native American names?" She shakes her head. "No, it's alright. If it's tough you want; Morning Star is also a very dangerous medieval weapon." I have no idea what it is. I look up the translation and it turns out to be a big spikey iron ball, attached to a stick with a heavy chain. It looks quite deadly. "Hm... I think I can live with that," I say. "What about Lian's story?" She starts laughing. "Oh that one was easy! She hikes in bright blue pants and she eats cookies all day." Lian laughs out loud. "Well, yes, I do eat a lot of cookies. I need to maintain my weight!" Snow White smiles, she's happy that we've accepted our names. We share some nuts and talk for a bit. This is so much fun. From this point on we will be known as CookieMonster and Morning Star. Now we fit in completely!

Soaking

"Look!" I say softly to Lian. She moves around a bit in her sleeping bag. "Huh? I'm still asleep." I open up the tent canopy a bit further and she looks outside. "Brr... I'm staying in bed for a bit longer." I get it, we've woken up in fog and drizzle, but I really have to pee. My bladder is exploding, and I can't hold it much longer. I shake out my shoes for scorpions, put my bare feet in them and walk naked to our designated 'toilet'. Outside the sky is grey. Cool drops of rain land on my skin. And while I'm peeing against a tree, I can see the sun trying its best to shine through the thick clouds. Hmm... maybe it'll get better, I think to myself. I quickly get back to the tent and crawl into my warm sleeping bag. This is definitely a morning to sleep in.

"This fog is like a fairy tale, the scenery doesn't in the least resemble a dry desert. Did you expect this?" We take our time getting up. Lian places her backpack against a young tree and answers, "No, not at all. It looks more like Norway out here." She pauses and then continues: "On a rainy day, with wisps of mist lingering in the fjords." I look around. It really does have a resemblance to Norway. We are surrounded by big, fat pine trees sticking up straight into the air. We can't see the end of them, which makes them seem even bigger. "Maybe the tops will reach all the way to the clouds," I wonder. In my mind, I picture myself flying closely over the clouds, with all these tiny little Christmas trees sticking out of it. This scenery also turns out to be quite typical of Southern California. And, yet again, it is something that we would never have expected when we pictured the 'desert part' of this trip.

"My pants are getting wet from those bushes," she says. I look down and find that mine are also soaking wet. Annoying. When we were preparing, we read that this part of the trail was always completely dry this time of year. "Maybe it wasn't such a good idea to send our rain pants ahead to our depot in Kennedy Meadows…" I sigh. Lian dispiritedly pulls the wet fabric free from her leg. "No, I guess that wasn't our brightest moment." Kennedy Meadows is located at the beginning of the Sierra Nevada Mountain Range; a high mountain area with snow and ice. But that's still a long way ahead of us. Luckily, we do have our raincoats and the umbrella also helps a lot. In the meantime, we hope the sun will come out soon.

But it doesn't.

"Yuk! Can't you drive a bit slower!" I shout. Yet another car that doesn't slow down, races past us and in its passing splashes a huge wave of water over us. We try to shake the water off. "Why would anyone do that?" Lian is getting angry too. Our pants are drenched and our feet are soaking in our shoes. It's day ten and this is our first horrible, boring, rainy day.

The trail to the mountain town Idyllwild is closed due to a fire that burned down the area a few years ago. That's why we have to go around for fifteen miles on a tarmac road. After a few hours of nasty wet hiking, a car pulls up beside us. The window doesn't go all the way down, as the driver tries to keep sheltered from the rain. "Can I give you guys a ride?" Lian and I have been pondering for the past hour if we would consider hitchhiking. We feel very conflicted. Our goal was to walk every single inch from Mexico to Canada, but right now the walk isn't much fun at all. "Where are you headed?" the man asks. "To Idyllwild," I answer, desperately trying to hide under my umbrella.

"Oh, that's a 20-minute drive from here. I can take you there if you want. I'm heading that way myself." Lian and I look at each other doubtfully. "What do you think? Should we give up our goal so early in the trip already? That doesn't feel right with me." She shrugs. "No, I feel the same way. This is no fun at all, but we're soaked anyway. Things couldn't possibly get any worse. These kinds of situations are part of the deal too." I turn back to the car. "Thank you very much but we're on a mission. We want to hike the entire PCT." He looks surprised. "What's PCT?" We explain briefly what it is that we're doing, and he listens to us in complete astonishment. "All that way? Why the hell would you want to do that?" That's actually quite a good question, now that I think of it. Why am I doing this? We say goodbye and before we know it, we're back on the wet tarmac alone, watching the car drive away. Was it a mistake to let him go?

That thought crosses our minds a few more times, when we see cars passing by full of hitchhiking hikers. Not everyone has the same goal as we do. One of the other hikers just told us this morning: "I'm here to be closer to nature and to meet new people; not to walk on a boring tarmac road. I'm not taking all those detours because of fires and whatever. By the way, if I want to take a shortcut and hike without my backpack for a day, I still will have walked the trail, won't I?" On some level, I do understand his point. Every year only 20% of the hikers reach the end of the trail and, knowing that statistic, everyone wants to experience the best parts of it at the very least. Most of the 20% of finishers have taken shortcuts or skipped a few miles. Only 5% of all hikers that make it to the end actually hike the whole trail from start to finish with a backpack on, all the time. That is our goal, to walk the whole thing, every inch, with our backpacks and without any shortcuts. Stick to the plan now André and don't give in to temptation, I tell myself.

"I'm so cold," Lian says a few hours later. "Another thirty minutes to the lodge. Hang in there sweetheart, we'll be warm soon." She's folded her arms around her body, like she's hugging herself. Her hiking poles hang loose from her wrists as she drags them along behind her. "I'm wet and my muscles are tight." She stops and turns around. I hold her tightly and try to warm her up with my hands. It helps a bit, even if only for comfort. She's in really good shape, which means she has hardly any body fat and that's why she gets cold quickly. I'm thirty pounds overweight and that layer of bodyfat keeps me nice and warm. I think of myself kind of like a seal, but less streamlined. I chuckle. No, not streamlined at all.

"We're here! Finally, I can have a hot bath!" she cries out when we see the first houses of Idyllwild. She's really very cold now. I look around at this cute, cozy little town. It's a fun small town with lots of wooden cabins, and a few inns and lodges. Slowly we walk further into the town and find beautiful wooden carvings and statues everywhere. "I could spend some time here," I say cheerfully. I love places like this. It makes me feel like I've gone back in time to the gold rushes of the 19th century. Lian is silent. She heads straight for the lodge that we booked online a few days ago.

We pick up our key and climb the stairs to our room. She opens the door and "Wow! What is this?!" With a huge smile on her face she steps into the room. I follow her inside and find a five-person jacuzzi in the room next to the bed! With water jets, bubbles, and a console to control everything. "Oh, I'm never leaving this place!" And before doing anything else, she opens the faucet. "Did you know about this when we booked?" I want to say yes, but I shake my head no. This moment is too special, and I don't want to ruin it by teasing her.

The bed looks amazing too. It's a canopy bed with beautiful curly posts that reach all the way up to the ceiling. Mosquito nets are draped stylishly from the sides of the bedposts. I fall onto the bed. Tomorrow we're taking a day off in this town to rest and to stock up on supplies for the next part of the trip. I sit up on the bed and see that Lian is already undressed. The bath is only half full, but she just can't wait any longer. Slowly she steps into the bath. "Oo, it's nice and hot. I think this is going to be the longest bath of my life!" I smile. "Enjoy it, I'll join you in a minute."

Contrasts

They're sparkling beautifully in the sun, like diamonds. The sun shines through them at a perfect angle, so every now and then we see all the colors of the rainbow shining through the ice. Icicles. Lots and lots of icicles, hanging from tree branches and bushes. Just a few hours ago everything looked so different. We left Idyllwild early this morning and are currently climbing the top of Mount San Jacinto. It stands tall at 10,834 feet, which makes it the second highest mountain in Southern California, and it is completely covered in snow!

"Nooooo, I didn't do that. The trees did it!" André is walking in front of me and he turns around with a stern frown on his face.
"Yeah, right, am I supposed to believe that?"
I push him softly.
"Well..." I say with a big grin on my face. He knows I'm lying through my teeth.
The ice is thawing now, and we are bombarded by falling icicles and piles of snow. Snow in the desert; we just can't get used to it. In front of me I see a couple of cacti with snow on them.
It looks a bit surreal, like something's not quite right.
Boom! I hit him right in the head and the snowball falls apart into a million pieces.
"What's going on?" André shouts and turns around cautiously.
"Hahahaha, got you there!" In the meantime, I've already made a new snowball and I throw it straight at him. It's a full hit.
"Nanananana!" I say provokingly. He won't stand for it and throws a snowball back. He misses!
"Snow attack!!" he shouts.
"No! No!" I run like mad, but he's faster. He catches me

and before we know it, we're rolling in the snow together on this narrow path.
"Gotcha!" He's on top of me, turns around and grabs a big chunk of snow. It's coming right at me. He pushes it in my face and it gets everywhere!
"Nooooo!!" I cry out, but it's useless.
"Oh no... it's all the way down to my bra!"
He smiles. "That's what you get for throwing snowballs at me!" With a big grin on his face he gets up and puts his hand out. I take it, and he pulls me up. "I'll pat you down." So, while he wipes all the snow from the outside of my clothing, I pull the last of the snow out of the inside. We look at each other smiling. I feel the same way I did when we fell in love in Iceland, thirty years ago. This is a great morning. The break we took yesterday did us a lot of good.

We're almost at the summit. John Muir, a famous American nature lover, once wrote: "The view from San Jacinto is the most sublime spectacle to be found anywhere on this Earth." So we're expecting a lot. We can't wait.

"Oh man, look at this view!" André whispers. He stops and looks at the horizon. It takes me just a few more steps to catch up and he's right. This is amazing! I start pointing at things. "Look, just below us, the city of Palm Springs." A small part of the summit blocks our view. He walks a bit further and stops again. "I'll be damned..." He turns around.
"Look at this. We just climbed up this mountain for almost two miles and it turns out there's a cable car here to bring people up..." It makes me laugh.
"Well, that was to be expected. The people of Palm Springs probably like this view as well." He nods.
"Yes, why wouldn't there be a cable car? Not everyone is able to climb a mountain like this. For them this must be an amazing place to have lunch!" He puts his arm around me and together we take in this beautiful view.

Our desert shoes aren't waterproof. They're not supposed to be, because they have to ventilate well in the heat. So, after hours of hiking through the soft snow, our feet are soaking and freezing, just like two days ago. We jump around for a bit at the summit to warm up. There's not much time to enjoy ourselves. The cold is taking over our bodies and we have to keep moving. After a few hours of descending, we arrive at a nice and flat piece of land with a few trees scattered around.

"What do you think? I think we've reached the 15-mile mark, don't you?" He looks around. "This is a good, level spot. Lots of room too. Let's make camp here."

I'm so cold, I'm shivering all over. What a difference compared to this morning. We're at 8500 feet now; it's bound to get even colder. I quickly pull the tent from my backpack, give it to André and while he pitches the tent, I start on a nice hot meal. I also change into dry clothes and sacrifice one pair of dry socks to try and warm up my feet. Although I don't think they will stay dry for long in my wet shoes.

Since we left early this morning, we are the first ones to set up camp in this amazing spot. We thought we would have all this space to ourselves, but that turns out to be an illusion. The first hikers start pouring in quickly and pitch their tents close to ours. The climb was long and hard for everyone and no one has the energy to continue today. I cling to my hot coco with both hands and finally start to feel like myself again. It's absolutely amazing how many people have poured into the site.

"Wow, it's really getting crowded here. Where did they all come from? It's starting to look like a campground. There are at least thirty tents up already." I say to André, he gets up. "I'm going to ask around," he replies and walks over to someone we know.

"Hey, do you know why there are so many hikers here, all of a sudden?" His name is Snowman, and he's just gotten his trailname. He didn't bring enough water up the mountain and now he's melting snow. "Hey, Morning Star. Yes, it has rained heavily in Idyllwild in the past few days. Lots of people decided not to climb the mountain. They all went up today." Aha, so that's it. There was an accumulation of people in the town and we didn't notice because we left early this morning.
"Do you know Dundee?" he asks.
"Yes, we do. Now that you mention him, I haven't seen him in quite some time. What about him?" Snowman carefully slides some more snow into his tiny saucepan.
"The day before yesterday, he was dead set on going up in the rain. We tried to warn him: if it's raining in Idyllwild, it's bound to be much worse on the mountain. But he went anyway! The next morning, he came back to the town. He was soaking wet and freezing cold." I follow the conversation from a distance and can tell that André's shocked.
"Dundee didn't manage to pitch his tent due to the strong winds. He crawled into a small cavity somewhere and wrapped the outer part of his tent around him. The wind rushed around him, and his bones ached in the freezing cold. He couldn't lie down or sleep and stayed like this all night. Finally, at dawn, he came all the way back down to the town." Snowman notices me and I wave at him. He smiles and waves back.
"I don't understand that at all. I thought he was an 'off-piste-skier'? You would think he would be able to assess the situation," André says. But now that I think of it: this is Dundee's first long-distance hike, and he too was inspired by the movie 'Wild'. It appears to be a rookie mistake. I wonder how many lapses in judgement these 'Wild walkers' are going to have on this journey.

The alarm goes off. It's half past four and it's still dark outside. The weather looks like it favors us today. I flick the tent wall with my fingers. "Look at that; there are ice crystals on the inside of the tent." It's still well below thirty-two degrees outside so we put on all our thermal clothing. The sky is crystal clear. "Look at the Milky Way We never see it like this at home," André whispers softly. We don't want to wake anyone. I look up and see an amazing purple band across the night sky with millions of stars in it, sparkling beautifully. He's right, with all the light pollution in our country, we never see the stars like this. This is stunning! We quietly start our descent and after an hour we take a break in the morning's first light. Time for breakfast. We purposely haven't had breakfast yet. We don't want to wake up any of the sleeping hikers with our noisy gas burner. They need their rest too, so we're having breakfast a bit further down the trail in the morning sun.

"Do you know what's funny about this descent?" I say to André a couple of hours later. "No? What?" I catch up to him. "It doesn't seem like it's ever going to end. Every hour or so we shed another layer of clothing. Who knows, when we get to the bottom, we'll be naked!" He turns around and grins at me. "Yeah, that would be something: hiking across the hot desert nude with nothing but a backpack on. I think the locals might have seen every kind of PCT-hiker by now, but I bet they haven't seen that!" I laugh out loud at that thought and say, "I don't think I'll do it!" He grins and shakes his head. "Neither will I, don't worry."

It's a 15-mile descent with lots of hairpin turns, but we've made it. We're in the valley now and it's scorching hot again. You can see the heat rising up from the ground, and there's not a wisp of wind. We're trying to hide under the reflective umbrella, but it's so hot now that it barely makes a difference. What a contrast! From freezing winter with snow and ice, back down to the scorching hot desert.

49

The Cocoon

A beautiful landscape stretches out in front of us: a brown greyish ground with rough, green bushes that grow up to our shoulders. A dusty narrow path sways between big pointy dunes and all around us are giant light-brown boulders, round, and oval ones. We're in the middle of this surreal landscape and we just don't know where to look. We decide to climb one of the bigger boulders, and when we get on top of it, we feel small and insignificant. We sit down and take it all in. Our minds are clear, there is only this moment of wonderment at this immense and uninterrupted space.

This is a place where peace and quiet roam and we are open to it. We feel it already, we are in the cocoon. Or at least, that's what we call it. It's a specific way of being and taking in your surroundings. A trance-like state, free of time, of just existing. It usually starts a few weeks into a hike. In the cocoon there is no such thing as time. There is no start and no finish. The nerves and stress we felt at the beginning of the trip are gone. There is no home in Belgium or friends in the Netherlands; there is only here and now. Observe, wonder, enjoy and let go.
Our daily western lives bombard us with impulses all day. It keeps our minds occupied and distracted every minute of every day: advertisements, radio, tv, internet, phone, news, conversations, work… These things are all absent on long hikes like this one, and we love it. There is no news, no Instagram, no Facebook, or any other diversions from where we are right now, at this moment. We see many hikers struggle with this, especially the ones that hike alone. They wear earphones, listen to music or books, talk to their loved ones on the phone and post pictures to Instagram as soon as they find a signal. It's fun, and very understandable. But it takes you away from being here. It takes your mind somewhere else.

We especially take care to go online only at set times. Like once a month, we write something to let our loved ones know what's going on. Or we might make a call to check if there's an emergency back at home. The rest of the time we turn everything off, and without these stimuli our minds become clear and free. When all the noise disappears, the world is so much more beautiful.

When the cocoon manifests itself, everything clears out and lost things come back up. It feels pure, almost meditative. Our minds are brighter, and our memories are sharper. We can even remember more things, back to our earliest childhood. Our senses heighten and we see and smell with more intensity. We literally surrender ourselves to nature. A simple thing like a ripple in the water can captivate us. Or the fine veins in a leaf, a salamander on the riverbank... we just observe and let it all in. Sometimes a thing can be so overwhelmingly beautiful, that it makes tears of pure joy bubble up from deep within us, and flow out like a waterfall. It is pure, immensely beautiful and one of the main reasons why we love long-distance hiking.

Sometimes traumas, dark and insecure thoughts that we've carried with us since our childhood, will come up as well. You can't escape it. They can stay with you for days on end, unshakably. Everyone has them; it can be something small, or something huge like abuse, losing a child, war violence... The noise at home constantly distracts us, so we never have to face these things. We completely or partially push them away, consciously or not. But now there are no more distractions. No apps or appointments that constantly need our attention. It's a direct confrontation and we are forced to look at our reflections in the mirror. For days and days these thoughts can weigh us down. Especially if we're hiking through dark forests and rainy weather for a few weeks. It makes you pull back into your raincoat, not looking at the horizon, just staring at the ground, putting one foot in front of the other.

Sometimes it can keep you captive all day for days. It can be impossible to escape the dark, painful thoughts. They're too forceful and take up all the space they can find. The trauma is relived and needs to be processed, to find a peaceful place in your mind.

Fortunately, we have each other. We can pull each other out of moments like these. We have all the time in the world to talk and work it out calmly. It helps, it processes and clears space. The solo hikers can have a hard time with this; they are more vulnerable. They tend to get together in groups after a while. We could look for distraction if we wanted to. But to experience deeply and intensely what we go through outside, and clean up the inside, is a million times more fascinating than any distraction could ever be.

Junkies at McDonald's

"Toooot!!! Toot-toot!" A deep foghorn-like sound comes rolling over the mountains. From higher ground we can make some sort of railroad train yard far away. It's an intricate design of tracks that looks like it might have been designed by a toy-train enthusiast. Long lines of extremely long train cars are pulled in the direction of the pass painstakingly slowly by diesel locomotives. "Toot-toot!!", we hear again. We get a bit closer and now we can clearly see how immensely long the trains really are.
"Lian, have you ever seen anything like it? I haven't." She stops and shields her eyes from the bright sun with her hand.
"No, I can't remember ever seeing anything like this, anywhere. Wow! They are very long, aren't they?"

The funny thing about the Cajon Pass is that in the past few days no-one has even mentioned trains. All the hikers we run into, only seem to talk about one thing: eating hamburgers at McDonald's! Like true fast food junkies, looking to score their next fix, some of them walked over 25 miles without stopping just to get there as soon as they possibly could. It makes us laugh, but we do understand why they want to go there. We've been hiking for three weeks. And with all that dry food, we could really go for something different by now. But McDonald's? Really? That mushy junk?

It's seven in the morning when we go in. It's on our route anyway, so why not have breakfast there? We join a few other hikers we know. Chilly Willy, the hiker sitting next to me, has already finished two breakfast meals and now orders another Big Mac, a Buffalo Bacon Deluxe and three servings of fries. "Hungry?" I ask. He grins. "No, I just like it." We talk for a bit and during our conversation, the young lady across the table called Rainbow, empties three huge cups of soda. She lets out a loud belch and immediately apologizes for it. Chilly Willy's food has arrived, and I watch in astonishment how he eats all of it. I smile. Well, we burn about 5000 calories a day, so I really do understand why his appetite's so big. We order breakfast, which turns out to be a questionable bun with a fried egg. Or at least that's what it's supposed to be. It's perfectly round and it doesn't look like egg, more like something made of powdered egg. And that's exactly how it tastes. It could just as well have been flavored tofu. The bun tastes like nothing and the coffee is lukewarm and watery. Still, the others are loving it. I think we may have different taste buds in Europe.

We're still hungry, but we really don't feel like going for a second McDonald's menu. We hear about a Subway sandwich shop a bit further down the road and decide to go there. The sandwiches there also turn out to be a bit different than we thought. Unfortunately, they're not the crunchy French baguettes with soft brie or pâté that we're craving; they're soft. But at least we can load them up with lots of toppings. We each order two footlongs and top them with roast beef, tomatoes, lettuce, and other vegetables. One for now and one for lunch. We now each have two footlong sandwiches, which should be enough. We leave the shop and hike towards a small tunnel that goes under the highway.

"Woah!" He startles me. Just before we reach the tunnel, a man suddenly jumps out of a RV. He leaves his door open and starts hiking along with us. He has a lot of fantastical stories about all kinds of things.
"What are your names?" he asks. He strikes me as a very strange man, but I guess we can give him our trail names.
"CookieMonster and Morning Star." He pulls a sharpie out of his pocket and starts writing our names on his arm. This is getting really weird. He has so many names written

all over his arm, there's hardly any space left. He shows them off proudly, like tattoos. He is very pushy, and he won't leave our side. We really don't trust him at all, and he follows us all the way to the dark tunnel. This feels extremely strange. This is the United States of America, the country where people get shot for no good reason at all.
"This is scary, isn't it? He could have a knife or a gun," Lian says to me in Dutch, so the man doesn't understand. Hmmm... this doesn't feel right at all.

Just before we reach the tunnel, we see Rob, an American marine. He's a retired veteran and he seems to sense our discomfort. He seems suspicious of the strange man too and starts up a conversation.
"Hey, CookieMonster and Morning Star, how are you?"
But before we can answer the man says:
"Hey, hello, what's your name?" He walks right up to him and pulls the cap off his sharpie.
"Rob," he says.
"That's it?" the man asks.
"Oh well, some people call me Rob Steady."

You don't meet many people like Rob. He's hiked the PCT before, and a number of other long-distance trails, like the Appalachian Trail and the Continental Divide Trail. Hiking has become a way of life for him. The comradery, the adventure, the outdoors. Since the military he feels most at home when he's on a trail.

The strange man looks at Rob and adds the name to his arm. "Rob Steady. Great."
Lian winks at me and looks at the tunnel.
"Quick," she whispers, "It's now or never. Let's go, while we can." I nod and we start walking at a quick pace. The man sees us go and now he's confused. He thought we would stop and talk to Rob, like him. He looks at Rob and then back at us and decides to sprint to catch up with us, but we speed up the pace. It's dark in the tunnel, not

pitch black, but it gives us an eerie feeling. Luckily, we can already see the light at the end of the tunnel. We stay silent and keep walking. We look behind us and see that Rob comes after us and catches up with the man.
Not long after that the man goes back in the direction of his RV. "Phew…, that was close. What a creep. I'm glad we lost him," Lian says softly.

On the other side of the tunnel we wait for Rob to come out. He comes up to us, smiling.
"Well, he was an odd, special kind of guy, wasn't he?" he says.
Lian checks the tunnel to make sure he doesn't come back. Rob laughs.
"Not every American is an idiot with a gun," He grins.
"He's just one of those special kinds of people you might find on the trail."

The Oasis

We take out our water bottles, have a drink and check our water supply. In this part of the trail, water is scarce. We're still carrying up to two gallons of water per person, per day on our backs, but every now and then we get lucky, like now.

"Hey, it's a bridge. What's that doing here?" I ask André. We're in the middle of a barren landscape on a tiny path, so a towering bridge is probably the last thing we would expect. We walk onto the bridge and look down.

"Wooow, this is beautiful!" André is already hanging over the side of the bridge.

"Yeah, and it's quite a long way down, too." I sound a bit concerned. The view out here is very unexpected and absolutely amazing. Down below us, a beautiful little creek runs between tiny sandy beaches, slowly rippling under the bridge. The banks are littered with bright green plants that look like they might be herbs of some sort. This is such a contrast compared to the dark green shrubs we've been seeing for the past few days.

"It's an oasis!!" I cry out. "Let's camp here!" He nods.

"Well, it's a bit early, but we'll make up for those miles in the next couple of days." We look for a way down and see a small path. We descend, find a nice level spot and put up the tent.

I take off my shoes and get into the water. This is so nice!! Tiny grains of sand squish their way in between my toes. It feels amazing on my bare feet. André gets into the water with me, grinning from ear to ear. The water is crystal clear and comes up to my knees. I slowly slide into the water backwards, lay down flat on my back and let the water wash over me completely. This is just delightful!

We take our time, relax, and finally give our tired muscles some well-deserved rest. We plan to enjoy this experience intensely. I feel like a small child, going to the public pool for the first time, seeing all the fountains. I feel radiant and I can't stop smiling. Slowly I wade through the creek. My hands just barely touching the water surface and leaving small ripples in their tracks. Large green and blue dragonflies dance around us just above the water, and on the riverbank we find fresh mint.

We feel a new kind of excitement, like bear cubs hunting salmon for the first time, frantically splashing around in the water. We're falling over each other, splashing water into each other's faces, running around and chasing each other hysterically, until finally I lie down on the sandy bank, with my feet still touching the water. I pull my sun hat over my face, close my eyes, and take a moment to relax, while André purifies the water. When he's finished, he sits next to me. At this point, I'm already dozing in and out of consciousness and I slowly open my eyes. He looks into my eyes peacefully, with big loving eyes and softly says, "I've made you some cold mint tea."
"Mint tea?" I answer just as softly.
"Yes, I picked some mint and put it in our water bottles."
I smile and take the bottle silently. Mint tea, my favorite. He's such a sweetheart. We drink our tea and stare at the beautiful scenery. So beautiful. Indescribably beautiful...

On Which Snake Will Lian Step?

"Woah! Another one!" I cry out in terror. I'm right behind Lian and even though it's hot, I'm extremely alert. We're standing right next to the snake, stiff as a poker, too nervous to move. "Should I move or not?" she asks me. I'm not really sure. It's so close to her ankle, it looks like it could attack at any moment. "What if I stepped forward in slow motion?" she says anxiously. The snake just keeps on rattling and I don't know what to do. Snakes are beautiful creatures, but I'm no expert on snakes. In the Netherlands, we have a famous television-biologist called Freek Vonk. He would grab this snake in a second and know exactly how to handle it, but I have no idea. She slowly picks up her foot and moves it a little bit forward. The rattling noise in the bush gets louder, but nothing else happens. I still have to make my way past it somehow. "Let's throw some rocks at the ground right in front of the bush. Snakes can't hear, but maybe it'll go away when it feels the tremors in the ground." We throw a few rocks, stomp our feet and eventually it finally decides to slither off. We can finally move on.

On which snake will she almost step today? This has been our reality for the last ten days or so. Apparently, snakes enjoy lying in the middle of a hiking trail between three and five o'clock in the afternoon. The first snake Lian almost stepped on was a rattlesnake too. Fortunately, she spotted it just in time. It was so well camouflaged, she initially thought it was an oddly shaped stick, but when she put her foot down close to it, it moved and slithered to the side of the road and started rattling. That ended surprisingly well, and it moved far away enough for us to pass it easily. Oh no, it's another one. Lian steps over a Common Garter Snake and not long after that she almost steps on the head of a Striped Racer. At least those aren't deadly. They blend into the environment so beautifully that you really can't see them until it's almost too late. "I really don't see the snakes! And they seem to have trouble seeing me too," she says, a little bit flustered. This is no fun for me either. Whenever Lian steps over a snake, it startles the poor thing and it shoots off the road or puts its head up in the air. It scares me every time. I'm walking right behind her and all these startled snakes keep jumping up right in front of my face. Fortunately, most of them aren't poisonous. I don't blame her, it's not easy to see them. I have trouble recognizing them myself. An hour ago, I was in front and I almost stepped on a Checkered Garter Snake as well.

By now we have encountered at least ten rattle snakes up close, and even though it scared us at first, most of them don't really make a move. If anything, both us and the snake want to get far away from each other as soon as possible. Lian is more perceptive and is really getting good at identifying the high pitch of the rattle. Sadly, I'm not able to do that. I lost my ability to perceive high sound in a diving accident in the army. In an emergency ascent, both of my eardrums ruptured because I couldn't clear the pressure. It's called a 'reverse block'. I'm lucky I can hear again, but I do need a hearing aid. I brought it with me on this trip, but I lost it somewhere in the first couple of days. This means that I have to be on high alert, because even when a rattle snake warns me to stay away by rattling its tail, I probably won't hear it...

It's getting later in the day and a thick cover of clouds is forming. We see less and less hikers around. The weather forecast says there's a hailstorm coming this way, so most hikers are hiding out in the towns around here. We assess the situation, keep an eye on the clouds and decide to go on. We think we'll be able to make it to a safe place, just under a mountain ridge, where we can ride out the storm.

We keep on climbing and around five o'clock we feel the first hailstones coming down. The wind picks up, there's no denying that the storm is here, and we really must stop. There isn't much space, but we manage to cut away a few branches under a thick group of shrubs with a small army knife. Our tent only just fits in this perfect little hiding place, sheltered from the wind. The weather takes a turn for the worst. This is the first time we've really had to secure the tent in its place, and it's a good thing we did. Sometime later we hear the wind howling on the mountain from inside our tent. Luckily, we're safe and warm in our sleeping bags.

We wake up in a thick blanket of snow. When I tap the canopy, soft chunks of snow slide down the front of the tent. It's pretty cold, so I put on a few layers of clothing and step outside. "Hey, look at this. Everything's covered in snow. Hahaha, snow in the desert... again! Who would have thought? Lian, it's beautiful! The sun is out and we're above the clouds!" I'm looking out at this amazing white landscape, and it's really astonishing. Lian comes out of the tent, she wants to see this for herself. The fresh snow creaks under her trail runners as she walks up towards me. She puts her arm around me and with her beautiful smile, she takes in the view. This is amazing. In our thermal clothing and our Gore-Tex jackets we walk the small path up to the mountain pass. The sun is still low on the horizon and it hits the white ridges perfectly, casting long shadows over the amazing scenery. The sky is bright blue. We walk over a ridge and below us we see tiny fluffs of clouds floating in the valley. What a phenomenal view. This is pure joy.

Ghost Town

"I've just learned something new," says André while he traces his finger across the screen of his phone. "It says here that in this region there are two types of desert: high desert and low desert. The amount of precipitation is used to determine whether an area is called a desert." I look at him. "So, not the temperature or the fact that it has sand dunes?" He shakes his head. "No, apparently there are many different kinds of desert." I look around. "Then, for the past few days we must have been hiking in the high desert. It is nice and cool here." I look at the ground. In front of me is a huge pinecone, and I pick it up. "Look at this!" André looks up from his phone, puts it away and walks over to me. "Wow, that's a good one." The pine trees here have enormous cones that look like they're armored with shark teeth. Some are even larger than my head. André picks another one up and it cuts his finger. "Wow, these edges are as sharp as a knife!" I chuckle.

It's my birthday today and I couldn't have picked a better spot for it. We are currently on top of Mount Baden Powell, at 10,000 feet, and the view is absolutely astonishing.
"Hey Lian, I think that's Los Angeles?! Can you see it? There. If you look closely, you can see the shoreline right behind it." He points to it. I'm not so sure.
"It can't be, can it? That's more than 50 miles away. It's impossible to see that far." He shrugs. "I think I'm right, though." I look at the map and it is, in fact, Los Angeles. "It's like a tiny paper model of the city. All the tall skyscrapers look so small from here," I say. André has already moved his attention to something else. He's looking the other way. I turn around and see what he sees. It's the enormous outstretching hot, arid plain of the Mojave Desert. It feels threatening and desolate. It won't be long until we have to go through it. I wonder what that will be like…

We descend and arrive in an area that was completely devastated in the Station Fire of 2009. This is the notorious 'Poodle-dog Bush area'. The poodle-dog bush is a plant that flourishes in burnt areas. It's very poisonous and causes skin irritations from a nasty rash to large blisters when you touch it. The blisters can take up to a month to heal, and they are said to be extremely itchy and painful, and to make matters worse: the toxic oils from the plant can get into your clothing and spread quickly over your whole body, causing your entire body to be covered in itchy, blistery rash. Our trail goes right through the middle of the burnt area and it's completely overgrown with this horrible shrub. We don't have a choice; we have to go through it.

"They smell quite awful, don't they?" André stops and sticks his nose into the air. I stop too, and together we sniff the air. I break into laughter right away. "Well, now that you mention it. It's like walking through the city center of Amsterdam." He frowns at me. "Yes, it is just like a bad marijuana scent." Now he's laughing too. "That city has changed so much from when I was growing up there. You're right, it smells kind of the same. Oh, hey watch out!!" I jump up, terrified and look straight at him. "Your pants are touching the poodle-dog bush, dopey!" I turn around to look at it, and in the process I also touch the top of the plant with my sleeve. André points at my sleeve. "Now what?" he says. "I'll take everything off!" I call out as I quickly put down my backpack in a small clearing. I carefully take off my clothes and put them in a plastic trash bag. I hang it on the outside of my backpack, far away from my other clothes. "What are you going to wear?" he says. He looks concerned. "I don't have a choice. My rain pants are in Kennedy Meadows and I don't have another pair of pants. I'll have to hike in my skirt." But truthfully, I'm too scared. This horrid plant is all around us. I put on my skirt and stare at the path hesitantly. He puts his arm around me. "Why don't I go first, and I'll call out when I spot the plants and on which side of the path I see them," he says.

We decide on a code; left, right, up, down, close, and far, and off we go. It's painstakingly slow, but after hours of bending and turning slowly and evasively through the dangerous shrubs, we finally find an alternative route over an old, weather-beaten tarmac road. We're extremely happy we found this road, because the constant vigilance was wearing us out. We follow the road and eventually we end up at an old fire station. Or what's left of it anyway.

Heat-bent, contorted pieces of metal stick aimlessly into the sky. Creepy blackened branches stand among the broken concrete. Three black beams standing tall, showing us that once upon a time, they carried a roof. Above the entrance and on the window next to it we see large black spots. That must be where the smoke and flames came out of the building. This is pure devastation. We walk into the street. It's not just the fire station, this is a tiny town where the fire-fighters and their families used to live. Now it's an actual ghost town. Our mood darkens more and more as we start to realize the intensity with which all this came about. It looks like a war zone: rubble and debris everywhere. We stop at a completely burnt out car. Even the color is no longer visible. Big black blobs lie under the rims of the car, that must have been the tires. It's surreal. We look around and see nothing but ash and blackened spots. We don't know what to say, so we stay silent. We try to imagine what these people must have gone through. In the cracks of the destroyed concrete, the first plants have started to grow, trying desperately to make this place beautiful again.

The intensity of it all slows us down. It feels like walking among the white crosses on a large memorial graveyard. It must have been awful. Slowly we walk through the town and end up at a monument looking over the valley. The rusty, steel letters on top spell 'Station Fire'. Underneath that, in a large circle is the logo of the fire brigade. People have hung baseball caps from the sides. At the foot of the monument are pieces of contorted metal. In the middle is a memorial box with a book and a notebook. We read about the fire-fighters that didn't escape the fire. This monument was put up to commemorate them.

I look up at the sky and see the mares' tails clouds. It's a clear sign that the weather is about to change. A thunderstorm is brewing, and this day is about to get even darker.

Casa de Luna

With her pants around her knees and her bum naked, she suddenly shows up right next to the guy taking our group photo. "Say cheese" he says from behind the camera. With big eyes we all stare in astonishment at her big bare bum. It turned out to be a very funny picture. We are staying with Trail Angels 'the Andersons' and this isn't the only funny thing to happen here. Casa de Luna, their house and territory, is said to be a place where everyone can have fun. A place where life isn't taken too seriously, and where you can have a little party. A place for goofing around. Well, that's exactly what it turns out to be. It is very appealing to many hikers and so they tend to hang around for a couple of days.

In the meantime, we have arrived in what is called 'the hiker bubble'. Even though the permits for the PCT are distributed evenly so that no more than 50 hikers can start the hike each day, some will walk a bit faster and some will be a bit slower. So now there is quite a high concentration of hikers on the trail. I was reluctant to go to the Andersons, because of its popularity. I like my space and I don't like crowds, so I don't feel very comfortable in this part of the trail scene. Lian is more social than I am and she really wanted to come here, so I let her talk me into it.

We go off the PCT trail and walk about four miles until we reach a large yellow house. I'm glad she talked me into it. I am so happy we came here. In hindsight I would not have missed this for the world. A big crescent moon wearing sunglasses hangs from the tree in front of the house. On the ground is an inflatable flamingo. On the porch there are big blue umbrellas with garden chairs and tables. It's a pleasant setting. On the patio are a few bearded men, who look like they might have come straight out of a 'Hobbit' movie. One of them is having a beer, and the other is smoking hash from a pipe. Hanging out comfortably in a white chair with blue cushions, a woman hiker is chatting away with some others, while her feet rest on the chair in front of her. She's wearing leather slippers and each one of her toenails has a different color nail polish. On the wall behind her, is a large white bed sheet. It's full of names and funny sentences. At the top, in giant 'flower power' letters it reads: 'Hippie Daycare'. We're back in the seventies.

We go up the steps to the front porch and knock. The door is already open. We step inside and find lots of people running around. A big woman with long, straight, oily hair turns around. She smiles abundantly as she comes towards us. "Hi, I'm Terrie, welcome to Casa de Luna!" Terrie and Joe Anderson are trail legends. It's so nice to meet them. "Hi Terrie, it's quite lively here," I reply. "Yeah, there's about fifty hikers here at the moment, it's great fun. Where are you from?" That's a very frequent question among Americans. It usually results in a conversation about the state they originate from and where they live and work now. "I'm André 'Morning Star' and this is Lian 'CookieMonster'. We're Dutch, but we live in Belgium." She smiles. "Aha, the Dutch-Danish-Belgians. Welcome." This surprises us a little bit. Does she know us? Is she expecting us? We don't understand. Lian asks her, "Why do you think we're Danish? We don't speak Danish. We've been to Denmark in the past, but other than that we have no link to it. In fact, this is the first time we've heard this. People usually refer to us as 'the Friendly Hikers'." Terrie lights up a cigarette and looks at us. "I'm not really sure. Two friends of yours came in yesterday. They asked me if you had passed through here already. The Dutch-Danish-Belgians thing stuck with me, that's all. They're still here by the way. I have no idea why they call you that. Why don't you ask them?" We wonder who they are. Terrie goes on and points us to a brightly colored poster on the wall.

"These are the Guidelines":

1. Hug Terrie.
2. Pick out a Hawaiian shirt and put it on.
3. Go through two gates and keep going, find the trail and a spot in the magical Manzanita forest.
4. Water on side of house.
5. No fire out back.
6. Please no hard alcohol, no drinking games.
7. Protect your food from critters.
8. Pancakes and coffee for brekkie.
9. Taco salad for dinner.
10. Wash your hands before meals and don't hold your plate over the pot!
11. No politics or religious banter.
12. F-word. Don't yell it, we have neighbors.
13. Please have your picture taken before you leave.
14. Class bandanas here!
15. Sign the banner!
16. Keep noise out front so others can sleep.
17. Quiet time 10 p.m.
18. MOST OF ALL, HAVE FUN AND MAKE BEAUTIFUL MEMORIES.

Followed by a collection of hearts.

We leave Terrie and walk onto the grounds. It's actually quite big and it's littered with red-brown shrubs that have small, oval-shaped green leaves, the Manzanitas. In the shade of the Manzanitas there are sandy lots everywhere, and many of them have hiking tents on them. We also find lots of fun little signs that say things like "What happens in the forest, stays in the forest." I smile and wink. "That's an interesting thought." She chuckles. "Men ..." We walk further into the forest and try to find a nice quiet spot. It doesn't take us long to find one and after we put up our tent, we set out to explore the terrain. We quickly find two familiar faces: Aquanaut and Little Bear.

They didn't give us the 'Dutch-Danish-Belgians' nickname. We continue and find a nice spot with the other guests on the patio. Our Korean friends He-man and Spontaneous are there too. We share our adventure stories and listen to theirs. We all agree, this place is so different. It's a different kind of oasis; one of friendship and fun.

A bit further onto the patio is a long table with arts and crafts materials. A few young women are painting each other's faces there. We decide to go and see what's going on. We've seen them before, but they were all hiking separately. Apparently, they got together, and they've been hiking as a group for the past two weeks. Next to the table, a variety of painted stones are lying on the ground. They've been decorated with patterns, words, and proverbs. Lian picks up a few bare stones and a brush, and lets her creativity run freely. All the while chatting away with the other girls.

Sometime later I see another two familiar faces. "Lian, look, it's Snow White and Wallstreet!" She turns around and looks in the direction I'm pointing. They must have heard me, because they also turn around and look our way. We all laugh and come together, giving each other big hugs. "I haven't seen you around for at least three weeks!" Wallstreet says. "Yes, that's right. We noticed you were a day or two ahead of us in the trail logs," Lian replies. Snow White looks at Wallstreet. "See, Ben, I told you they were behind us." She turns to Lian and continues, "We asked Terrie if she'd seen you, but she hadn't. We didn't see your names in any of the logs, so we thought maybe you'd quit." Aha, so they're the ones who asked about us! "What's with the Dutch-Danish-Belgians? What's that about?" I ask Wallstreet. "Well, you were born in the Netherlands and you live in Belgium. But when we hear you talking to each other in your own language, it sounds a bit like the cook from the Muppets. 'It's all Danish to us!' so we started calling you that." We all laugh about this.

"But why are you still here?" Lian asks. Wallstreet replies, "Today is Snow White's birthday and we thought this would be the perfect location for a birthday party." We nod. "It sure is," Lian confirms. So, we wander to the chairs under the umbrellas together where we have a beer and share our stories.

After a great afternoon with wonderful people, it's getting closer to dinner time. With our Hawaii shirts and our wacky hats on we stand in line. There is a communal dinner, which is something these Trail Angels do every day, for all these hikers, from the goodness of their hearts. The macaroni and cheese, beans and taco salad are very tasty, and with our bellies full we crash down on the sofa among the other hikers. We meet even more hikers and listen to their wonderful adventures for hours. I'm getting quite tired and look at the clock. "It's getting quite late. Our alarm is set for five o'clock. Let's go to bed." We quietly walk past the tents. We hear some soft moaning coming from a few of them. "That doesn't sound like snoring," Lian whispers. We giggle a bit and with the phrase 'What happens in the forest, stays in the forest' firmly planted in our minds, we go to our own tent.

Mission to Mars

Mars, the red planet. A wild, rugged, and inhospitable environment where nothing seems to be able to survive. In the last couple of days, we have been seeing glimpses of the Mojave Desert and it looks just like the space pictures from NASA. Impressive and frightening at the same time. Rugged rock formations are intertwined with huge outstretches of empty sand plains on which absolutely nothing will grow.

Now the time has come; we have to go straight through it. We decide to hike at night, to escape the scorching heat of the day. At night we consume less water, and water will be our greatest problem here.

"What time do you think we should get up?" André asks. "I don't know. How about two o'clock, and then we can set off at three?" He's bent down over his backpack, his head shoots up immediately. "Excuse me? I know that you want to start early, but four or five a.m. would be fine, right?" He tries to read my expression. "Get up at three then? Leave at four?" I reply. He nods. That time seems to work a bit better for him. Three o'clock should be early enough. It really is necessary; this place is very hot and extremely dry. In the next couple of days, we'll be carrying around two gallons of water each in our backpacks. That sounds like a lot and it should be enough, but we still worry we might run out. It's a matter of life and death. Not enough water could have fatal consequences.

It's pitch-black when we get up. Above us, we see the amazing blue-purple Milky-Way. With our headlamps on, we set off: two tiny flickering lights, merging with the stars in the night. After a few hours of hiking under the crystal clear, never-ending star-filled night sky, an orange glow begins to emerge from the east. One by one the fading stars are swallowed by the glowing horizon. It feels like we're in a fairy-tale. The first outlines of the desert are visible now. A few lonely Joshua trees stick their prickly leaves proudly up into the air. The sun comes up. It starts out, just a thin orange line shining on the mountain ridges, but soon its light floods the desert at full strength.

We keep walking until the sandy trail reaches a deserted old bridge over a dry riverbed. It's around noon. We sit down in the shadow of the bridge and have a siesta. André takes a nap, but I can't sleep at all. It's way too hot for me. And although the sun is still blistering hot, we decide to set off again at four o'clock. We really want to make as many miles as we can, so we can leave this desert behind us as quickly as possible and get to our planned tent spot. At eight o'clock p.m. we stop in a deep valley, and it has a tiny little stream. Water. Yes! At last! Finally, I can have some peace of mind. We're almost out of water. Now at least we can hydrate properly. We set up camp, drink as much as we can and have dinner. By now, we've covered more miles than a marathon.

After a few days of beautiful night-hikes and amazing sunrises we arrive at the small town of Tehachapi. We pick up the resupply package that we sent here in advance. In the next couple of days, we will be heading into the toughest section: 43 miles without a single watering hole and we have no idea how to tackle this.
"We could do the whole thing in two days? But then we would have to carry 4 gallons of water each…" I suggest.
"Umm… I don't think that'll work. The volume of our backpacks is only 36 liters and they can't carry more than 40 pounds. We also have a new five-day food pack to carry. It's never going to fit, and even if it would, I don't think we'd be able to move comfortably with all that weight." I agree with André. This isn't light-weight hiking anymore, it's more like trudging through the desert like a mule. I'm sitting on a bench, moving my legs around nervously. No, the heat and drought really aren't my thing at all.

How about walking at night and sleeping during the day? No, that won't work either. "We could presume that there will be water out there. The word is that Trail Angels have made two water cashes, and that they keep them stocked up," I say impulsively, but I immediately notice the contradiction of this to all our principles of safety, and I take it back again. André looks at me calmly, silently. He knows, just as well as I do, that the desert is no place for presumptions and that preparation is key. The blackout from day one is still fresh in our memories. It is our responsibility to figure this out. We shouldn't go in blindly and put all our faith in water cashes, that could very well be empty.

In Tehachapi we meet Aquanaut and Little Bear again; two able-bodied professional offshore divers who have both quit their jobs to go on this six-month adventure. They invite us to share a hotel room with them. It's got more than enough room, they say, so why not. We find out that they're facing the exact same predicament.
"We're considering hiring a car for a day, and making our own water depots," says Little Bear. André and I look at each other. That is a brilliant idea! We nod in agreement and before we know it, we're discussing how we're going to do this. Their plan is already quite elaborate, and on the map they show us the tiny sandy dirt roads that are close to the trail.
"If we make water depots in these locations, we only have to hike 15 miles a day, and that means we can do the dry section in three days. It looks doable," says Aquanaut.
We're all very excited about this plan and to celebrate, we spend the rest of the evening in a bar, playing a few rounds of pool, after which we return to the hotel quite tipsy.

The next morning the alarm goes off at a reasonable time for a change. We rent a small car for fifty dollars. The guys get the deal done quickly and before we know it, we've loaded it up with a dozen or so one-gallon plastic bottles full of water. We soon arrive at the first tiny dirt road. The poor little car, it's not really suitable for this kind of terrain. With all that water, plus four people, it bounces and hops around all over the place. We try to carry on and get as far as we can, but at a certain point the firm sandy country road turns into a loose sand path. To drive over it you would really need a decent four-wheel drive car. We're still quite far from the trail, but the car won't take us any further, so we decide to make the depot here. To make sure no-one can see it, and maybe use it for themselves, we hide the gallon-size plastic bottles in the bushes. Not that we expect anyone to be wandering out here in the middle of nowhere, but still. We don't want to leave anything to chance. Without water, it's impossible to survive out here. In the next days we hike from depot to depot together and thankfully they are all intact. Even though it adds extra miles to the already long hike, it's worth every step. Especially the can of coke the guys sneaked into the stash. So good!

We run into a few hikers who didn't feel like carrying extra water. It's the middle of the day and the sun is scorching hot. They don't hold siesta and they ask us for water. They are running out and still have another twenty miles to go to the next watering hole. We don't have much to spare, and although it sounds harsh, we can't give them a lot. André and I have both done rescue training and the number one rule is: "Personal safety first!" As a rescuer, it is important that you monitor your own health and safety, because if your own safety is jeopardized, you won't be able to help anyone else. And what's more, it's their own fault for not wanting to carry more water. But hey, sending them off to die isn't such a good idea either, so we give them what we can spare.

After twenty miles we arrive at a water cache that was made by a Trail Angel. A large group of hikers is lying around, waiting in the shade of a Joshua tree. The plastic gallon-size water bottles are empty. "Stupid Trail Angels! There's no water here! Now I have nothing!" someone shouts. A few others also cry out angry and foul language. We stay silent and keep our distance. They are definitely not happy. They're acting like spoilt children, like it's their right to be supplied by Trail Angels. As if the Trail Angels' job is to make sure they have enough water. They don't get it. These hikers, too, didn't feel like carrying extra load and put their blind faith in the Trail Angels' never-ending stock.

"Guys, this water supply is a gift from the Trail Angels, not a public service. You made the decision to walk into a desert, where there's no water for more than 40 miles. Nobody made you do this; this was your choice. Be responsible for your own life and make sure you're well-prepared! Stop complaining about these wonderful people!" André says a bit upset to one of them. They decide to wait for another Trial Angel to come out with water. When? No one even knows if it's going to happen at all. We keep on going. Personal safety first.

The Vortex

"The end of the desert!!" I shout, as I point to a small stream in front of us. Lian walks right up to it and steps into the water, clothes, and all. "This is soooooooo nice!!! It's so cool! Come in!!" She doesn't have to ask me twice. I get undressed, spread out my arms and fall face-front into the water. This is amazing! After this wonderful break we hike on, and not much later we see a few wooden buildings in the middle of the vast emptiness.

Kennedy Meadows; it's right in front of us. We've made it through the desert section. Five weeks it's taken us; it's just a speck of dust if you look at the whole map of the PCT. But at least the drought, our area of non-expertise, is almost over.
"Hey, that's the General Store. That's where we're going!" Lian says happily. I look in the direction she's pointing. A few wooden pillars holding up a crooked roof. It's straight out of a western movie. Above the small roof is a wooden screen, like the ones in the old movies, where a cowboy would come out from behind it, ready to shoot someone from above.
There are groups of hikers everywhere. Some are playing around with a frisbee, others are having animate conversations. On the right side of the building is a large wooden veranda. I see someone walking in front of the veranda with a big inflatable donut around his waist. I laugh and wonder why. There's no water here, right? What is this funny little place?

We come closer to the building and suddenly we hear a huge applause! Everyone starts cheering and we're welcomed in like we're heroes or something.
"What's all this for?" Lian asks.
"I don't know, maybe we're the 200th hikers to come in?"

Humble and a bit uneasy, we walk into the crowd. After a few heartfelt pats on the back from numerous hikers we finally come to a standstill at a broad-shouldered young man. He's wearing a funny t-shirt; it says, in big green letters: "For a bear, sleeping bags are like soft tacos." A very appropriate text for the next part of the hike, I think to myself.
"To what do we owe this honor?" I ask him. He smiles.
"Oh, we do that for every hiker that arrives here. It's an homage to your victory over the desert! That part of your journey is over!" And as he says that, he puts his right arm, with his fist clenched, high into the sky.
"My name's Buttplug. What's yours?" I burst out into laughter.
"How on earth did you get that name? And why would you keep it?" He chuckles. "Well, I got the name because I couldn't shit for five days." We can't stop laughing.
"And I kept the name because it always makes people laugh. Nobody ever forgets me!" I pat him on the shoulder, still laughing, and together we walk towards the house.

On the veranda we see mostly young people, having lively conversations with each other at small tables. Many of them have a large hamburger in front of them, and a cold beer next to it. Against the wall are a couple of joined tables. On them are five huge crates with discarded stuff. "Hiker Box" it says in big letters on the wall behind them. Interesting, we should check it out later. The party mood is contagious. We decide to go along with the flow and talk to a bunch of people we met on the trail. Our well-earned hamburger arrives, and we enjoy the cheerful company. Everyone shares their greatest adventures here. It's unbelievable how many different stories there are, from people who have all just hiked the exact same trail.
The craziest story is the story of Mary Poppins, a young man in his early twenties. He got the nickname because he brought way too much stuff. It didn't matter what you asked him, he pulled it all out of his backpack. From a

huge machete to fishing line, he's got it. He's a good talker: "Yes, well, and then I went hitchhiking and out of nowhere, I got offered a helicopter ride!" he recounts with large gestures. "Aren't you the one we met right at the start of the trail in Wrightwood? You're the guy with the huge triangle tent, that had to be fixed on the trees with big lashing straps, aren't you?" Lian asks. "Yes, I am! It's a very strong tent, and it fits up to six people." His tall tales seem to have gotten taller with every mile he's hiked.

"I'd like to get sponsored by this tent manufacturer, so that's why I'm going to carry this enormous tent all the way to Canada! That's bound to impress them."

All right then... I think to myself. "I don't know if you've heard, but I changed my trail name recently. I didn't care for Mary Poppins so much. A woman with a magic purse and an umbrella; it doesn't really support my image. From now on I will be known as 75. Which stands for 75 pounds, the weight of my pack without food and water."

Excuse me? 75 pounds? That's the base weight of his pack? And he's proud of that? Not exactly ultra-light. It's a miracle he's come this far. Although, if I think about it... if you add water and food, he allegedly would have walked through the desert with 100 pounds on his back. Um... I think he may have had a few more of those 'helicopter' rides.

Places like Kennedy Meadows and Casa de Luna are also referred to as a 'Vortex'. A tornado-like wind that sucks you in. Whenever you run into a hiker on the trail who says he's behind on schedule, all you have to say is: "Vortex?" and they'll mostly answer, "Yep, got sucked right into it." Especially solo hikers tend to stick around. They are especially vulnerable to the magnetism of togetherness, fun, stories, and friendship, after being alone on the trail for some time. It helps them gather their strength and it boosts their morale for the next part of the trail. Despite all the fun we're having here, we've already decided to set off again today. We're on a mission! We are four days ahead of schedule and we intend to keep that advantage for as long as we can. Having fun is great, but if we lose our discipline this could turn into a whole other kind of journey; and we still have a very long way to go…

We finish our delicious hamburger, round off our conversations and now it's time to run our errands. We start off at the only shop in town, that also functions as the local post office. We pick up our resupply package and our 'bounce-box'; a special box full of equipment, that will be bounced forward during our entire hike. Back in San Diego, when we sent our resupply packages and maps to key locations along the trail, we purposely sent the bounce-box to this place. It contains our winter gear. Starting now, we're going into the high mountains and we need to change our equipment. Extra layers of clothing, ice axes, crampons, gaiters… It's all in there. A lot of fresh snow has fallen in the mountains a few weeks ago, but it might not be so bad now. So the question is; do we need it all? It is a whole lot of extra weight for us to carry.

Lucky for us there's a National Park Ranger in town today. We hope he can answer some of our questions. We see him at a table in the back. He's wearing a beige hat, there are dents in the top and a leather band around it. On the left sleeve of his shirt is a brown-green shield. It depicts a tree and a bison. Pinned to his chest is something that looks like a police badge. Yep, he's the real deal. "Sir, we're going up into passes that are 14,000 feet high. We don't want to sink down to our waist in the snow. Could you please tell us what the snow depth is in the various passes? Do you think we'll need our ice axes for the traverses on the steep slopes?" He is eager to help us, and seems to be afraid he might forget something, so a fountain of words streams out of his mouth. He looks me in the eye from under the brim of his hat and says, "Most of the snow is already melting. It's going to be a dry year in California." He takes a calm breath and continues, "Most passes are already open to experienced and well-equipped people, and by the time you get there, I don't think you'll need your ice axe at all." Wow, that's good news. "Do we need our crampons?" He shakes his head. "No, no need for crampons. But did you bring microspikes? The snow melts during the day and freezes up at night. Without microspikes it can get pretty slippery on some parts of the trail." Good thing we put those in our box too. Great! We nod. "Yes, we brought them. Thank you so much for the advice!"

We look for a quiet place in the shadow and cut open our bounce-box carefully. We empty it completely and examine the contents. Yes! Finally, there they are: our Gore-Tex rain pants. It's curious how intensely you can long for the strangest things. Lian goes straight for the extra layers of Merino wool. That'll come in handy. She doesn't want to get freezing cold again. My brand new half-high Gore-Tex mountain boots are there too. Those will take some getting used to. They weigh a bit more than our airy trail running shoes, but we're definitely going to need them. The support they will provide for our ankles, as well as dry feet, is absolutely essential where we're going, up into the snowy mountains. Among the contents of the box I also find my hair clipper. It is about time I had a haircut; it's grown more than an inch. I open up my compass, and as I look into the mirror, I move the hair clipper over my head quickly. There, all done. It might not be fashionable, but it sure is practical.

We decide to leave the ice axes and the crampons in the box, to save weight. But the umbrella... um... It's great in the rain, but in the strong wind on the mountain passes it'll probably break. We have to choose; we can't take everything. We end up putting the umbrellas in the box. The desert shoes and the hair clipper too. We look at the contents of the box carefully one last time, and then we tape it shut. We forward it to South Lake Tahoe, a small town north of the high Sierra Nevada mountain range. It will be summer when we arrive there, and we'll need to change our gear again. We leave the store and outside we notice the crates again. "This is the biggest hiker box I've ever seen. Look at it. There's all kinds of stuff." I look through the crates with Lian and find half-empty tubes of sunscreen, old shoes, spare food, and plastic bags filled with all kinds of stuff. I laugh and say, "If you close your eyes, this is like the biggest grab bag you could ever imagine. You never know what you might pull out of it!"

Just like us, many other hikers have chosen this place as a key point in their journey. This is where they replenish their food supply and switch their gear. Weight saving is essential for ultra-long-distance hiking. So, everything that's superfluous, is sent home or dropped in a hiker box. Another hiker passing by might have forgotten or broken something and could be in dire need of whatever you leave behind. It's a proven way to help each other out.

During the first five weeks of the trail, statistically around a third of all the hikers have already quit. They quit for all kinds of reasons: physical problems, mental problems, homesickness, shortage of money, issues at home with family or work... However, the biggest fall out will be in the next month, hiking straight through the middle of the high Sierra Nevada mountains. The main feature being the 14,505-foot-high climb of Mount Whitney. It's not mandatory to climb it, but it is the tallest mountain in the contiguous United States and the Sierra Nevada, so most people, like us, want to climb it anyway.
When talking to the other hikers, we've noticed that not many of them are experienced hikers in this environment. We're curious to see if they'll all make it. For us, this is like coming home. We feel very at ease in the mountains, so we decide to extend our daily hike with an extra four miles to a grand total of twenty miles a day. Within that distance we will climb and descend at least one mile every day. We know what this will entail. If the snow conditions are mild, it's definitely doable. And what's more... we can walk during the day and we don't have to carry gallons of water anymore!

Part Two
High Altitude

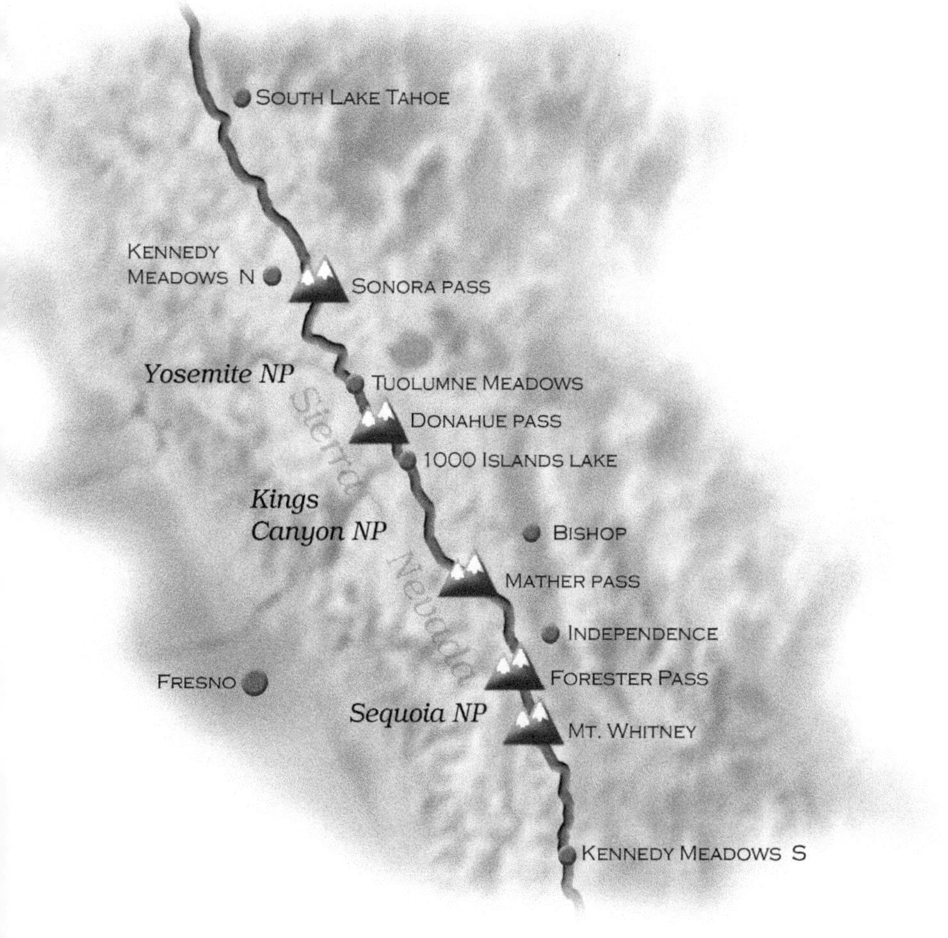
South Lake Tahoe
Kennedy
Meadows N
Sonora pass
Yosemite NP
Tuolumne Meadows
Donahue pass
Sierra
1000 Islands lake
Kings
Canyon NP
Bishop
Nevada
Mather pass
Independence
Fresno
Forester Pass
Sequoia NP
Mt. Whitney
Kennedy Meadows S

Bear in the Night

A full moon rises tonight. We watch in awe as the big red ball climbs slowly up into the sky; it's an amazing sight to see. It isn't completely dark yet, but even though the sun isn't visible anymore, the hills and mountains in the distance still have a beautiful purple-orange glow. It's seven o'clock at night, we leave Kennedy Meadows in good spirits and start our first six-mile hike towards the Sierra Nevada Mountain Range. The moon climbs higher and higher into the sky. The purple sky turns into a deep blue-grey color and the detailed outlines of the mountains disappear. There's no need to switch on our headlamps. There is enough moonlight for us to see the trail and everything around us. We slowly ascend. All the other hikers are spending the night in Kennedy Meadows, so there are no distractions out here. It's quiet and peaceful, serene even. Shadows dance around us playfully, and there are no distractions at all in this black-and-white landscape.

A twig snaps, there's rustling in the bushes. Lian is alarmed instantly. "I hear something.
There! Something's moving!" she calls out. Right in front of us, in a small gully, we see a shadow moving. It shuffles towards us. The light of the moon is enough to see where we're going, but not enough to see what's out there. "I have no idea what that is. Let's turn on our lights," I say. We get the headlamps out of the side pockets of our backpacks, fix them on our heads and turn on the lights.

"A bear!" Lian cries out.

A big, broad-shouldered black bear is crossing our trail, and he's growling at us intensely. It's getting pretty close and we can clearly see the outlines of its body. We shine our lights in its face. The bear's eyes are wide open, and they

reflect the light, like two giant, glowing glass marbles. We look it straight in the eye. It looks straight back at us and all three of us are completely still, frozen in this moment in time.
We start yelling,

"Hey bear, go away bear!"
"Yo, bear!"
"Hey, bear!"
"Go away bear!"

We grab our hiking poles and bang them together loudly, repeatedly. The bear lowers its head a bit, shakes it side to side and moves out of our lights slowly. Suddenly it takes off very fast and runs right into another gully. We can't see it anymore, so we have no idea if it's moving away from us or if it's circling back around. Our hearts are in our throats.

"Hey bear! Go away bear!"

We shout until our voices are hoarse. There it is again, in the beam of one of our lights. Fortunately, the bear is now running away from us, up the hill. We follow it with our lights and continue walking, cautiously, looking out to see if it may want to follows us. A grizzly bear can occasionally follow you for days, to see if it can get a meal from you, or perhaps even turn you into a meal. It hardly ever happens though. Black bears normally don't do that at all but you never know. Better safe than sorry.

The bear doesn't show up again, but we keep shouting loudly in this otherwise silent night. We increase our pace and shine our lights everywhere. Lian keeps looking behind her, she doesn't feel secure at all. We're too scared to stop so we don't set up camp for another hour. We've run into bears before, but always during the day and usually in an open environment, where there are escape routes for both us and the bears, so there was never any reason for tension between us.

What an exciting nightly adventure! I doubt we'll ever forget this and we certainly don't want to repeat it ever again. Sometime later, we're lying in our tent, still on high alert, reacting to every little sound we hear.

The next morning, after a restless night, this encounter made us laugh a little. It's a funny thing; we took a bear-behavior training course in Alaska once, where we were taught by National Park Rangers how to deal with bears. Because of that, even though it's not our native language, we shout at bears in English automatically. As if they could understand us better in English…

We spend the next few days walking in a transitional area. We're getting higher and higher, and slowly but surely all the cacti and Manzanitas are replaced by tall pine trees. They are Bristlecone and Foxtail Pines, the oldest living beings on Earth. Some are more than four thousand years old. The landscape is surreal. Many of these pines are twisted in strange ways, like spirals. It's like they've tried to follow the sun, around and around. Most of the trees don't have much bark left on them. If you didn't know any better, you would think that they're either dead, or dying. You couldn't be further from the truth; it is their natural form. Right next to their bare, sun-bleached beige wooden interior, there are dark-brown pieces of bark, with tiny twigs and needles on them. The tree takes its time to grow, and lives in its own momentum. It is amidst these ancient beings that we set up camp and marvel in amazement at everything we see.

Mount Whitney

It's getting late when we arrive at the foot of Mount Whitney. We've had a long day and I'm exhausted. The high altitude takes some getting used to. André is tired too, but he appears to be a lot fitter than I am. We ran into a friend today, Cloud Rider, an excellent hiker who walks at a much higher pace than we do. He covers more ground too. Without realizing it, we've adapted our pace to his and although we had a great time, it probably wasn't such a good idea. I feel drained. This day was too long, and there were too many miles in it.

The next morning I feel beat. I wonder if I'm the right state of mind to be climbing a summit. The trail runs along the foot of Mount Whitney, not over the top. It's not mandatory for the PCT but we're here now anyway and the men really want to climb it. It's such a long way up. My body says no, but my mind wants to go. It's still early, I might feel better in a little while. The guys are packing their backpacks, and I start packing mine as well. It's a long climb, and we want to get there and back in one day, so we're not staying at the summit overnight.
We leave the tents where they are, and since the weather's good, we decide not to bring an air pad and sleeping bag. We're thinking lightweight and quick. If the weather turns bad, we'll turn back right away. Unfortunately, there's no way of checking the weather forecast because there's no cell phone reception out here. So, we'll do it the old-fashioned way: staring at the clouds. I ask André if it's okay if I leave my backpack behind, and if he'll carry rain gear and lunch for the both of us. I don't tell him how I feel. "No problem," he replies cheerfully. A few moments later he swings the backpack on his back. Cloud Rider is ready to go too and we're off. At first it's all nice and easy. The trail is reasonably level for the first hour and we pass a few

lovely lakes, but pretty soon I can see the trail winding up a rugged rock face in front of us. I start the ascent, which is okay for now. So far, the path isn't very difficult. I look up and estimate that it'll be another two hours or so until we reach the snowy cliffs. We keep going and we're having fun talking and taking in the view.

"This place is amazing! Look at this view. It's astonishing!" André says. He is truly in his element here in this pure, rough open space. He's right, it is unbelievably beautiful out here, but on the inside, I feel empty and I can't genuinely enjoy it. Could it be the high altitude? I've been up in the high mountains before, but that doesn't always mean anything. If you're not fit, a higher altitude can surely have an effect on your wellbeing. But I am extremely fit, right? Maybe it was the long day we had yesterday, or just that I didn't get enough sleep to recuperate properly. Hundreds of thoughts like these run through my mind. I'm climbing slowly, as I should. It's like André always says, "I…am…a…snail…" Take one step for each word, in super slow-motion and monitor your heart rate. As soon as you start to feel out of breath, slow down. I'm not out of breath and my heart rate is fine, so that's not the problem. What is wrong with me? The guys are conducting a lively conversation. They look like they're having fun and they don't seem to have any problems. I'm starting to fall back. My head starts to drop. They don't notice. I decide to speak up, "Hey guys, please wait up. I need to sit down for a minute." I've already made up my mind, but they have no idea yet.

Halfway up the mountain we stop. André looks at me and immediately sees that something's not right. "What's wrong, sweetie?" he asks. "I can't do it. I feel drained and I don't know why," I reply. He takes off his backpack and sets it down next to me. He crouches down and gets me something to eat. Jellybeans, sweet candy. I put a few in my mouth and start chewing.

He hands me a bottle of water. Cloud Rider has arrived too, so we switch to English.
"Are you okay, CookieMonster?" he asks. I shake my head. André examines my expression. The candy helps, and I feel a bit better. Apparently, I needed some extra energy and water but the overall ill feeling is still there. They really want to go up there. How am I going to tell them that I can't go on? I think about it for a second, but then I look them in the eye and say, "Guys, I don't think I can go any further." They stay silent, it takes a minute to sink in. "I think it would be irresponsible for me to go on." I explain how I feel, and that my mind isn't in the right place for a climb like this. Especially further on, when we'll have to defy the steep snowy slopes near the top, without an ice axe. What if we fall and our only way to keep from sliding all the way down is to use our hiking poles as brakes... I need a clear mind for situations like that. We take a long break and talk a lot. They are so nice to me and André even proposes to walk back down with me. "That isn't necessary. You guys can go on, the weather is still great and the people that spent the night at the summit will be coming back down soon. I'll hike back down with them. I don't feel so poorly that I need someone with me at all times." The guys stand around, hesitantly.

"Go, I'll be fine."

So, our paths divide halfway up the mountain. The men ascend at a good pace and try to get back as soon as possible. I'm taking all the time I need to go down. There's no rush and I feel much better with this weight off my shoulders. When I get back down to the foot of the mountain, I look up and spot André's bright red raincoat easily against the snow-white slope. They're almost there. I take a long break and talk to some of the other hikers. Slowly I follow the trail down to our campsite. When I arrive two hours later, I go straight to bed and fall asleep instantly.

It's already evening when the guys wake me up. They're back and they've made me a wonderful bowl of vegetable broth. Delicious! They made it all the way to the summit and enjoyed the amazing view up there. They show me some pictures on their phones. It looks incredible, it's so high up that you can see lots of mountain peaks far away in the distance. The picture of the two of them smiling ear to ear, standing next to the plaque at the summit sticks with me the most. I feel a bit sad about not making it there myself, but I'm glad I didn't go. Also, I'm very happy that everyone is back in one piece, and there's bound to be another brand-new adventure waiting for us tomorrow.

Euphoria

"WooooW! I feel like I'm tripping!!!" I call out to Lian. One of the most beautiful views I have ever seen in my life reveals itself in front of me. Tears well up from deep down inside me. The pureness of the untainted landscape pierces through every pore of my skin and the overwhelming magnificence of what I'm seeing is almost too much. This pass is, without a doubt, the highlight of the journey so far. I feel deep emotions surfacing. I'm exhausted; there's no shield to stop them from flowing freely, even if I wanted to, so I let it all go. Tears of bliss stream down my face and I can feel every fiber in my body fully engaging in this experience. It's so intense!
I look back for a second. Behind me I see the steep trail winding up over the sharp, pink granite. Two bright blue lakes lie peacefully in the valley beneath us. It's almost a tropical kind of blue, like two sapphires in a rugged, rocky landscape. In the far distance we can just make out Mount Whitney. Oh man, this is amazing!! I turn back around. Lian is a bit further down and she's waving at me. She is enjoying this as much as I am. Right next to her is a small sign: "Sequoia National Park, Forester Pass, Elevation 13,200 FT." This is the highest pass on the PCT.

It's the surprise of this moment that makes me so emotional. After a very steep and difficult climb, we finally arrived at a narrow pass, and suddenly we were there, completely unexpected, right on the edge of Kings Canyon. The immense scale and the pure beauty of this impressive landscape in front of us, makes me feel humble, and intensely happy. A beautiful sharp mountain ridge stretches out before our feet. It dives almost straight down on the right side, on the left it levels out into the deep valley below. We can see all the high peaks, it's like looking at an impressive mountain range from above. The sky is blue and clear as a bell.

Towards the valley we notice a few light, thin clouds that look like they're on a quest to climb the mountains too. Slowly, the wisps of mist crawl up the mountainside, only to disappear into thin air when they reach the top. It's a magical dance of inception and disintegration, repeating itself over and over again. There's snow out here, a lot of it. It's a good thing we brought our microspikes. As it turns out, we really need them. Our good friends Snowman, Cloud Rider, Little Bear and Aquanaut are here with us. We've been hiking as a group for the past couple of days and it's been great! We're sharing this amazing moment together, having wonderful conversations as we put on our spikes.

The first part of this trail has a steep side slope, so we start zigzagging our way down through the snow. Fortunately, it's not too bad. We're glad we decided to start early today, because there's still a thin layer of ice on top of the soft snow. We don't sink in very deep and it doesn't take long for the trail to level out. At this point we've reached the sharp ridge that we saw from the pass. It looked quite difficult from above, but it turns out to be wider than we thought, and the snow isn't much trouble either. Like a bunch of bearded dwarves, we follow our princess Lian. It looks like a movie scene straight out of Hollywood; five dusty, fully packed hikers on an epic quest, out on the mountain ridge, dramatic landscape in the background. It even feels like a movie scene, too. Slowly we descend and one by one we vanish into the mist. What an adventure.

Hollow Inside

I still don't understand what's wrong with me? My thoughts keep drifting off. I look around at my surroundings. Sand has been replaced by blocks of granite, steep cliffs, and deep crevasses. We are in the Sierra Nevada Mountain Range. This area has the largest concentration of high mountains in the United States, aside from Alaska and it's absolutely amazing, so why am I not enjoying it as intensely as I thought I would? Ever since Mount Whitney, I've been feeling tired, sluggish, like I have no energy at all. It's depressing. I'm walking the miles, but it's not going as smoothly as it was in the beginning. Maybe I shouldn't worry about it, but still…

"What do you think? Could it be the distance, or the altitude? After all, we have increased our daily distance and we often go over 10,000 feet high," I ask André. He frowns and says, "I don't know, sweetie. It might be the altitude, because it's not like you're not eating enough, and we take enough breaks. You don't have a fever, do you?" I think about that for a moment. No, I don't. It feels like I'm hollow inside, run-down and weak. I make a decision: "Our food is running low, so we have to go down tomorrow anyway, to resupply. I'd like to go and see a doctor." It doesn't take him a second to think about it and he nods in agreement.

We've been high up in the mountains for a week now and we're arriving at Kearsarge Pass. This is where we say goodbye to Little Bear, Aquanaut and Snowman. They have enough food for now, so they're going to keep going. Cloud Rider is coming down with us since he needs to resupply too. The PCT runs through pure wilderness here and there's nothing out here but bears, ground squirrels, birds, fish, and beautiful plants. There are no towns nearby.

To restock, you have to take a hard turn off the trail and walk down the mountain. Kearsarge Pass is one of the few places that has a passage out of the wilderness. We hike down the mountain for an entire day, hitch a ride for the last part and end up in the small town of Independence. We pick up our resupply package at the post office and find a cute little inn. We quickly discover that there's no doctor here. There is a hospital in a town called Bishop, which is about twenty-five miles down the road. We leave everything in the hotel room and hitch-hike to Bishop.

It's a quiet little town that looks like a set from a Wild West movie. It wouldn't take much to make it look that way: remove the cars, put in some horse carriages and you're done. Fortunately, the hospital looks modern. I talk to the doctor and he wants to do a complete blood count. We have to wait for the results to come in, which could take a few hours, so we decide to go for a walk around town. The houses are nice. Many have wooden verandas, decorated with hanging baskets full of colorful flowers. We find an outfitter store and decide to go in.

There are lots of bears on the trail, so we need to protect our food. Right now, we're using a 'Bear Proof Food container', which is a solid, strong synthetic cylinder. A bear can't open it or break it. It's mandatory to use them in all the Sierra Nevada National Parks. They are quite heavy though, so we don't carry them on the entire trail. There are far lighter alternatives you can use to protect your food, like an Ursack: a white bag made of Kevlar, a material also used in bulletproof vests. We're curious to see if this outfitter sells something like that. We're in luck, they have a few in stock and we buy the biggest one. We leave the packaging behind and head back to the hospital. A friendly lady opens the door for us. "The doctor is expecting you," she says. We go inside. The doctor shakes our hands and points us to the two chairs in front of his desk. We sit down.

"Okay, I think we've figured out what the problem is." He looks at me with a neutral expression and says, "We've found something in your blood count, certain indications, which could explain why you've been experiencing fatigue lately." I tap my fingers on the desk a bit nervously.
"You said you've been hiking up in the mountains for quite some time now. What have you been eating?" What have I been eating? I answer him as truthfully as I can, "Well, mostly freeze-dried food. Usually we eat lots of dried vegetables with pasta, rice, or mashed potatoes. It's lightweight and nutritional. We hydrate it and cook it. We often have broth or noodle soup as an appetizer."
I explain our food schedule to him, including the sweet snacks in the morning and salty nuts in the afternoon. "And whenever we come across a town, I eat pancakes with maple syrup or a hamburger and fries, one more if I'm able to, with large dessert. When I get really hungry, I can eat all of that in one meal," I say grinning. Every day we burn about three times more calories than an average person and I need to maintain my weight.
"Well, that is probably part of the problem as well, you see," He pauses for a second, then continues, "It's not that you're not eating enough food or that it's not varied enough for the trail, but you wouldn't be the first hiker to come in here with some kind of malnourishment. Your electrolytes are out of balance, or in other words: quite a few of your reserves are completely empty."

I look at him, flabbergasted. What? No illness or infection? Electrolyte imbalance? Huh? "But, how? We take a multi-vitamin pill every day, and we take electrolytes, too. It even tastes good," I blurt out. He pauses before he answers, "Still, it looks like this is the problem. It's possible that what you're using is in fact not suitable for what your body needs. We've discovered a clear deficiency in potassium and magnesium, but your blood work also shows low levels of phosphate and chloride." He goes on to explain how a shortage of these minerals relates to my symptoms and tells me he's confident that the electrolytes he's prescribed for me will be a good supplement. We thank him and leave the doctor's office with peace of mind. This is not a scary illness, it's a fixable problem! We've been on the trail for about six weeks, and apparently the physical exertion, combined with my eating habits have completely exhausted my body.

At the pharmacy we get the prescription filled and buy four big boxes of electrolytes, because André is going to take them too, just in case. We treat ourselves to a Mexican meal and then hitch a ride back to Independence. Although, that doesn't quite go according to plan.

It's pitch-black. We're sitting down on the side of the highway. Hours go by, fewer and fewer cars drive past us. We hold our thumbs up for every car, but so far no one will take us. I rest my head on André's shoulder. I'm worried. "What do we do now? We can't sleep on the side of the road, can we? All our stuff is back at the hotel. We didn't bring anything." He puts his arm around me and says, "Let's not think about that just yet. We could still find a ride. Sometimes it takes a while to get lucky."

It was easy to hitchhike to Bishop, but that's not the case hitching out. It's been a nightmare ever since the town center; we couldn't find anyone by sticking our thumbs up in the air. After an hour, André started approaching cars at the traffic lights. It still took quite some time to find someone willing to take us. They were very friendly Native Americans, on their way back home from a shopping trip. They dropped us off on the side of the road in the middle of nowhere, at the exit towards their reservation. We got out of the back of the pick-up truck and said goodbye. That was four hours ago, and we haven't moved an inch. We're seriously starting to lose hope.

It's eleven o'clock at night. From the other side of the highway a car turns off the road. It turns around. The headlamps are coming straight at us. We jump up and start waving excitedly. The car passes, turns right, puts on its warning lights, and comes to a standstill in the emergency lane. We run up to the car. The window comes down slowly. A young man, with a sun-kissed face sticks his head out. "What are you doing on the highway at this time of night?" he asks. I start talking and he listens to our story. "Hmmm... I thought you might be in trouble, so I figured I'd pull over and see what's going on. Actually, I'm going the other way, to Bishop." Our faces dropped in an instant. Oh no, this can't be happening! He notices our disappointment. "Where are you staying?" he asks. We tell him the name of the town and the hotel. He takes a doubtful look at his back seat. "I'm not sure you'll both fit," he says. We look, too. The entire back seat is loaded, like he has everything he owns back there. As it turns out, he's moving to another town. "Don't worry, we'll make it work. We'll fit!" André quickly replies. The man smiles and says, "You know what? I'll take you. It's only twelve miles." André and I are overjoyed.

Our driver turns out to be a hiker too and he knows how hard hitchhiking can be. We move some stuff out of the front seat and André sits down. I climb on his lap. "Pull your head in, squeeze in a bit, and I can just close the door," André whispers softly. I'm folded up, squished against the ceiling. Fortunately, it's not a long drive. When we arrive at the hotel, we thank him again, the car door closes, and he disappears into the night. It'll take him three hours to reach his destination. We go up to our hotel room, collapse onto the bed and fall asleep instantly. What a day.

The Ravens

The next day we feel better than ever. It's a beautiful day. Lian is in a great mood and I'm setting up the first Skype connection of our journey with my best friends Chrétien and Anton. It's nice to see their faces again and listen to their stories. Proudly, I take the phone outside to show them where we are: in a hot valley with huge cold mountains on either side. We're headed for those mountains next. Several other hikers are getting ready to leave. We talk to a family called 'the Ravens'. Two parents with an eight-year-old girl and an eleven-year-old boy. They're hiking the entire PCT as a family. We've run into them a few times already, they're very friendly people that have become quite an inspiration to everyone on the trail. The children are home-schooled on the trail by their parents and we often see them doing fun stuff, like building a dam in a small stream, or playing a game in the shadow of a bridge. These parents have a lot of experience in the mountains. It's so nice to see them passing that on to their children.

Unfortunately, where we live, not many people have outdoor experience and therefore – understandably – they fear it, which leads to overprotective parenting. The Ravens' children, however, experience the outdoors in such a way that it enriches their lives. They don't have to look at a picture in a schoolbook, or a YouTube video, to see what a mountain, a bear, or a rattlesnake looks like. They live among them, experiencing the landscape, smelling the flowers, face to face with wild animals, and they are curious about everything they see. Like the children of the ancient tribes used to do, they learn how nature affects them and how to handle it. This will strengthen them and enrich their lives forever.

These parents are also teaching them solidarity on the trail; being there for each other and helping other people whenever you can, even if you've never seen them before. To treat everyone with respect and dignity, even if they are completely different from you, no matter their nationality, skin color, religion, or sexuality. Here they will learn that none of those things matter and that every human being is beautiful and amazing. It will balance out the input from the mostly negative and sensation-focused television broadcasts. These parents have the courage to give their children this amazing gift, and it's a wonderful process to witness. They will grow up to think for themselves, experience for themselves, and not to act rashly out of fear or ignorance.

We clean up and re-pack our backpacks. The lady who owns the hotel is nice enough to offer us a ride to a parking lot closer to the trail. From there, it's a one-day-hike up to the pass. Once we've crossed the pass, we set up camp near a small lake, with enough food to last for another six days. We take our time to fully enjoy the mountains, the deer, ground squirrels, birds, trout, and the pretty reflections on the water.

Lian is getting noticeably stronger every day. The doctor was right. It's amazing what a shortage of a few minerals can do to a person. She's still tired at the end of the day, but now it's a satisfying kind of tiredness, from hiking in the fresh air all day. The hollow feeling is gone and her face lights up like it always did. She smiles and marvels at every little thing she sees, like a child chasing a butterfly. I'm glad she's back.

Rescue in the Snow

The lake is completely frozen, except around the edges. The only sound we can hear is the soft creaking of the small sheets of ice scuffing up against each other. Actually, it's more like a soft ringing sound. We get a bit closer and see that this friction forges tiny crystals, standing straight up, like miniature ice peaks rising up from the lake. We feel like we're in the Antarctic, instead of the Sierra Nevada.

A small gust of wind picks up the fresh snow and twirls it up into the air. Other than that, it is quiet, silent even. A lot of snow has fallen in the past couple of days. Almost every afternoon, around three o'clock, clouds start coming together, only to unleash rain and thunder a few hours later. Usually, we see it coming just in time to set up camp but sometimes, like when we were climbing Mather Pass, the timing couldn't have been worse.

Dark clouds quickly come together and there's no shelter we can see anywhere. "Bang!!" The deep, loud thunder in the distance rolls over the rocky plains. We haven't seen any lightning yet. In front of us, far ahead, is what looks like an amphitheater of mountains, which amplifies the sound of the thunder. It's deafening and extremely humbling. It feels like we're small, naked, and alone in this immense open landscape. There's not a soul in sight. At the top of the resonating mountains we see the pass. Lian stops, looks at it and asks, "Shall we go on and take the pass or try to find emergency shelter somewhere?" Thick snow starts coming down from the sky and sticks to my pants. "I don't know... It will take us an hour-and-a-half to get to the pass, and who knows what the conditions will be up there tomorrow," I say doubtfully. It would be wise to find shelter here, but we're high up in the mountains and we don't see a safe place to make a shelter anywhere.

"Bang!!" Out of nowhere, the overwhelming loudness of the thunder takes us by surprise. Like cannon fire it blasts right through us. Visibility starts to wane, which makes us even more cautious.

"This is no place to put up a tent. If it turns into a full-scale thunderstorm we'll be blown to smithereens," I say as I scan our surroundings. "There's not even a ditch or a snow mound anywhere." We've seen plenty of safe places to hide in the past few days, but there's a fierce wind on this plain. Lian searches with me, her eyes fixed on the ground. "The snow is too thin to build our own wall," she says. She looks at the map. "There are lots of ditches on the other side of the pass. It's a lot steeper down there, and even further down there are trees. Maybe we can find a safe place there?" Our eyes lock and I nod in agreement. We decide to keep going. It doesn't feel completely right, but it's definitely not an option to stay here.

It doesn't take us long to reach the foot of the wall and we keep climbing up towards the pass. The wind picks up even more. Bang!!! This time it's ear-splitting and right next to us. Are we doing the right thing? The first lightning bolts shoot down from the sky. Until now, we hadn't noticed the strange deep-pink-grey color of the clouds around us. My warm down-filled beanie is covered in snow and the warmth of my head is making it melt, so the down is getting wet. Why didn't I think of that sooner? I pull the hood of my raincoat over the beanie. And it's a good thing I do, because we haven't even come halfway up the wall and the snow is coming down like crazy. We can't call it a blizzard just yet, but the snow is flying into our faces horizontally now. I'm still not sure about this. We can't see the pass anymore. "What do you think? Should we turn back?" I ask. Lian is carrying the altimeter; she looks at it and shakes her head. "No, if the height on this thing is still accurate, we'll reach the pass in about half an hour," she says.

I like the sound of that, and with our raincoats pulled closed tightly around our bodies we climb the last few feet up to the pass. Quickly, we make our way over the pass and it's true: this side is steeper. The only problem is that there is a thick layer of snow here. On the other side we could still see parts of the trail, but here it's nowhere to be seen! We turn on our smartphone and open the GPS app. Lightweight hiking is always about finding a balance between weight and necessities; it's a matter of compromise. If we had been in the mountains guiding a group, there's no doubt we would have brought more stuff. Like professional GPS equipment, that can always show us where we are, even in a deep crevasse that's sealed off by plants and trees. Now we have no choice but to put our faith in a cell phone. The app is thinking… a detailed area map is loading… no signal yet… we wait… and there it is, finally, the red arrow. It's found us, even under the thick snow-filled clouds, great! This probably saves us from making an emergency shelter in some shallow ditch. Just to be sure, we compare what's on the screen to the shape of the terrain; it matches.

Nevertheless, we can't see much in the snow, and it turns out that it's not so easy to follow the trail with only an app to guide us. "I don't like this at all," I say to Lian. "What do you mean?" She turns around, her backpack facing the wind and walks closer to me. "I may be 'Old School' or whatever, but I prefer a map and compass to find my way in these circumstances. I'd rather rely on the contours of the terrain than on a red arrow pointing to a trail I can't see." She stays quiet, waiting for me to continue. "Let's do this the old-fashioned way. I'll draw lines on the real map, and that way I can lay out a course through the terrain using waypoints. I can't really do that with this app. All I can do is follow the arrow and hope we're following the trail. It's not getting us anywhere and it's draining our phone battery." Lian knows exactly where I'm going with this and answers, "Let's do that then." I nod, draw the coordinates from the GPS onto the map and lay out a course.

We're heading for the tree line, that isn't visible yet in the dense snowfall. My arm is stretched out in the exact direction we need to go. I hold the compass in my open hand, I look over the top of it and see Lian ahead of me. With my other arm I show her which way to go. She moves from side to side and when she's perfectly aligned with my compass bearing, I signal her to stop. I walk over to her and we repeat the same process. It's slow, but it feels right. It's something we've done before, and we know it works well.

"What did you say?" Lian shouts to me from a distance. I look up from my compass. "I didn't say anything!" I call back. She stops and listens, and suddenly she raises her head up. "I hear someone yelling!" My arm drops. Yelling? Now? In this weather? It must be the wind. I don't hear anything. She points and says, "Over there!" I make a big cross in the snow with my feet, hoping I might find it again when we come back. Together we go in the direction she's pointing. Now I hear it too, a faint call in the distance. We look around and from far away we can just make out a young woman running down the mountain.
She keeps on screaming and shouting, and she's coming straight towards us. There's a terrified look on her face when she finally reaches us; her pupils are dilated, she's sweating and panting and cries out, "I'm so happy to see you!" She's completely wet from the melting snow and the sweat. Her open trail-runners aren't waterproof, so her feet are soaking wet and she's freezing cold. "What's your name?" Lian asks. "Sweetums," she answers, her face as white as a sheet. "Hi, Sweetums, we didn't expect to run into anyone out here in these conditions. Are you okay?" Lian asks, putting her arm around the poor woman. "I've been looking for you for so long! I'm all alone and then the lightning started. I got so scared and didn't know what to do. I found your tracks in the snow and started running like crazy to try to catch up to you." Her words fall out of her mouth like a runaway train.

She takes a quick breath and continues, "But after the pass, I lost your tracks. I couldn't find the trail either and just decided to walk down, hoping to find you. I've been calling out to you for about half an hour."

She's clearly very upset. Lian talks to her and tries to comfort her. In the meantime, I've picked up my compass again. I'm never going to find my cross in the snow, so I lay out a new, more direct course down to the trees. I want to get her out of this weather as soon as possible. Together we make our way down, this time just winging it with the compass in my hands. It's less accurate, but it's a lot faster.

After about an hour we reach the tree line, and we soon find a nice semi-circle full of man-high pine trees. It's still snowing quite heavily, but the trees break the wind, so it's a good place to set up camp. Sweetums is exhausted, so we help her with her tent. She is a textbook example of an 'ultra-light-weight-hiker'. Someone who covers super-long distances, carrying only the bare minimum. "It's always sunny in California, so I left lots of things at home," she tells us. It sounds a bit naïve to us. Warm sunny plains and beaches have nothing in common with the mountains. The mountains have their own weather systems, so you can never rule out snowfall in summer, especially at this altitude. We decide not to tell her this, because it wouldn't do her any good right now.

She's still very cold and she's having trouble getting warm in her sleeping bag. A sleeping bag doesn't produce any heat, it's an insulator. It only captures the warmth that your body generates. When you cool down too much, or when you're weak, you can still freeze to death in a good-quality sleeping bag. Her feet are ice-cold. She tried to save weight by not bringing any cooking equipment, so she's living primarily on protein and granola bars. There's nothing in her backpack to warm her up.

I look at her; she looks exhausted, confused, freezing and she keeps falling in and out of consciousness. If I don't do anything now, she might not make it through the night.

I use our own cooking gear to warm up a cup of coco for her, and she ends up drinking three of them. Immediately, she feels better. Her body is warming up, and her state of mind is definitely improving as well. Lian and I wait – in the falling snow – in front of her tent and make sure she keeps talking. She's comfortable now in her sleeping bag, that's getting increasingly warmer. She even laughs at my cheesy jokes and slowly she falls asleep. I wait a little longer, for my own peace of mind, until I hear her breathing regularly. Then I also go to bed.

The next day, she hikes down with us until we reach the snow line. We take a long break, dry out all our wet gear, and hang out our sleeping bags until they're all fluffy again. After the break, Sweetums feels like herself again. In high spirits and with a big smile on her face, she parts with us. Her pace is clearly a lot higher than ours and we never run into her again on the trail. I wonder if she made it to the end.

Our Morning Ritual

"It's funny to see that we're such creatures of habit," André says, as he stuffs his sleeping bag into its cover. Did he really just say that? That's not at all how I know him. I know I can be like that, but he doesn't really seem to have a schedule at all at home. He usually does whatever he feels like, or whatever he thinks of at the moment. I like stability a bit more but on trails like this he is different. It's nice to hold on to certain routines when you're in desolate places for long periods of time. It calms your mind. We have a clear division of tasks and a rhythm. Some kind of unwritten discipline that we hold ourselves to.

Our morning ritual starts with the alarm clock, which goes off at five o'clock these days. Whichever one of us is most awake, gets up first and tries to wiggle into their clothes, half-upright in bed. Then, the sleeping bag is packed, and the air pad is rolled up, so the other person has more room to get dressed. Once one of us gets outside, we put on a pot of water. While that's heating up, we fetch fresh water from the stream to sterilize. We use a Steripen for that; it's a small device, with a strong ultraviolet lamp on the tip. You stir it slowly in water for about 90 seconds, and it kills all the bacteria. André is responsible for hanging our food in a tree, and taking it back out, but at the moment there's no need for that since we're using a Bear Proof Food Container, which I usually retrieve from a remote location. I'm responsible for cooking, which includes breakfast. It's often quite simple, like oatmeal or granola, but that gets a bit boring after a while. On a long hike, it's important to keep the mind and the senses stimulated. For example, I like to make delicious, surprising breakfast packages up front with bits of dried apple and cinnamon, for example, or filled tortillas.

Today it's time for my tropical oatmeal recipe:

1 cup rolled oats
⅓ cup dried pineapple
⅔ cup shredded coconut
¼ cup chopped pecans
¼ cup chopped almonds
Powdered milk

While I cook, I divide the snacks and our trail food for the day. They are also varied, so that we eat something different every day. Energy bars, nuts, dried fruit, dried meat, candy, M&Ms, Oreo cookies. When we buy it, we basically go through the local supermarket's entire product range. While I'm busy preparing the food, André takes down the tent.
Because of bears, we always eat away from the tent. Usually we walk to a place where we have a good view of our surroundings, so we don't get surprised by nosey bears. We always try to find a spot with a nice view or a small river.

For the past few days, it's been pretty cold and morning frost covers the leaves. Nice and warm in our down coats and down beanies, we enjoy the delicious, beautiful beginning of this day. After breakfast, I make a nice cup of hot tea. This is how it goes, every day. Many hikers live on protein bars and other simple meals. They stuff it in and off they go. It's important to us to enjoy a nice breakfast and it makes for a wonderful start of our day. Since we've divided our tasks equally, it doesn't really take a lot of time, so we do it every single day.

André gets up in a rush, looking for the toilet paper and the scoop. Pooping in a hole in the ground is also an important part of the morning ritual. There isn't much time because his colon has started working already. He runs into the woods, finds a decent spot, and starts digging like a maniac.

According to wilderness etiquette, a poop hole should be about six inches deep, but that's a long dig when you're in a hurry! Especially in rocky soil like this. Normally we dig the hole in the evening, just after we set up the tent, but yesterday we forgot. I watch him hacking fiercely into the ground, desperately trying to hold it all in. We never have to wait long; our metabolism is in perfect condition, a welcome side-effect of a high-fiber diet, combined with lots of exercise.

To preserve and protect the wilderness, we don't leave anything behind, not even toilet paper. That is the law and that's how it should be. Used toilet paper doesn't go into the hole in the ground, we put it in a scent proof, waterproof plastic bag. We carry it with us – sometimes for as long as a week – all the way back to civilization where we can throw out our trash.

The ritual also entails washing ourselves in water from the creek. Not too much, just enough to stay clean. We hardly ever use soap and we never use deodorant; it'll only attract bears. Some hikers we meet don't really wash at all. Especially the men tend to take pride in their often troll-like appearance. It seems to be part of something called 'Hiker Trash'. We usually look pretty fresh, because we clean our bodies and our clothes regularly, which is also good for our mental state.

André also shaves, not every day, but regularly. The Hiker Trash scene often mistake us for day-tourists or weekend-hikers. We often hear them say, "You are way too clean to be real 'Thru Hikers'." It makes us laugh. We've been hiking through the wilderness longer than they've been alive. What we think they don't understand, is that hygiene is just as important here, as it is at home. Maybe even more important.

Hiker Trash don't shake hands on the trail, they 'fist bump'. When we came across this phenomenon for the first time, we asked them why they did it. "You never know where that hand's been," was the answer. Umm... we prefer to do things a bit more hygienically.

We finish our morning ritual by brushing our teeth and putting the last few things into our backpacks. The whole ritual, from waking up to leaving takes us about an hour and fifteen minutes on average. With food in our bellies and our minds in the right place, we're ready to go. We put on our backpacks and get back on the trail, towards another beautiful day with new and exciting adventures.

Pure Wilderness

The water is up to our knees. The current is strong and the cold cuts through our skin like a knife. We shouldn't linger here. Maybe we should have crossed the river side by side. In a flash I spot a trout, racing past my feet. My eyes want to follow it, but I don't let them. I focus all my attention on what I'm doing, as I lean on my hiking pole and take a step forward. The current grabs onto my leg and tries to pull it in, like a creature trying to pull you under. Just in case it succeeds, I've untied all the straps on my backpack. If I should fall, I can always escape and swim to shore, without the backpack pulling me down even further.

I put my back into it and my sandals touch the bottom, sending tiny pebbles up from the riverbed. The current sweeps them away, and they tap softly against the side of my foot. Lian calls out to me, "Are you okay?!" She's behind me, still in the shallow part. She's not as tall as I am, so she'll go in even deeper. I take another step. "The current is very strong here in the channel!" I call back, "Push back hard with your legs, you'll be okay!" Lian sticks her pole firmly into the riverbed, tests it for stability and then goes deeper into the water. I can't watch for long; the water is extremely cold and it's draining all the energy from my body. I have to keep going while my muscles still work. "It's getting very deep now!" I hear her say behind me. I look back; the water is almost up to her waist. She's got one pole to her right and the other to her left. She looks at me and asks, "Is it going to get any deeper?" The water splashes up against her right side, and on her other side a tiny whirlpool appears, with white tips that leave small ripples in the water. "No! This is the deepest part!" I answer. Her eyes stay fixed on me for another moment and she takes another step. For a second it looks like the current will sweep her away, but she finds her balance again. Strength takes over, uncertainty fades. She slams her poles into the riverbed and fiercely she pulls her body through the water. It doesn't even reach her thighs anymore, and she takes another step. I turn around and head for shore. Not much longer, she joins me on the riverbank. This is not our first river crossing, but this one was quite a bit wider, deeper, and wilder than the others.

The Sierra Nevada Mountain Range is a lot like a roller coaster; every day we ascend almost a mile and then descend just about the same. By now we've made it through the highest peaks and passes, so we rarely come across snow anymore. Most of it has melted, its water has run off into lakes and rivers, which we have to cross every day. They slow us down a lot. Shoes off, sandals on, wade through the water, sandals off, dry your feet, shoes back on and still we manage to hike at least twenty miles a day.

The landscape is changing; the bare, rough rocky terrain has more vegetation now. There are pine trees everywhere and you can smell 'green' in the air. No more desolate wilderness, everything is alive here.

"Hey, look at this. If we go up here, we can camp at a small lake," Lian says, bent over a map pointing at something. Behind her is an unbelievably phenomenal landscape. An impressive outstretched mountain, with patches of snow, rises up in the distance. On both sides, the ridges sink smoothly into the ground. In front of it, is a beautiful lake with an infinite number of small islands floating peacefully in the bright blue water, not a gust of wind, not a ripple in the water. We are on the banks of 1000 Islands Lake and it is breathtaking. We take it all in, enjoying every second of it.

After a short break we take the route Lian pointed out. There's no path so we scramble up the small wall, we step into a small ditch, I look up and suddenly freeze right then and there.

"I'll be damned," I blurt out. Startled, yet still calm we lock eyes for a second. Yellow, almost orange eyes stare straight at me. Grey-brown fur glistens in the sunlight. It's no more than 30 feet away from us, quietly, curiously, calmly watching us; one ear fixed on us, the other pointed to the right. It looks away, and then back; we stand there motionlessly. We've never seen a coyote before and we had expected to see them in the desert, not around here. It blinks slowly, lowers its head, and pretends to smell something interesting in the grass. The left ear is still fixed on us, registering every little move we make. The head lifts up quickly, but there's no change in posture, no fear or aggression. The coyote decides that it's time to part ways after this lovely interaction, and calmly trots away in the direction we're going. We see it off and then quietly follow it.

"Wow," I hear Lian say. The lake appears magically in front of us. "This is amazing!" I grin. Yes, this is a truly amazing place. We set up camp and take a walk around the lake. The view from the opposite side is spectacular. The pine trees reflect beautifully, almost life-like in the water, as if they were growing upside-down. The rocks and the tiny clouds also have razor-sharp reflections in the serene water. On the bank, on the other side of the lake, we can see our tiny little tent in the bright-green grass with the huge, rugged mountain ridges in the background. We take off our clothes and go for a swim. The water is cold, but the sun keeps us warm and dries us off quickly. We have the place to ourselves, except for the small creatures we hear all around us. It's incredible, like living in a Bob Ross painting.

Summer in Yosemite National Park

It's early in the morning when we arrive in Yosemite National Park at 11,066 feet. We are on top of Donahue Pass, looking out over a wide valley that stretches out as far as our eyes can see. To our left and right there are pine trees; through the middle there is only grass, with a lovely creek twisting and winding through the landscape. Yosemite is one of the most famous national parks in the USA and we've heard everyone talking about it on the trail for the past few days. It's supposed to be heaven on Earth. We visited this area a few years ago, and it's true: El Capitan, Half Dome, the Valley and Cathedral Peak are all amazing in their own way. But if we're honest, we think the Ansel Adams Wilderness and the John Muir Wilderness – that we just hiked through – are far more beautiful. The phenomenal landscapes we saw there every day were completely overwhelming and we could lose ourselves in them completely. We can't stop talking about it.

"It's like wandering around in 'Skyrim' or 'The Witcher' in real life," André says. He's talking about the adventure games he plays on his game console all through winter. The hero in those games always roams around immeasurable landscapes, trying to solve near impossible tasks. They always come across the strangest creatures and animals too. I chuckle, because I never made the connection until now: In winter he can't go on adventures like that in real life, so he makes do with virtual ones. I wonder if he realizes this about himself.

At the far end of the valley we spot a few hikers. It's been a while since we've seen anyone on the trail; in our last break all we saw was a couple of rainbow trout. It was very quiet there. But now that we're leaving this amazing valley, things are about to change.

"It's like a circus, full of people," André says as we walk into Tuolumne Meadows. He doesn't like crowded places, especially when we're fresh out of the wilderness. "Look at all these people, cars and buses. I don't remember it being this busy." He looks around, while the smell of fuel, fast-food and freshly bathed people threatens to overwhelm us.

Yosemite is the most visited park in the USA. In summer, millions of people travel here to go on day hikes, many of which start in Tuolumne. It's very busy with all the traffic but then we see a lot of friendly faces as we get closer. I love it! André and I are clearly out of sync here; he wants to leave as soon as possible. This is way too crowded for him. I want to stay; talk to people we haven't seen in weeks and listen to all the adventures everyone's had. This place is packed with PCT-hikers and we know why: there's a campsite here and a hamburger place, so it's a great spot to recharge. Some stay for a bit longer and take the bus to Yosemite Valley to see the rest of the park.

"Hey, that's Cuban B," André says. I look in the direction of the white hamburger place and see a small, thin man walking around with a huge burger in his hands. Yes, it's him alright. We start waving enthusiastically and walk up to him. Cuban B is an American nurse with Cuban roots. Whenever we see him on the trail, he always makes us smile. With his short legs, he walks at a surprisingly high pace, and he talks even faster. He's a big happy chatterbox. "How have you come this far already?" he asks us. "I haven't seen you since the desert and you've caught up with me already. I didn't think you hiked that many miles a day?" He seems a bit surprised. "Well, we didn't at the beginning of the trail. We wanted to ease into it, but we decided to speed up towards the end of the desert and here in the mountains, we can cover more ground than most people," I answer. It's good to see him and we have fun catching up on things or rather, he tells story after story and I listen.

In the meantime, André gets us a couple of burgers. When he returns, Cuban B is still talking lively about all kinds of things: about hikers he's seen recently, some of whom have quit by now. He also tells us about a hiker who hit her head on the rocks when she fell and had to be rescued by a helicopter. This friendly chatterbox just keeps on talking. Sometime later we end up talking to a few other hikers as well, like the Australian Wallaby: a funny man in his sixties, strong and tough, then Teflon: a young woman in her early twenties. I ask them about everything and I am so happy. The hamburger does what it's supposed to and I feel completely satisfied. Not just by the food, but especially because of the lovely, warm atmosphere and the wonderful conversations. I'm all caught up on everyone's lives.

In the distance I see someone coming this way, in his unmistakable white outfit and cap. "Cloud Rider!" I call out excitedly. We guessed that he'd be a day or so behind us and now he's here already. He laughs and says, "CookieMonster and Morning Star. I haven't seen you since Bishop!" He gives us both a big hug and then turns to me, "How did your visit to the hospital go?" We sit down at a table and I tell him the whole story. "Wow, that's quite the adventure!" He's been through a thing or two himself and I love listening to all his adventures. He's making a quick stop here, just like us. "I have to walk a lot of miles per day to get to South Lake Tahoe on time. It's about another 150 miles and I only have six days to get there," he explains, "My wife has booked a nice weekend for us and I really have to get there in time." He's hiking on his own and she's flying in from home. South Lake Tahoe is quite far from here, so I see why he's in a hurry. André and I spend every day together and share all our experiences. It's nice that his wife can be with him a few times during his six-month trip. We give him a final big hug and say goodbye. As it turns out, his daily mileage eventually gets so high, it's impossible for us to catch up.

In the tiny shop, a long line of people are waiting at the counter. "Oh boy, it's like a carnival in here," André says. Day-tourists and PCT-hikers wait patiently for their turn. André looks at the shop assistant, who is extremely busy doing multiple things at once: phone in hand, writing stuff down and listening to customers, all at the same time. He looks quite stressed out. Hikers' boxes in all colors and sizes are piled up against the walls, hundreds of them... It turns out almost every PCT-hiker sends their resupply package here – sometimes more than one. It seems like a smart thing to do, because it's a very practical point on the trail. So clearly, this is chaos. Another shop employee picks up three boxes, puts them on the counter and gives them to a customer. We get in line and wait for our turn. "André, I hope they have a system, because I don't see our box anywhere," I say a bit nervously. He looks at the piles of boxes. "You stay in line and I'll go and see if I can find our box."

We always put something we can recognize on our boxes, in this case huge red Smiley stickers. We can usually spot our box from a mile away, but this time we can't. André returns after ten minutes and says, "I don't see it anywhere." It's beginning to make me nervous and I answer, "We have six days to go to the next resupply-point. What do we do if it's not here? We can't survive on a couple of burgers and whatever cookies and chips they sell in this shop." André grins and says, "Then we'll buy up the whole store and eat the same thing every day." Yeah, we probably will, but that doesn't make me feel better at all. It's a good thing we're almost at the front of the line.

"How can I help you?" Even with all this stress the man at the counter remains friendly. "We are Lian and André de Jel. There should be a package for us. We're PCT-hikers. There are a couple of large red smiley stickers on the box." I stop talking and wait anxiously for an answer. He looks at me and asks, "Do you have an ID? A passport or something like that?" We show him our passports, and he starts looking through a notebook that looks a bit like a register. "One moment, please," he says. He gets up from his seat and talks to someone else. The other man leaves. "My co-worker is going to take a look. Can you wait?" Of course we can. The line seems to be getting longer and longer and he goes to the next customer. More hikers start pouring in. Apparently, a bus has just arrived with hikers returning from a day trip to the valley. Some of them buy food. I hope they leave enough for us to buy if our package isn't here. We've heard stories about packages not arriving... My mind is filled with all these anxious thoughts. It's nerve-racking. After about five minutes the co-worker is back, with a box, our box! Happy and relieved, I take the box from his hands. Apparently, it was stashed somewhere in the back.

We empty the box into our backpacks and go to the hamburger place next door to get an enormous ice-cream with chocolate chips on top. André is getting restless; he wants to get going, away from this crowded place. We fill up our water bottles and put on our backpacks, which are heavy with food now. That'll take some getting used to again: from an empty backpack this afternoon, to a full one now. In high spirits we set off on the trail. It doesn't take long for the crowds to disappear, and a few hours later we're alone again. We find a nice open spot, level and green. A bit further on, a marmot is munching on a few red flowers. A nice creek flows right by us and we're surrounded by green pine trees. This feels like the trail again. We're home. We set up camp and go to sleep.

Bzzzzzzzzzzzz

"What kind of freaky creature is that? It's like something out of a science-fiction movie," Lian says. She's on one knee and with large eyes she's following this little critter crawl across the ground in front of us. I laugh loudly. It's stumbling along a bit clumsily. Its long lower body has black, yellow, and white rings on it, with pink dots on the sides. Its upper body is short and plump with big black flaps on the side, also with pink dots on them. Its head is made up entirely of yellow fluff, with very wide antennae on top. Lian bows down closer to the ground to get a good look. "I have no idea what that is," she says, and looks at me like I might know. Slowly the creature hobbles on. It's about three inches long, and it's the strangest insect I've ever seen in my life. I make a short video with my phone and post it in our PCT-hiker group with this question in the caption: "Look who decided to come over for coffee. Who knows what this is?" It doesn't take long for the first hilarious answers to come in. "Aliens have landed.", "Nothing you want to run into at night!", "Stuff of nightmares! That's why I won't go cowboy camping ever again!" We have a lot of fun reading these, but there is someone who actually knows what it is. "Great footage man! I've never seen one filmed like this before. It's a Sheep Moth that's just crawled out of its cocoon. I've only ever seen it in pictures. Cool man, thanks for sharing!"

The moth isn't the only thing undergoing a transformation; the landscape is changing too. We've left the Sierras for the most part, and it's clearly noticeable. High pointy mountains and deep valleys slowly give way to lower, more rounded hilltops with wide rivers and lots of lakes for us to swim in. We won't encounter much snow, with the exception of maybe one or two higher passes, but it's mostly beautiful alpine meadows covered in flowers.

The growing season is quite short here, which is why flowers appear everywhere, like an explosion and within a week the whole place is completely covered in them. We notice another big change that takes place here. The wild array of flowers and the many lakes practically give it away: Mosquitos are everywhere and you can hear hundreds of them, day and night...

Bzzzzzzzzzzzzzzzzzzzzz. "Where is my mosquito net?" I look around, but I don't see it and I really have to go outside to pee. Each day now begins with packing up everything inside the tent, because, they're already waiting for us outside. Lian helps me look for it, and I finally find it. The net somehow managed to get under my air pad. I put the net over my head, put the bottoms of my pants in my socks and quickly open the inner tent. The canopy is littered with mosquitos. Like tiny black vultures they perch on the fabric, waiting for their prey. The first ones are already flying into the inner tent. I quickly open the outer tent and make a run for it. Lian closes the inner tent as fast as she can and goes on a mosquito-killing-spree.

"This is not working!" I call out, frustratedly. It seems to be even worse today. "What's wrong?" Lian says from the tent. "Have you ever tried to pee with hordes of mosquitoes flying around you?" I answer. "Yes, what do you think? Last night, my bum was covered in bites! And it's quite itchy!!" she shouts back. It's true, and the warmth of the sleeping bag only made it worse. She couldn't stop scratching. But I can't focus on that right now, like a mad man I move around and try to pee at the same time. I really don't want any itchy bumps on my penis!!! One of them goes for it and lands. I try to shake it off and wet my pants as a result. Arrgggh... now this again. I really feel the urge to crouch down and go number two, but I quickly decide that it'll have to wait. I return to the tent, feeling like I've got a cork up my ass.

Lian has finished getting dressed in the meantime and with a mosquito net over her head she comes rushing out of the tent. We put 90% DEET on our hands, which is basically a modern kind of DDT. It's carcinogenic, but it's the only thing that works out here. The insects are extremely aggressive and hungry, and they don't react to organic repellents at all. This highly concentrated DEET will keep them away for a few hours.

Having breakfast is hard; with every bite we have to lift the net, and that's when they make their move, so our necks have quite a few bites on them. It's not so bad during the day, but from about four o'clock in the afternoon until eight in the evening we each have our own personal black cloud hovering around us. During breaks we try to find a windy place by a creek, which helps a little.
We've been hiking for two months now and we've passed the 1000-mile point. That's approximately the distance from Amsterdam to Barcelona. What a milestone. This has also been hard on our hiking shoes. Lian's first pair were worn out after 500 miles, her second pair started losing its profile after only 180 miles, so these are her third pair of shoes. They are high-mountain boots and the sole of one of her boots has started to come off. The only thing holding them together is a thin, fragile layer of Gore-Tex.

She's sitting on the ground with one shoe in her lap. With a needle and iron-thread she's trying to save it. "This is the third time I'm fixing it. It's hopeless," she says. Sighing deeply, she pushes the needle through the fabric. We're in the middle of the mountains and it'll be another five days before we can buy her new shoes in South Lake Tahoe. That's more than a hundred miles to go. Mine are wearing out as well and I'm on my third pair too. I bought a new pair 250 miles after we started, because I kept getting blisters. 380 miles later, in Kennedy Meadows, I changed shoes to the same ones she's trying to repair, and mine are starting to show the same problems.

Everything wears down out here. The tips of my hiking poles have broken off. I've been hiking without the tips for days now and I hope I can buy new ones in South Lake Tahoe. I've gone through three pairs of socks, Lian's pants are full of holes and repairs, and her backpack has torn on the titanium seam for the third time; we've bound it together with pieces of string. We still have warranty, so the manufacturer is sending us a new one for the fourth time. It may sound crazy, but all three pairs of my paper-thin underwear are still holding up, and I thought they'd be the first to go.

I look at Lian, putting on her shoes with a doubtful look on her face, I hope they'll make it to South Lake Tahoe.

The Atomic Bomb

A large column of smoke rises up from the ground and forms a huge, mushroom shaped cloud. From a distance, we see black and brown strings of smoke drifting slowly into the air to join the larger column. "It looks like an atomic bomb explosion," André says. It's impressive and daunting at the same time. We are on Sonora Pass: a beautiful pass with amazing outstretched views. It's one of the highest places in this area and we can see snowy mountain peaks absolutely everywhere on the horizon, sitting in the landscape like giant panda bears. We hike through a few small snow fields and then descend. The trail is wider here so I can walk next to André. "I hope it's nothing bad," I say a bit concerned, as I look at that cloud.

The trail ends on a tarmac road. The PCT continues on the other side of it. There's a warning sign on the trail here. Large black writing on a yellow sign tells us: "Pacific Crest Trail Notice. A lightning-induced fire has closed both highway 4 and highway 89. Both roads will remain closed until further notice." Excuse me? That is quite vague. It says the highways are closed, but those highways are days from here. "It doesn't mention the trail, or conditions on the trail. There's no police ribbon or anything closing the trail. Can we go through here or not?" André says. I understand what he means: it's unclear and it doesn't feel right. "They didn't put the sign up for no reason, right?" I reply doubtfully. We talk about what to do next: do we keep going, or not? We clearly don't agree on this. He wants to go on, I really don't. We need confirmation on what's actually going on and what this means for us. At least we can agree on that. He's always more the risk-taker than I am, but he weighs his risks carefully. Fortunately, he doesn't want to hike in a fire either, so we turn on our cell phone and wait. There's no signal. Shit! What do we do now?

We hitchhike to the nearest ranch, which is, coincidentally, also called Kennedy Meadows. We talk to the owner. He's got a radio and agrees to contact the Forest Ranger, a forester that also has police authority. He turns in his chair, reaches forward and picks up a black, square microphone, which is attached to the radio by a coiled cable. The microphone fits his hand perfectly. He pushes the button on the mic and starts talking, "Kennedy Meadows for Ranger Station, Kennedy Meadows for Ranger Station, over." A soft white-noise comes from the speaker. He repeats his call and we wait. Suddenly we hear, "Ranger station here, over." The ranch-owner starts talking again. "Hi, Kennedy Meadows Resort and Pack station here. Say, I've got a couple of PCT-hikers out here. What's the current situation on the fire? Can they go up north? Over." He lets go of the button on the microphone and waits. The voice on the other side answers, "Well, it looks like the wind is in the right direction for now, away from the trail. We're still fighting this fire round the clock. I think they're okay to pass through. There's about 250 acres that's still blazing, but it's at least twelve miles away from them, over" André looks at me and smiles. I know that look, it means we're going. I'm not completely reassured, but if the Ranger says it's okay, then it'll probably be okay. We thank the ranch owner and set up camp nearby, because as it turns out, he also owns a couple of cabins, a campsite, and a good restaurant.

We set off early the next morning, in high spirits. Just to be safe, we want to cover a lot of distance per day to get through this area as soon as possible. We hike 27 miles without smelling anything remotely like fire. Maybe it won't be so bad. The second day we run into a Native American. He's wearing a backpack and going the opposite way. We hadn't seen any people until now, which was a bit unsettling. "How is the trail further on?" I ask, "Do you think we can get to the road?" I realize later that I didn't even take the time to introduce myself. "Today it'll be

okay, but tomorrow you'll experience a lot of smoke. It's quite unpleasant." He puts the tip of his drinking tube in his mouth and drinks from it calmly.
I want more information. "What do you mean by 'unpleasant'? What's out there?" He takes a few more sips and puts the light-blue tube back on the chest strap of his backpack. "The smoke really irritates your eyes. Sometimes visibility isn't very good, especially in the valleys. Tomorrow you'll be able to see the fire from one of the hilltops." Wow, that'll be scary, we're closer to it than we thought.

In the evening, the wind settles down, the air cools and the atomic cloud disappears. We hear the fire helicopters flying in and out of the area. I listen to it in my sleeping bag, afraid to fall asleep. What if it comes our way? What if we have to run suddenly, run for our lives away from the fire? What if the fire blocks the trail on both sides? We'll be forced to go straight through the wilderness, find a lake and dive into it. My thoughts are everywhere. Suddenly it's quiet outside. Is it over? André is already asleep. I wish I could sleep that easily sometimes, but this fire keeps me up all night.

The next morning, it's still quiet. No atomic cloud and no helicopters. "That's a good sign!" I say with a big smile on my face. The doubts in my mind have vanished, and we climb the hilltop enthusiastically. But when we reach the top, oh no… smoke rises up through the trees. "That's only three miles from here! Not twelve!" I sound angry and frustrated. My mind goes into overdrive. André looks at the red band of fire that stretches out across the horizon. Red hot flames and they're so close. "The smoke appears to be coming our way," he says, calm as a cucumber. He's in 'action-mode' now. He takes the map from his pocket and looks at it. "If the wind picks up and continues to come in our direction, we're going to have a problem. There won't be any roads for the next three days, we're still in the wilderness. I don't see any side road we can take if things take a turn for the worse," he says. I stay sheepishly silent. I thought this might happen; I looked at the map yesterday evening and couldn't find any side roads. We have no choice but to keep on going. Turning back would take so much longer.

I have no idea where all this energy is coming from, but I'm off like a rocket. "My goodness, woman, can you take it down a notch?" André calls out from far behind me. He can't keep up. "I like this pace!" I say, teasing him. Normally we hike at about the same pace, but not now. Maybe it's the nerves, I don't know, but somehow, I'm 300 feet ahead of him. We keep going and we only take breaks when it's absolutely necessary. Sometime in the afternoon we reach the valley the Native American talked about – I still don't know his name, I should have gotten his name.

The entire valley is filled with smoke, like a thick, dark fog. We descend into it and smell the wood-fire. Our eyes start itching and the smell grows stronger. Is the fire close-by? I don't know, I can't see much. Don't think about it and keep going, I try to tell myself calmly. Breathing is hard, we cough a few times. I suddenly think of all the cigarette-smokers; this is probably how they feel all the time, blegh, not my thing.

After a while, the wind picks up. The thick smoke starts to open up and we get a few welcome whiffs of fresh air and finally, we have some visibility. Phew... I don't ever want to go through this again. We keep hiking and after 34 miles, the evening sets in. We've passed the fire and the atomic cloud is out of sight. We're exhausted, but it looks like danger has passed. We stop.

I'm in my bed listening for sounds. André's fast asleep and it's silent. I can't hear a single creature, no peeps, no creaks, no movement. How can that be...

Flowers, Flowers, Flowers

Large flower buds are fighting for a spot in the sun and they look like they're all in a rush. One hill after another, field after field; They are all covered in huge yellow flowers, small white ones, orange 'Indian paintbrush' flowers and blue lupines. There's not a gardener in the world that could get it to look this rich, colorful, and full of life. The air is thick with a wonderful flowery fragrance. We are in love with this miracle of nature, just the natural beauty of it. Wild lilies, one even more beautiful than the other. The trail even runs straight through a field full of wild blue irises. They are all around us, as far as the eye can see. The area we're hiking through now is a lot like the European alpine meadows. There are so many butterflies too, dancing around until the warm summer evening sets in. And fortunately, the mosquitos have almost completely disappeared.

What we don't have in the European Alps, are hummingbirds. One just flashed right by us, bright green and sounding like a fat bumble bee. Not long after that we spot another one hanging in mid-air right next to us. Its beautiful red-orange neck glistening in the sun. Its head, with its delicate little beak moves from side to side. Then…zoom… as suddenly as it appeared, it vanishes. "I always thought they only lived in tropical areas?" I say to Lian. "So did I. I only know them from the Caribbean." It feels a bit strange, watching them flying around the pine trees like this. We look it up in our bird app. It appears to be either an 'Allen's Hummingbird' or maybe a 'Rufous Hummingbird'. These days are idyllic, timeless, a single moment of pure bliss. We're laying in a field of flowers, side by side, hand in hand; we're staring at white, woolly clouds in an otherwise clear blue sky. Our imagination runs freely, and like eight-year-olds we find the funniest figures in the clouds. "Hey, an elephant with tiny wings." I look at

Lian. She's pointing up at the sky. I follow her finger with my eyes. "Hahaha, you're right. Look at that dolphin over there." We stare at the clouds for another hour, calling out strange formations and laughing. Sometimes we don't say anything for a while and feel the happiness of the present moment flowing through us. This is such an intense and absolutely beautiful moment!

Not long after that, we're on a mountain ridge, looking out over a valley with four lakes. "Which lake shall we swim in today?" I ask Lian with a big smile on my face. It's quite warm so a nice dive in a cool mountain lake would be very refreshing. We found a waterfall with a deep blue lake underneath it yesterday. Cliff jumping!! I wonder if that's possible here. We hike down and find a great spot at lake number two.

"Aaaah…this is so good!" I say as I come up after my big splashy jump into the water. Lian comes in as well. Carefully, she steps over the rocks and then she jumps in. "This is wonderful!" she says. We swim around and splash water at each other. At some point Lian stands up. "Hey, what's that? Something bit me!" She jumps up and starts swimming. We don't see anything. A snake is the first thing that comes to my mind. "Where did it bite you?" I ask. "Well, on the top of my foot." The water is very clear, so we both put our heads under water and start looking. Apart from lots of small brown fish, we don't see anything. I pull my face out of the water and ask, "Are you okay?" She stands up again and pulls one foot out of the water.

"I don't see any bite marks. It wasn't very painful anyway, more like a tickle. There it is again!" I look under water and see a large school of small brown fish moving around her foot. I come back up and burst out laughing. "Hahahaha, they're cleaner fish. They're eating the dead skin off your feet! Do you have any idea what people pay for that in a wellness resort? Hahaha!" She sets her other foot down in the water and starts giggling, "It's actually quite nice."

I stand next to her and together we relax and enjoy our free cleansing treatment. Our very own wellness experience surrounded by nature.

Part Three
Fire Hazard

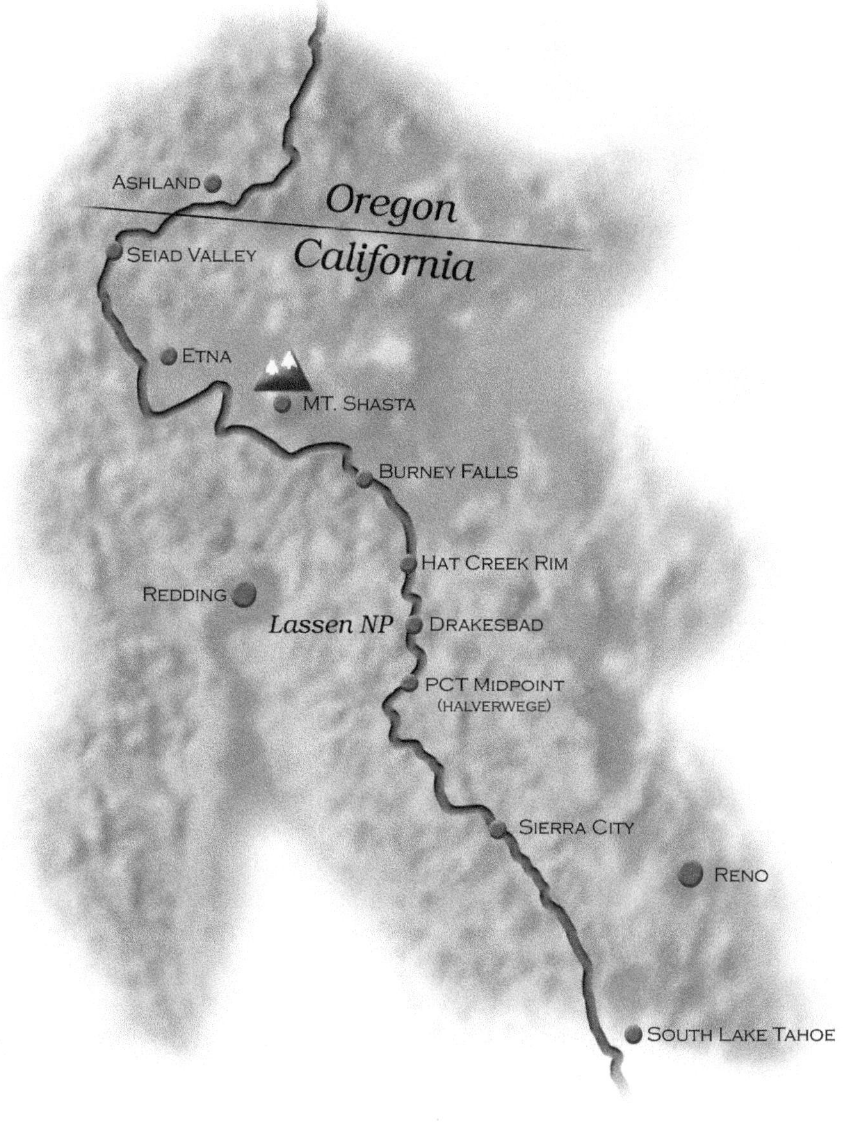
Ashland
Oregon
California
Seiad Valley
Etna
Mt. Shasta
Burney Falls
Hat Creek Rim
Redding
Lassen NP
Drakesbad
PCT Midpoint
(halverwege)
Sierra City
Reno
South Lake Tahoe

Hiker Hunger

We arrive at our next big stop: South Lake Tahoe. It's popular place, where many tourists like to spend their summers by a huge lake. It's like an American version of Lake Garda in Italy; there are zip-lines, water scooters, cinemas, casinos; you name it, it's there. A lot of outfitters too. For us, this place is a two-day stay in which we'll have all our gear repaired and buy new gear, like shoes. We'll also be doing a lot of grocery shopping, since this is where we make the ten new resupply packs for our entire Northern California journey. Also, there are other packages waiting here for us. Like our bounce-box and Lian's new backpack. Our reasons for being here are mostly logistical and organizational.

We've started to suffer quite severely from a condition known as 'Hiker Hunger': a unique feeling, only known to long-distance hikers that have been on the trail for a while. Imagine having an insatiable appetite, like you're trying to fill a never-ending emptiness inside. We're hiking a marathon a day on average at the moment, which roughly translates to five to six thousand calories per person, per day. We need and want to eat constantly. Our friend Little Bear told us about the 'all you can eat' buffets in casinos; eat as much as you want for the whole evening. We'd like something like that! So, we decide to go there tonight!
As it turns out, casinos are just really big hotels that have a huge casino covering the entire ground floor. We open the door and step inside. The thick fumes of cigars and cigarette-smoke hit us like a wall. "Huh? What's this?" Lian says surprised. It's not something we're used to anymore. It's quite dark, it's almost like the lights have been dimmed purposely. "It's like walking into an old pub," I say. A small sign tells us that the restaurant is on the top floor.

We walk across the thick red carpet towards the elevator, astonished by all the nervous people anxiously tapping on the slot machines. We never go to casinos, so we expected a James Bond kind of vibe; roulette and poker tables, with people standing around them, dressed to the nines in tuxedos and evening gowns. Maybe it is really like that in some casinos, but this is not one of them. All we see is rows after rows of flashing neon machines and people in everyday clothing trying their luck. By the time we reach the elevator we smell like two stinky cigars. Yuk! What a shame for our freshly washed clothes. I guess we'll take a shower again tonight and air out our clothes.

There's something funny about this city; it's in two different states: California and Nevada. California is a bit like Scandinavia: social, polite, clean, well-organized and there are a lot of healthy laws, like no smoking in public buildings. You can walk down the street here and literally fifty feet after you cross the state border into Nevada, it's like walking from Scandinavia straight into an average southern European country. Not-so-well-organized, dirty, and other people's cigarette smoke flying up your nose constantly. Casinos have much stricter regulations in California, but in Nevada they are free to do whatever they like, so all the grand hotel-casinos are located just a few feet across the border.

We come up to the restaurant and the first thing we see is enormous amounts of food. All the continents are represented here; Asian, European, Mexican, American... We imagined it might look a little bit like this and the thought of it alone was great, but this tops everything. Such extravagance, an Eldorado of food and all the enticing aromas! "What shall we start with?" I ask Lian. Speechless, she simply replies with a shrug. We take a plate and have a look around. "What do you think? Shrimp or steak?" Lian's question makes me laugh. This isn't a very difficult choice to make. "Let's have both!" We laugh and start with shellfish. No pasta, rice, or burritos since we have that all the time on the trail. We pick a nice spot by the window with a beautiful view over the lake.

We go back for seconds, fill our plates, and sit back down. I'm in the middle of taking a bite when Lian says, "I just can't eat anymore, can you?" I'm enjoying my freshly poached vegetables, I cut off a piece and notice that I'm also starting to feel quite full. "Now that you mention it." She takes another bite. "I really feel like I'm stuffing it in and it's making me nauseous." I'm not completely full yet, but I think by the end of this plate I'll have a genuine Christmas feeling. Like I'm an over-stuffed turkey that's ready to explode. And there's still a big dessert bar!!! What an anticlimax. Lian looks a bit disappointed. "We've come all this way to have an 'all-you-can-eat' dinner but then we get here and see all this wonderful food, and we can't eat any more after only two plates! We can't eat any of the other nice things we see!" Her eyebrows go up, her shoulders go down. "But I want dessert!" she says, pouting her lips.
I think about it for a moment. We eat a lot on the trail, but they're small portions every hour to keep the motor up and running. "I've noticed that the food is much greasier here. It has lots of oil and butter. I don't think our stomachs are used to these amounts of fat anymore, so maybe that's why we feel full so soon?" I say. She shrugs. We get a cappuccino, take our time, and still decide to have some dessert. Once again there are too many choices. We stare at the delicious-looking chocolate cake, but in the end we go for the light strawberry cottage cheese.

Even though we couldn't eat as much as we wanted to, we have still had a wonderful evening, and a delicious meal. Funny thing about Hiker Hunger... as the expression goes: "your eyes are bigger than your stomach." But because our stomachs are gnawing at us constantly when we're on the trail, our eyes had become humongous compared to what our tiny stomachs could actually handle.

Intensive Care

When I wake up the next morning, Lian is already in the shower. I start coughing straight away. I've had this cough for a few days now and I haven't felt very fit for a while. Electrolytes? Nah, I don't think so, they seem to be under control. Maybe I have a cold. While I'm thinking about this, something else comes to mind. A while back we hiked together with someone for a week, who also had a cough and eventually had to quit because of lung infection. With that thought in mind, I decide to see a doctor. Maybe I need antibiotics or something.

Lian is packing resupply boxes; they have to be posted this afternoon. While she does that, I walk over to the nearest healthcare center. I take a number and sit down. It's clean and modern, with soft cheerful music playing in the background. I hear a 'ping'. Number 26; yes, that's me. I go up to the small reception desk where an older woman asks me some general questions.
"Do you have health insurance in your home country?"
"Yes, I do."
"Do you have additional health insurance for the United States?" I have that too. She asks me a few more questions. The most important one being: "How do you wish to pay for this visit?" Pay? Oh right, I'm in the USA.
I give her my credit card, she swipes it through a machine and just like that, I've already paid the doctor, without even seeing him. I sit down in the waiting room and after half an hour, the doctor calls me in.
"Good morning, my name is Bill. How can I help you?"
I tell him what I think is wrong with me and how I feel.
"So, you have a cough and you're feeling short of breath?"
I nod in agreement. He gets out a blood pressure monitor and attaches it to my arm. He pushes a button; the pump starts and the cuff swells.

He looks at the number and says, "You have low blood pressure and your heart rate is 52. Do you feel tired sometimes?" Ha, yes, what do you think? "I have been a bit tired lately. I also get lightheaded sometimes when I stand up." I explain to him that we're hiking the PCT. "That sounds like an intense sport, doesn't it?" I don't really see it that way. I'm just having fun and I get tired at the end of the day, who doesn't? But from where he's standing, we're packing quite a bit of weight and we're hiking in the mountains a lot. "Yes, well, I guess that's one way to look at it," I answer. He looks at me quizzically. "Do you get stomach-aches?" Well, yes, especially after last night. "I do feel a few cramps actually, now that you mention it."
He writes something down. "Can you take off your shirt, please?" I do as he asks. He gets up and puts his stethoscope on my chest. While he listens, he asks me to take a few deep breaths. "Have you ever had any problems with your heart?" I look him in the eye. My heart? Where is he going with this? In fact, I did have some heart arrhythmia 25 years ago. It vanished after a minute or so, but it was very strange. Back then I had just got out of the army, where we worked out a lot. When I came back to civilian life, I stopped working out. I had some tests done and they found out that I had an athlete's heart, which had started shrinking. Could this be something similar?
I tell the doctor honestly what happened back then. He sits down and takes some more notes. "I'd like you to have a bit of testing done in the nearby hospital." Ah, now we're getting somewhere. "How far is that on foot?" I ask. "It's too far on foot. I'll order you a cab, that'll be easier. Could you wait out in the hallway, please?" I walk out of the office, but before I can sit down the receptionist comes up to me and hands me a pile of paperwork to take to the hospital. "Where should I report to? I ask her. "The driver will know where to go. Oh, there he is already." Wow, that's fast.

A bit stunned, I get into the cab. The driver speeds off and before I know it, we're at the hospital. He drives up to a special entrance that says 'Emergency'. Good, this looks like the quickest way in. Still, no warning bells are sounding in my head. Sometimes I wish I was more like Lian; she would have realized what was going on from a mile away. We get out of the car and the driver asks me to wait as he goes up to the reception desk. He talks to the nurse; her head turns quickly, and she looks right at me. She gets up immediately and walks up to me. Politely, she asks me to accompany her. Now this is service, I don't have to wait at all. At home, going to hospital always means waiting around a lot. This thought turns out to be pretty naïve.

Together we walk down the hallway, past all the people who do have to wait. A second nurse comes along with us and before I know it, I'm in a bed with a hospital gown on. "Excuse me, Madam, I only came up here for a few tests. Blood tests, I think. Are you sure this is necessary? She rolls a small cart closer to me. "We'll take some blood later, Sir." She's holding a big bunch of wires in her hand, she opens my gown and starts sticking all kinds of sensors on my body. The second nurse comes back in. She's brought a pole on wheels, with a big bag full of clear liquid. She works fast, because within two minutes she's taken multiple blood samples and there's an intravenous drip in my arm. I'm beginning to wake up from my ignorant state, so I start asking all kinds of questions, which they politely and evasively answer. "A doctor will be with you shortly. He will explain everything to you," is the answer to everything I ask. Then they leave and I'm left there, in Intensive Care, with a machine that beeps all the time and that spits out an electrocardiogram every now and then. I look at the needle in my arm. I can see the clear drops falling into the tube right next to me.

An ECG? IV drip? WHAT IS GOING ON HERE?!!

Six hours go by. Yes, six and I'm still lying here. In the meantime, three different doctors have come to see me, asking all kinds of questions and then looking at the machine. The drip bag has been replaced once. I'm bored to death. They did let me call Lian once on their phone. To keep our weight down we only brought one phone on this trip and she has it. Nothing much else happens.

After another half an hour, another doctor comes in. "Good evening, how are you feeling?" I try to be funny and say, "Like a moose that's bored to death." Either the doctor was trained well or my joke wasn't funny. His facial expression didn't change a bit. "We've tested you for everything we could think of and there's good news. You are perfectly healthy!" A big smile appears across his face. I look back at him, dumbfounded, and blurt out, "Uhm… I already thought I was. I was just a little tired and I had a cough. Why was all this necessary and what about my blood? No infections or something like a mineral deficiency?" His smile stays on – probably well trained. "No, nothing like that, we didn't find anything. Your heart is perfectly fine and your bloodwork is fine too. You can get dressed and go home." They remove the stickers and the drip. Before I know it, I'm at the reception desk to pay the numerous bills; they won't let me leave before I pay them all.

Apparently, I'm fit as a fiddle, nothing is wrong with me. I'm hungry and I still have that cough. They didn't say a thing about that, nor did they give me anything for it. I step outside. Nothing has changed, except that I'm down 2200 dollars…

Have You Seen My Dealer?

This is the first thing he says to us. Unshaven, with black, curly hair that doesn't move, even though there's wind. He's deadly serious and I'm a little intimidated. He's staring at me with big, hopeful eyes. "What are you talking about?" I wonder if I've heard him correctly. "Wild Monkey?" is the only thing he says. I don't understand, but I don't think he's in his right mind. I try again, "I don't understand what you mean by that." A thin layer of dust covers his face, just like it does ours. The trail has been dry and dusty for the past few days. We've been eating dust, especially whoever was hiking behind.

His head swings sideways and he tilts his head inquisitively. "Don't you know who Wild Monkey is?" His hand finds a rectangular plastic bag in his pocket. "No, doesn't ring a bell," I answer. "This is all I have left." His fingers fidget in the bag and pull out a small green ball. "He's my 'provider' and I missed him a few nights ago. I didn't get my package. I think he might already be a day ahead of me." He seems kind of sad. "Have you got any? I'm totally bummed out. I really need it or I won't make it over those mountains." I look at the ball. There's a typical, sweet smell coming from it that reminds me of 'Poodle Dog bush'. "That's pot." André grew up in Amsterdam and instantly recognizes it. Wild Monkey must be a dealer who's somewhere on the trail. Funny name, I wonder who gave it to him and why. André looks at the man, and answers, "No, we haven't met him at all on our trip. I haven't seen his name in the trail logs either. Maybe he's behind us." That seems to lift the hiker's spirits. He sits down, we say goodbye and walk on.

We had noticed before how many American hikers use marijuana on this trail. It's like it's infused in the hiker scene, especially in the desert section. Whenever we sat down with a group of people, we noticed they were regularly passing joints around. Or at Casa de Luna, where the hash pipe was used a lot. We've never seen this on any of the other US trails that we've hiked. Some time later we ask a couple of stoned hikers sitting on the side of the trail about it. It seems to have come from the Appalachian Trail, another long-distance trail on the east coast. That trail seems to have more of a party element, with lots of places that function as a vortex; 'happy places', that suck everyone in completely.

Two days later we run into the guy again or actually, he almost runs right past us. Glassy-eyed, he approaches us, "Heeeeey, I'm gonna get that mountain! I'm gonnnnnnna get that moutainnnnn!! Yes!!" You can smell the sweet smell on him clearly. I don't know what's in Wild Monkey's stuff, but he sure is wild. Passionately, he swings his hiking poles back to front and he races up the mountain at high speed. We stop and watch him go. "I wonder how many people need drugs to reach the end of this trail," André says, more to himself than to me. "It's so strange; they're walking through these beautiful landscapes, one more beautiful than the other. Instead of taking in, and experiencing all these miracles of nature, it seems that they need to take this shit just to get through it." I nod and answer, "I think some people have a completely different trail experience than we do." My eyes look out over the winding mountain trail, where I can still see the guy running like a madman. I wonder how long he'll keep that up. That was the last time we saw him, so who knows, maybe he made it.

No Food, What Now?

It's the middle of the afternoon, we are on the road to Sierra City, hungry and weary. We can keep up the pace because our backpacks weigh next to nothing. We've run out of food. At five o'clock this morning we had breakfast and that was it. The thought of food makes us walk faster and faster. We arrive at the post office just in time to pick up our resupply package. I go inside and quickly discover that our package is not here. We have no food for the next five days. What do we do now?

There's a small shop that sells hamburgers and there's a restaurant here, so we won't have any trouble finding food for today. But how are we going to solve our food-problems for the next few days? I take a look in the small hiker box. "Well, it's been properly cleaned out. It's all but empty... We always leave whatever we can spare in the box, and now that we need it, it's empty. Figures. Just our luck." I say to Lian, exhausted and disappointed. "Now what?" she asks. "I don't know, let's get something to eat first." Lian looks in the hiker box one last time. "There's a lot of shampoo in here, maybe I can wash our clothes with that tomorrow. They have some of those pay-per-use washing machines here." She takes a bottle from the box and we walk up the steps of a white veranda. We push open the door to the small shop and go inside. The walls are covered with racks full of fishing gear: rods, reels, and lures. There's lots of canned food – not something we would bring on a hike. There is also some bread, a small variety of vegetables, tortilla chips, candy and a few more things like that. We look around and eventually take comfort in one of the enormous hamburgers they sell here. We go for the 'Gut Buster': one pound of meat with everything on top. They taste amazing and we feel the energy returning to our bodies.

Sierra City; before the Goldrush in 1850, only a handful of Native Americans lived here. Once gold was discovered, around 3000 people moved here within a few years to find their wealth and happiness. It used to be a thriving city, but as quickly as it came into existence, it also disappeared again. Now it's a quiet town with about 200 residents. The atmosphere and the houses make it feel like time has stood still here since 1850.

The postal worker is also from 1850. Seriously, I'm not kidding. Although I don't think people were that sizable back then, they could very well have been just as rude. There he is, behind the counter, behaving like he's some kind of demigod. The image he has of himself is clearly not the same as what we – and other hikers – see in front of us. Unshaved and slouched in a chair that's obviously too small for him, thick slabs of fat push through the sides of the chair. He's stuck, like he's being held there by a suction cup. A hairy flap of skin sticks out from under his t-shirt, which is way too tight. The fluffy navel; it's staring at me like an evil eye. I don't want to look at it, but my eyes are drawn to it somehow. In front of him on the counter is an XXL coke with a bent straw. Crumbs are scattered all around it, mixed in with various papers and envelopes.

"Next!" The young hiker was in the middle of a sentence when he's sent away. I'm next. I was here yesterday, too, with nothing to show for it. I'm going to try a different approach this time.
"Good afternoon, Sir," I say. He seems to be working on something, so he ignores me. I wait. After about thirty seconds he finally pretends to notice that I'm there. There actually is a line out here... "Yes, what do you want? Didn't you come in yesterday? I told you, your package isn't here!" Hmmm... This is not the quality of service I usually get from the US Postal Service, but I try to stay calm. "Yes, that's true. You also told me that there were a lot of packages you hadn't looked at yet. It's the next

morning now, so I hoped that you might have found a moment to look at them by now." He lets out an annoyed sigh. "What do you hikers think? That you own the post office? Do you see how many boxes there are here? I'm not about to go and wrestle through that! I work from ten to two and then I close up. You're just out of luck. You need to stop sending so much stuff out here!" I take two deep breaths and answer, "I don't mean to burden you, but I really need that package for the next part of the trail. Would you mind if I checked the boxes myself? Mine has a huge red smiley sticker on it. Maybe that way I could help you out?" He pushes himself forward in his chair and bows over the counter, quite intimidating. "What do you think, mister. I'm not authorized to let anyone behind the counter. So, if you don't have any other questions, you can leave. Come back tomorrow, maybe I'll find some time." He looks right past me to the next customer and waves him over. In his world I'm yesterday's news. I decide that this is not a good time to let things escalate, so I go outside.

The next morning at ten o'clock, I'm back there for the third time. He sees me come in and sighs, "No, I haven't looked yet and a new load just came in." In my nicest voice I say, "I have another idea. I have a track-and-trace number. After our conversation yesterday, I tried to find out where my package is on the USPS website on my cell phone. However, I'm confused, because it looks like my package is somewhere else completely, somewhere around San Diego? Would you please check your system to see what's going on? There might be an explanation for all this." He looks me in the eye, puts down the letters he's holding and walks over to his chair. He squishes himself into it, turns around, bends over his keyboard with an arched back and starts typing very slowly. The monitor lights up half his face with a brownish glow. Somehow this whole scene makes me think of Looney Tunes cartoons. I wait patiently and after about a minute he sits up straight. I hadn't seen the tiny pearls of sweat on his wrinkly forehead until now.

"Your package isn't here at all and it hasn't been delivered anywhere." I'm really confused now; Lian sent it a while back when we were in South Lake Tahoe, when I was in that stupid hospital. It should have arrived here ages ago. He notices my confusion and says, "Your package was sent to the wrong zip code. The post office there received it, noticed the mistake, and sent it back to distribution. From there it should come to me, but that's not what those idiots did. They sent it back to the wrong post office again, it's been back and forth six times now." This country does not cease to amaze me, although this time it's not because of its beautiful nature. "Uhm, isn't there anybody in the distribution center who actually reads what is on the box? After one or two times, someone should notice that something's wrong, don't you think?" His eyebrows move up. "You don't think we actually look at all these packages, do you?" Well, apparently, they have a different system and a different work ethic than back home but OK, different country, different rules. "What do you propose we do?" I ask. He picks up a piece of paper, looks at his screen and writes down a number. "Call this post office. They have to change the address, so it'll go to another location." I'm getting ready to ask him if it's not his job to do that, being a USPS worker. If he can't just make a call and fix this problem right away. This is their mistake after all, not mine. But I decide to swallow my words. I think it might be better if I sort this out myself.

An extremely friendly lady picks up the phone. She is very helpful and the whole thing is fixed in no time. She's sending the package to Etna, a small town that's on our route about three weeks from now. We were planning to buy food in a shop there, because we hadn't sent a box there, so now that problem's fixed as well. Now all we have to do is get food for the next five days.

I put an advert in our PCT Facebook group and immediately a number of great responses start coming in. Like someone who has quit the trail, but his resupply package is already at this post office. We can have it! Unfortunately, it quickly turns out that we can't because you need to identify yourself on the spot to collect a package. It's a good rule: you have to prove that it's yours, to make sure it's not taken by some other person. Anyway, this won't work. After many more responses like this, we decide to buy all our supplies in the store.

There's a tiny grass field behind the small white church in town. PCT hikers are allowed to camp there. It's very crowded; eight little tents standing completely wall-to-wall. We quietly sneak into bed, carefully so we don't wake anyone. It's ten p.m. by now. We've only just tucked ourselves in nice and cozy when the church organ starts playing. Beautiful melodies fill the night sky. "Lian, is it time for some kind of holy mass or something? Is it a special religious day?" I don't believe in gods, but Lian was raised Catholic, so maybe she knows. "I don't think so. It's quite late for something like that anyway. It's beautiful though! Who could be playing so beautifully?" Her curiosity takes her outside in her underwear. She opens the church door and to her surprise she finds a group of hikers sitting in the church benches, while another hiker passionately plays the overture. She closes the door quickly and runs back to tell me what she's seen. It makes me laugh. I turn over on my pillow. The word 'pillow' might be an overstatement; it's a pile of clothes that I've stuffed in the bag of my sleeping bag. My nose touches the fabric and I smell the wonderful scent of shampoo. Ah yes, the inventive laundry detergent from the hiker box. Now all we can do is hope that there aren't any bears around this town. We've been through enough for one day.

Thick Clouds Gather in the Sky

It's a beautiful morning. The sun has only just come up on the horizon and is shining great beams of light throughout the forest. There's a light mist that makes it look like a fairy-tale. As if gnomes or fairies could emerge from the shadows at any moment. Small, green plants with white flowers grow beside the narrow trail. It's still so quiet and cool. We walk through this mesmerizing scene with our down-coats and hats on. Slowly the animals are starting to wake up and when the sun is a bit higher up in the sky, we spot a ground-squirrel. It's very busy, digging up something that looks like a little ball. It turns the ball around, checks it out and then starts munching on it. Maybe it's a nut, left over from last fall? After a while it notices us, looks up at us and then continues eating, undisturbed. It's clear to us that many hikers have quit by now. We hardly ever pass anyone anymore and almost nobody passes us while we're on a break. We can experience the wilderness completely undisturbed too.

Around eleven o'clock we arrive at a spectacular view. André gets up on a rock and I take a beautiful panorama picture. All you can see is his silhouette and the beams of sunlight coming from the clouds behind him. Underneath him is an enormous outstretched valley filled with pine trees. He's standing there like a lonely hiker in an immense landscape. Amazing. My man.
The sunlight disappears and thick clouds start gathering when we slowly hike up a mountain ridge. It's covered in groups of low-growing green plants with large yellow flowers. They're everywhere and the feel a bit velvety. They look like large 'woolly hedgenettles' or 'lamb-ears'. We've almost reached the top, when... kabooooooom.... In the distance we hear the low rumbling sound echoing through the valleys. After about thirty feet, we reach the summit

and see a giant dark cloud right in front of us. Underneath it, gray vertical lines shoot down towards the ground. It's raining heavily down there. Uh oh, that doesn't look so good. And at the exact moment this thought hits my mind, a lightning flash appears out of nowhere. The loud bang scares us. "Hmmm... Interesting. We're on a lonely mountain ridge and now this is coming right at us," André mumbles. The large cloud is rapidly coming closer and the flashes are getting more intense. They're striking the trees right in front of our eyes. We quickly put down our backpacks and get out our raincoats. I really don't like this at all. This kind of brute force is not my thing. This whole area is wide open, and the blunt force of nature is king here. There's nothing you can do. The threatening energy of it all makes you feel humble, small, alarmed, and frightened all at once. It makes you feel like you're an ant, watching a horde of elephants coming right at you. I swing my backpack on and start up a quick pace. We have at least another seven or eight miles to go on this ridge and there's no shelter anywhere around here. There is a big chance that we'll be struck by lightning out here, so there's no time to lose. Let's go!

Not long after that, water comes streaming from the sky. The wind picks up, the rain is gushing down now, and our legs are starting to get really cold. For a few scary hours we hike over the mountain ridge in the pouring rain. Flashes of lightning are followed quickly by rumbling thunder. It's right over our heads. I cringe every time I see a flash and the thunder feels like it's roaring right through us! Slowly the cloud seems to move over us and the mountain ridge starts to descend very slowly. Every now and then we come across a few trees, so we can catch our breath for a few minutes. Which is really not smart at all, seeing as they are the only things sticking out into the sky here and they could very well attract lightning. We have to keep going, going, going. Down the ridge as quickly as we can to safety.

The rain has turned the trail into a muddy creek. Under normal circumstances we would probably try to go around it, but it doesn't matter now. There's no use, our shoes are soaking wet already anyway. It's getting colder and later. "Hey, I think it's turning away to the left!" I call out to André. "What?" He can barely hear me in this strong wind. I stop for a moment and he comes closer. "It looks like the lightning won't be striking right over our heads anymore. Look, the core of the cloud is moving to the left." He looks up. "Finally, maybe the rain will stop too. How are your shoes holding up? I'm soaked." I look down. "So am I. My socks are drenched and with every step I take, brown blubber squishes up the sides of my shoes up to my ankles."

It finally calms down around five o'clock. The thunder has gone, the trees and bushes are still dripping with rainwater and we hike on down the mountain, hoping to dry off a bit. It's not an easy descent. The wet bushes give off a lot of water. My pants and my shoes seem to be getting even wetter than they were in the rain! It's like buckets of water are being emptied onto our legs. Fortunately, it's stopped raining when we put up our tent at seven o'clock. We quickly take off our freezing wet shoes and pants. I jump around a bit in my sandals in an attempt to get warm. We have a quick bite to eat. My feet still feel like icicles. "Why don't you make yourself a hot water bottle?" André asks. I had thought of that myself, but it means I have to use more gas, which I don't want to do. However, I can't possibly get any sleep if my feet are cold. "OK, a hot water bottle does sound nice," I agree and while André crawls into his sleeping bag, I heat up some water. I pour the hot water into my water bottle and put a sock around it, so my feet won't burn. It's now warming up the bottom of my sleeping bag, while I get undressed. I get in bed and feel the warmth rising up from my feet. This is wonderful.
I snuggle into my warm bed and fall asleep right away.

Woohoo! Halfway There!

"It's got to be here somewhere?" Lian says. "Yes, according to the map it should be right here," I answer. We're looking for a small sign, so we're walking very slowly, afraid we might miss it. "How big is it anyway?" She's looking on the left and I'm looking on the right side. "I don't know, I haven't seen a picture of it, just a dot on the map, that's all I know about it." We're walking over a narrow path. To our left are pine trees and to our right is a small grassy hill. It feels like an old forest. This area probably hasn't changed much in the last couple of thousand years.

"Yes, that must be it. We're here!" Lian shouts. A small granite signpost sticks out between the rocks on the left side of the trail. Small letters have been chiseled out. On our side it says: 'Canada 1325 miles.' On the back it says: 'Mexico 1325 miles,' and on the side it says: 'PCT midpoint.' Yes, this is it. "Woohoo!! We're halfway there!" I shout out with a big smile on my face. We laugh, kiss, and take a picture.

1325 miles, that's 2132 kilometers. This really is halfway. What a milestone. We feel euphoric. We've been looking forward to this for days and now we're really here. Lian looks at the imprint again. First on the left and then on the right. "Hang on a minute?!" she suddenly says with a frown on her face. "This means something else, too..." She stops talking and takes a deep breath. She waits, her face looking a bit sad now. "André, we still have so many miles to go!" She sounds surprised, like this is the first time she's realized this. Yes, I've had the same realization. It's almost unimaginable. We've been on the trail for exactly three months now, and we've had so many adventures already. I can't wait to see what the next three months will bring.

I think about home for a moment and dig up a memory. "Do you remember when we were back home, looking at the total distance?" The entire PCT was as if we were hiking from our home in Belgium all the way to Moscow, turned around there, and walked all the way back home again. She looks a bit lost, and mumbles, "Yeah, we're only halfway there..."
"Sweetheart. Think back to what you told me at home. Your version of 'it's only a mountain'. Remember? You told me, that instead of feeling overwhelmed by looking at the entire length of the trail, we should split it up into twenty-six different vacations. Every time we pick up a new resupply package is the beginning of a new vacation. Small bites for the mind, remember? I thought it was genius! Twenty-six vacations joined together feels a lot less scary than a six-month-mission." This seems to make her feel better, and she smiles. "Of course! I'm so stupid, I forgot my own words of advice. Thank you for reminding me!"

We've been on the trail for ninety days now and we've been in a great mood for the past few days. We wanted to do something fun, to celebrate our arrival here. We decided to sing, and we quickly came up with an idea: our own lyrics to the song 'Living on a Prayer,' by Bon Jovi. Lian puts her hands on a hiking pole. She holds it in front of her mouth like a real microphone and we go for it. In our best voices we sing:

> "Ooooooh, we're half way there.
> O, ho, living on the trail.
> Take my hand, we'll make it out there.
> Wo ho, living on the trail.
> Living on the traaiiilllll"

A few other hikers are right next to us, laughing heartily at our performance. They obviously think it's hilarious and we can't stop laughing either. Finally, we step aside and make room for them to take their picture with the sign. We say goodbye and get back on the trail, to the next milestone. We can start counting down now.

After about an hour we suddenly lose the trail. It's disappeared underneath chaotic piles of broken branches and small downed trees. It looks like a giant came through and pulled all the trees out of the ground and flung them around in a fit of anger. It's quite extraordinary. We decide to split up and go in different directions and try to find the trail that way.
"Can you find it?" I call out to Lian. "No, not really," she answers. I can't see her. Somewhere between the fallen trees, she's looking for the trail. It's almost like a huge storm passed through here. Maybe it was the same storm we encountered a few days ago. She's looking on the left, I'm looking on the right, but after a while we give up. I point in the direction of the trail. "Lian, we've been searching for half an hour, we really can't find it. Let's just go straight through there." She takes a last look left and right, hoping to catch a glimpse of the trail, and then we make our way through the terrain. One moment we're walking over tree trunks, the next moment we're crawling underneath them. After half an hour we finally see the trail lying ahead of us. We crawl our way through a few more feet of forest and then we find ourselves back on a neat-and-tidy-looking trail.

It's nine o'clock in the evening. We've just experienced the most amazing sunset and we're lying comfortably in our sleeping bags. The temperature is lovely and we've put up the tent without the outer tent. It looks like a giant mosquito net now. Like almost every day, I fall asleep instantly. Lian is still dozing a bit and at one point she quietly shakes me to wake me up. "I hear something." Her voice is soft. As I open my eyes, I'm still a bit drowsy. "Huh?" With glassy eyes I look around a bit. In my dream, I was having a wonderful time kayaking on a beautiful river. Slowly my fingers find their way to the cord on the hood of my sleeping bag. I fidget with it to make some space and stick my head out. "What's wrong?" I yawn. "Shhh, listen." I'm trying, but I don't hear anything. "What is it?" I really just want to turn around and go back to sleep. "I hear something scrabbling around the tent," she whispers in my ear. I sit up, my sleepy head is starting to wake up. Then I hear it, the sound of small twigs snapping. "It's coming from the left," I say, still too loudly. Lian looks at me and puts her index finger in front of her mouth. "Sshhhh..." She points at something. I look past her on the left side and spot a deer sniffing around our tent. It's a young female with a beautiful beige-brown coat that shines in the moonlight. It scratches the ground with its hoof like it's looking for something. Slowly it circles around our tent. What a wonderful encounter. I continue to look at the deer for another five minutes and then I feel the sleepiness pull me back into bed. Almost as soon as I lie back down, I'm off to dreamland again. Lian tries to get some sleep too, but the deer doesn't stop scrabbling about, and the noise is keeping her up.

After an hour, she's finally had enough of it. She gets out of the tent and yells, "Go away, deer!" I wake up and see her walking right up to the deer, it makes me laugh. It's kind of funny; a naked woman yelling and waving at a deer in the middle of the night. That's not something you see every day, is it? The animal isn't shy though. It calmly watches Lian coming, its head bent towards the ground and its legs slightly apart. Eventually it jumps off, takes a few steps, and then stops again, its big brown eyes fixed on Lian. Maybe the deer is thinking what I'm thinking: It's not every day you see a naked lady waving around in the forest! This is so funny. The animal is quite stubborn, because no matter what Lian tries, after a few steps the deer jumps aside, then calmly trots back towards our tent. Lian finally gives up and comes back to bed. "Just my luck, at home you hardly ever see a deer and here they won't leave you alone!" she mutters. We still haven't managed to scare off the deer. It keeps lingering. When Lian lies down, the deer suddenly starts licking something off the ground vigorously. It's even smacking its lips. "That's the sound I kept hearing when you were asleep!" Suddenly she bursts out laughing. "Hahahaha, do you know why it's standing there?!" She points. "That's the exact spot where I peed earlier!" The animal licks, smacks its lips and then starts scraping at the ground with its hoof again. It wants the salt and it's licking our urine!!

It's such a wonderful thing, to experience animals here in the woods that don't see people as a threat. At home, in the forest where we live, it's a very different situation. Unfortunately, we have hunters there. They're mostly older men, often sitting side by side, shooting anything that moves. They even have a celebration for it: the Saint-Hubert festival. After the hunt we see all these animals, that had been roaming freely just a few days earlier, hanging upside-down from racks, being auctioned off for charity. I don't understand what could possibly be charitable about this. I would much rather see them alive in the forest. Hunting is forbidden on our property, but in the rest of the forest and the meadows behind it, it isn't. We hardly ever see deer, rabbits, or pheasants anymore and if we do see them, they run away instantly. It's been at least six years since I've seen a fox…

Rotting Eggs

Hot steam rises from the ground and in little mud pools, bubbles slowly come up to the surface. The whole place smells like rotting eggs. We've walked into Lassen National Park and we're standing at the 'Terminal Geyser'. A large cloud of hot steam shoots up high into the air. At the bottom of the geyser, between the stones, we can see the water literally boiling. It pushes its way through the stones and is thrust out in irregular pulses. The rocks are covered in red-grey colored minerals and we can't hear a thing over the loud rushing sound. It's a little bit strange, to be standing in the middle of a volcanic hot spot all of a sudden. This is such a big change compared to the long stretches of forest we've been seeing the past couple of days.

The trail twists and turns and suddenly we arrive at a lake and not just any lake. This is Boiling Spring Lake and it looks like an otherworldly planet. It's surrounded by pine trees. From the surface, water vapor rises into the air and... it's bright green! "This is amazing!" André is in seventh heaven right now and gets out the camera. Geology, and more specifically volcanology, is one of his biggest hobbies, besides plants and animals.

"Look at those shores!" Like a kid in a candy shop he gets closer and closer. The shores are red and littered with brown mud pools that spit out large chunks of mud. A red ring has formed around them where the mud drops down. "It's like they're erupting mini-volcanoes," he calls out with a huge smile on his face. He's down halfway on his knees, trying to capture this moment on camera. I smile back. It makes me happy to see him like this. It reminds me of the stories he used to tell me about his childhood.

When he was a small boy, walking around with a big hand net. Showing off his first, self-caught salamander from the ditch behind his home. Right now, he's that same small boy again, only forty years older.

You couldn't make this up if you wanted to. We take our time to admire this miracle, but the sticky, half-dried-up red clay isn't making it easy for us to stay on this shore. We both slip and have two big red-muddy butts because of it. We laugh about it, and we're thankful that we didn't slide all the way into the water. "This is so different from what we've seen in Iceland and New-Zealand, isn't it?" I say as I try to wipe the red clay off my hands. He nods, puts one hand down on the muddy ground and stands up. He helps me up as well. Then his eyes drift back to the lake. "Yes, it is, and Chile was different yet again. Less trees, less vegetation too." We bring back memories, but it's a difficult comparison. Every volcanic area is completely different and they're all beautiful in their own way.

Lassen National Park is seen as a smaller, more compact version of Yellowstone and it is every bit as stunning. We're entering the park from the south, and we're headed straight for Drakesbad: a lodge with a restaurant and we've gotten up extra early, especially for that restaurant. We put the pedal to the metal this morning and hiked an additional six miles just to get there in time for lunch! There's a rumor that PCT-hikers can get a good discount on lunch there. If what we hear is true, the lodge guests get first pick at the lunch buffet and then the PCT-hikers get a signal to join in. We can eat whatever we want and it's supposed to be exquisite, too!!! Hiker Hunger; it's taken over our brains again.

When we get there, we find out that all the rumors are true. The food is amazing and we eat until we're full. It's very relaxed here. We decide to take an extra day to rest, and we pitch our tent in the nearby campground.

It's a small lodge with a spectacular view. There aren't many tourists here, which is a sharp contrast with Yellowstone. There's even a swimming pool, filled with naturally warm water that's high on minerals. This is what most of the guests have come for: an amazing wellness experience in the midst of nature. After a certain time PCT hikers are also allowed to go in the pool. A sign tells us: "The water is collected straight from the hot spring. It has soothing and softening qualities." Well, that sounds great.
"Do you mind if we join you?" I ask one of the other guests. "Not at all, come in." The vibe is pleasant. I sit on the side of the pool, stick my toes in the water and then slowly sink my legs in. "Ooooh, this is nice!" I say. The man nods and says, "We've been coming here for over ten years and now you know why." My arms are resting on the poolside. I turn around and slowly slide all the way into the pool. "This is amazing!" That man is completely right. I'm grinning ear to ear, I look at André and pull on his foot. "Come on in!" I don't have to tell him twice. Before I know it, he's in the water with me and we spend the rest of the day enjoying this wonderful place.

The people are so friendly, they even let us join in on their enormous barbecue. Such wonderful abundance! We are always surprised by how happy this ordinary food makes us feel after eating dehydrated food for so many days. It feels extravagant. Food that would be totally normal at home, tastes divine out here and it helps you put your feet back firmly on the ground. Aren't we just incredibly lucky to have what we have? Sometimes I don't understand why people complain so much back home or on TV. It's little things like these that make you realize just how wonderful life is. It's amazing what a period of abstinence can do!

The next morning, André goes out alone. He's going to visit 'Devil's kitchen', a geological area, about an hour's walk from here. I'm going to relax and lie around in the grass, in the sun, and now I finally have some time to read on my e-reader. When André returns, he tells me that it was small, but very beautiful. He's had a great time, too. After yet another nice lunch, André is looking at a rack with postcards. A card catches his eye. He takes it from the rack and shows it to me. "Look how beautiful this is. I wonder if it's near the trail." I see a big black volcano with pretty colored lava around it. "I don't know. I've never seen a picture like that in any of the trail books." He turns the card around. Cinder Cone and Painted Dunes, it says on the back. "Never heard of it," he mutters. He goes inside and strikes up a conversation with the lady at the counter. She explains that it's not near the PCT. She points to where it is on the map and which trail you have to walk to get there. He comes back out. "It's a five-mile detour, give or take. If we take this trail, we'll go right by it and then we can take this one back to the PCT. It looks really cool. It would be a shame if we missed it. What do you think?" I totally agree and after another good cup of coffee, we thank our kind hosts and hit the trail again.

A spectacular, pitch-black, crumbly lava-covered plain opens up in front of our eyes. In the distance we can see the volcano. There's no road, or parking lot anywhere. Not a soul in sight. We leave our backpacks at the foot of the volcano. We take a bottle of water and follow the path up. The volcano lives up to its name. It's a perfect cone, completely made up of cinders: small grains of ejected lava. It's like walking on pieces of black coal, that are made of solid rock. With every step we take, we sink into it and then slide back a little. Still, it doesn't take us very long to reach the top. Before we know it, we're on the edge of the crater and the view is phenomenal.

"Oh man, oh man, this is stunning!" Why isn't this a part of the PCT?" André is ecstatic again and I completely understand why. This view is absolutely amazing. "I don't know. It's just a small detour. Maybe it's because of the tricky footing or maybe it's quite fragile?" We don't understand it, but we're fully enjoying it! We're on the edge now and to our left we can see a deep crater. It's kind of a rusty-brown color, and it's oval-shaped. The edge is nice and smooth, as if it was made yesterday. To our right, below us, are the 'Painted Dunes'. It's actually the end of a lava plain, but from a distance it really does look like dunes. "Pretty, isn't it?" All those red, yellow, beige and black spots," I say, pointing in that direction. André turns around. "Wooooow! That is intense!" His jaw has dropped and he's speechless. Behind the colored dunes is a small plain full of black sand and behind that, the green forest begins again. Far away in the distance we see the great volcano Mount Lassen, standing tall above all the other peaks.

The sun is low and paints pretty shadows in the landscape. We're up high. We feel like birds, flying high in the sky, all alone. We're side by side, admiring this beautiful, surreal landscape. He takes my hand and says nothing. We are so happy we didn't miss this.

Kangaroos? Really?

Here we are, in a big dark cave with black walls. Something moves, and it catches my eye. I look up and see a bat, dropping from the ceiling. It's not very big; its body isn't even half the size of my hand. It's a small little brown ball of fur with wings. As it flies by me, its little mouth opens up, like it's yawning. The inside of its mouth is bright pink with tiny, bright white teeth. It flaps towards the exit: a large round hole. Outside, the sun is blazing, trying fiercely to break through the cave walls.

It's five o'clock in the afternoon and outside it's scorching hot, over 104 degrees Fahrenheit. The ruthless sun is trying vigorously to get to us, but there's no way she can. It's nice and cool in here, and it's staying that way. Subway Cave isn't actually a cave, but a lava tunnel. A large, long tube winding through the Earth's crust underground. Lian looks up and says, "I can hardly imagine that liquid lava used to flow through here." Her headlamp shines on the ceiling, and it creates a spotlight, in which I see small sharp points facing downwards. "I think the sharp points are from the left-over lava, dripping down after the rest of the lava cleared out of the tube." She's thinking the same thing. There are a lot of them. They run across almost the entire length of the tunnel. It looks like the whole ceiling is covered in tiny stalactites, no more than an inch tall. They are a different color too; a rusty sort of brown, while the walls are black and smooth.

We walk the entire length of the tube. Sometimes the ceiling is right above your head, but at other times, like now, it's up to fifty feet above you. We can't see the entrance anymore and it's pitch-dark. We clamber over the fallen rocks and stand up on top of them to look around. It's quite humid here, and our headlamps leave behind a long trail in this otherwise empty space. There's nobody else here. "I feel like we're in a Hollywood picture. Like we're in a Jules Verne story, on our way to the center of the Earth." My imagination is on a roll now. Lian laughs. "Hahaha, yes, all we need now is dinosaurs."

In the coolness of the tunnel, we take our time and wait for nightfall. Northern California is extremely hot this time of year. Above us, just outside the tunnel, is Hat Creek Rim. One of the hottest parts of the PCT. We knew this difficult section was coming up. Around noon we talked about it while we were eating a huge ice-cream in the nearby town Old Station. "There's a campsite here. We could take a shower, pitch the tent and then get up really early. Like around three o'clock?" I suggest. My ice-cream starts dripping all over my fingers, and I quickly lick it all off. "That way, we'll be well on our way before it gets really hot." Lian listens. Her fingers are covered in ice-cream too. She licks the bottom of the ice-cream and says, "Yes, and then we'll be sweating and struggling the rest of the day, won't we? I really don't feel like hiking through that heat. There won't be any drinking water for the next 25 miles and there won't be much shade either. It's said to be an oven out there!" No, it's not a nice temperature to be doing anything active in during the day, I totally agree with that. So, we decide to hike the entire section at night.

Right now, it's about seven o'clock in the evening. I'm looking out from inside the cave, and I can clearly notice the light getting less and less bright and a bit more yellow too. The bats on the ceiling have noticed it too and are starting to get restless. They're getting ready to go hunting. The first ones are already letting go and flying towards the exit. The rest of them follow soon after. It looks like it's time to go. We get up and go outside. By the entrance is a small water tap. We fill up our water bottles and start our hike. The orange-red sun dips behind the horizon and by the time we're out, the sky has changed from orange to purple. We're on top of a mile-long cliff. In front of us is an immense barren valley with volcanoes lined up as far as the eye can see. It's an extraordinary view. After about an hour's walk, only the outlines of the mountains are still visible. The world looks like a black-and-white pencil drawing, with a thick orange line hovering just on the horizon. Above it, is a deep dark blue sky. To our left we can see a small crescent moon just over the top of a volcano. We're not sure, but we think it might still be Mt. Lassen. Next to it, Venus is shining brightly. What a wonderful night. Somehow, I feel sad. It's such a shame that it's getting dark now, because this is a very special place. We're walking precisely on top of a fault plane. One million years ago, this valley was all level, at the same height, but because of underground forces, the Earth's crust sank down along a very long crack. The valley is now almost 1000 feet below us. During the day, the views are said to be spectacular, but the decision has been made and I really think it was the right one. If I had been ploughing through the heat, I probably wouldn't have been able to enjoy it anyway. After an hour, we turn on our headlamps. It's pitch-dark now, and we can't see the trail anymore.

"What kind of strange animal is that?" Lian says suddenly. She's hiking in front of me and she's stopped in her tracks. She turns halfway around and points at the ground in front of her. I aim my headlamp at her feet and then I see it. A small dark-grey animal with a huge tail jumps onto the trail in front of her. Its fur glistens in the light, like silk. "Look at its huge feet!" I come closer to see what she sees. It has a slim, pointy face with large whiskers and under the chubby abdomen are two enormous feet. They are in no way proportionate to its tiny front paws. "What about the tail, it's at least three times the size of its entire body. I've never seen anything like it," she says excitedly. The animal stands still and looks our way. With its large dark-brown eyes, it's staring at us. "I think the body is about two or three inches tall. What do you think?" But before she can answer, the animal runs away. It's going down our trail, so we follow it. "It looks like a kangaroo," Lian says. "Look at it, hopping!" Yes, it does. It's like a miniature kangaroo, big ears included, and it's not alone. "Look! There's another four or them! They're so cute!" She says. They're all hopping along in front of us. Like a small family, we're easing on down the road together. We take a few steps, and in turn they take quite a number of hops. They're trying to stay ahead of us. They stay with us for at least ten minutes and they won't go off the trail. We decide to leave them in peace. We leave the trail and walk around them. "Byyyyeee, sweet creatures!" I hear Lian say. In the meantime, I'm checking the animal app on our phone. What are they? It doesn't take me long to find them. They're called kangaroo rats. Fitting name.

It's now two a.m. and we accidentally interrupt a group of PCT-hikers. We almost step on them. They're lying on a groundsheet like sardines in a can. It's a group of about six bearded men without a tent. "Umph, huh?" one of them moans, and another one sits up. We quickly whisper that we're hikers too and that we're just passing by. They lie back down. They weren't expecting anyone to come by this late, so they laid down on the trail. Seeing those sleeping hikers gave our bodies a signal. We're getting tired and not long after that we decide to take a 'power nap'. Like the hikers we passed, we don't put up our tent. We lay down our groundsheet, inflate our mattresses and crawl into our sleeping bags. Two hours later, the alarm goes off and we get back on the trial. A little bit of sleep can really pick you up. Even though we're not super fit, we have enough renewed energy to hike out the last ten miles. Slowly, the sun comes up and the end of the cliff is in sight. We hike through some shrubs into the valley and not much longer after that, we arrive at a river. There are tall trees here and even geese on the water. The sun is starting to heat things up quite a bit already. We decide to have a meal and get a few hours of sleep. We made it!

Unexpected Love

André is staring into nothingness. He seems distant and a bit moody. It's been a tough week for him. His shoes aren't very comfortable anymore. The sole looks OK, but there's something wrong with the inside. The result: two huge, long blisters on the edge of the sole of his foot, near the heal. "Can you get me that jar?" We're standing still and I open the zipper to one of the side pockets of the backpack. He's been hiking on the painkiller Ibuprofen for days now. Hikers sometimes jokingly call it 'Vitamin I'. We all carry a box with about 200 pills on us. "A few more and I'll start naming them...," he says, taking a small white pill out of the box. He puts it in his mouth and drinks it down with a big gulp of water. Half-ring-blisters, that's what he's calling them now. As if they were individuals. Little devils, constantly nagging him all day long. "I'm good for another hour," he says. He smiles, but not really. His head drops slightly and he takes a step. His face cringes. "I just need to start up. The pain is unbearable," he mumbles. Whenever we stop for a moment, it's always the first few steps that hurt him the most.

He hasn't been able to enjoy this at all in the past couple of days. It's a shame because Burney Falls is one of the most extraordinary places we've passed. At this waterfall, the water doesn't fall over a rock; the wall consists of porous, black lava. At the top, the water sinks into the porous stone, only to come out at the front, like white veils on a pitch-black backdrop. Underneath the waterfall is a small, blue lake surrounded by green vegetation. It's magnificent to see, but it doesn't really get through to André. Every time we stop to take a picture, his face cringes with pain when we start up again. Still, for a second, he looks like his happy, excited self again, when he notices that at the top of the waterfall, on a branch, is a large nest, that belongs to a bird of prey. Thankfully, his introverted mood changes completely when we arrive in the small town of Mount Shasta.

"There they are!" I yell and start waving. They are unmistakable with their two Australian leather hats. They smile and start waving back. Our good friends from the Netherlands are here! I walk up to them as quickly as I can, open up my arms and embrace Thea. It's like I'm hugging her to death. This is not something I normally do with Thea, but in this moment, I feel so much emotion surfacing. Way more than I expected. "It's so good to see you!!!! How are you?! How was your journey?" I have too many questions and I want to know everything. André gives René a big hug and they smile big smiles at each other.
"This is great. What a surprise!" I've only known they were coming for a few days. Back home, they told us they were planning on exploring the north-west of the United States. We had looked to see if our plans could somehow intertwine with theirs, but it was pretty doubtful at the time. Up front, we couldn't say for certain, if we'd be far enough along on the trail by now. Also, we had no idea how it would fit into their itinerary. And now they're here!
"How long was your drive?" I ask, and Thea starts telling.
"Well, it wasn't so bad at all really. It was about a three-hour-drive from Crater Lake." I give René a big hug too, to which he says smiling, "But it was absolutely worth it! We wouldn't want to miss this!"
We all nod in agreement. Together we walk into town and catch up on things. We have a bite to eat and a few drinks on a cozy little patio and have a wonderful time.

Later that day, we go to an outfitter store together. As soon as we open the door, we see a small, young woman, in her early twenties standing at the clothing racks. Her hand is holding the sleeve of a blue down coat. "Hey, that's BC," André says. She hears her name, turns around and smiles. Today she's not wearing her huge, dark-brown, square sunglasses. You know, the kind some people wear over their regular glasses, with dark, hard plastic sides on them. BC stands for 'Birth Control'. Other hikers decided that she'd never find a partner with those sunglasses. It's hilarious how some of these nicknames come about. In the store, we run into even more people that we haven't seen in a while. Aquanaut and Little Bear are here too. They're happy to see us and I introduce them to Thea and René. All of us hang around, talking and sharing adventures. However, André steps out quite quickly. He's on a mission. He ordered new gear on his phone while we were on our way here. It should be somewhere in this store. Joined by a shop assistant, he goes off somewhere and after fifteen minutes he's back with a huge smile on his face. He points to the floor. "Look, new shoes and new insoles!" That grin on his face is ear to ear. "Maybe this will mean I'm finally done with these blisters!" I hope so too. Even though he's tended to his blisters daily, a deep blood blister had formed under the layer of callus.

This was such an amazing day and we feel fully re-energized. Thea and René give us a ride to the point where we left the trail. We say loving goodbyes and wish them lots of fun on the rest of their trip. "You guys have a wonderful journey too. We hope your feet feel better, André!" We wave them goodbye until René puts his head back into the car, and the window closes. They're headed back to Crater Lake. We'll be there in about three weeks. I wonder what it will be like.

Here we are again, all alone, in the same spot where we left off, where the trail goes off into the bushes. A strange, empty feeling comes over us. We start walking and to our great surprise there's a young woman in the bushes. "Hey, hello. How are you?" André says enthusiastically. She looks up from the shade. She's holding a hiking map. She folds it and stands up. "Hi, my name's Fire Cracker." She's nice and spontaneous and looks very fit.

"Hello Fire Cracker, I'm Morning Star and this is CookieMonster." Her eyes open wide. "You're the Dutch Danish Belgians!!" We laugh loudly. "Yes, we've been called that before, but it's been a while. We haven't seen the people who called us that in quite some time." She straightens her back, smiles and then starts speaking a language that's completely unknown to us.

André and I lock eyes. She's telling us some kind of story and we don't understand a word of it. What is this about? When she's done talking, she looks at us inquisitively. Apparently, she's waiting for an answer. She hesitates and then asks in English, "You speak Danish, right?" A frown appears on André's forehead. Surprised, he says, "Uhm.. No, we don't speak Danish. We do speak a little bit of Norwegian. Why do you think we speak Danish?" She stares back at us, quietly and blankly. Like she's frozen until she's processed this. After about three seconds the corners of her mouth drop.

Her shoulders hang down and her straight back slouches forward. She starts speaking, in a soft, disappointed voice, "Some people on the trail told me you speak Danish and I was really looking forward to speaking my native language! It's driving me crazy, speaking English all the time. I'm all alone, and I've been trying to find you for weeks." She takes a deep breath, we're dumbfounded, waiting for her to finish the story. "I've started hiking more miles a day to catch up to you. I saw your names in the trail logs and I knew you couldn't be far ahead of me!" She sighs. "And now you don't even speak Danish..." We feel sorry for her. André steps up to her and puts his arm around her. He starts speaking a few sentences in Norwegian, hoping to sound somewhat Scandinavian after all. Maybe similar sounds will make her feel better. But it has the same effect as someone speaking German to a Dutch or Belgian person. Nice try, but it's not really what she needs.

After seeing Thea and René, we know exactly how she feels. Even though initially, we thought it would be nice to see them, it turned out to be much more emotional for us than we had anticipated. We are never really homesick. We're focused on this adventure now, but we're not hiking all by ourselves, we have each other and we speak Dutch to each other. Fire Cracker can't speak Danish to anyone and being a foreigner, all alone in another country, she's a lot more isolated than we are. We have come across many PCT-hikers from the USA, that meet up with family or friends along the trail, to have some fun together. Like visiting Yosemite together or taking a detour from the trail to go to Las Vegas for a weekend. Just to be together for a little while and recharge the batteries. For foreign hikers, who hike alone and don't have family or friends in the US, this is extra hard.

To us, seeing our friends was like coming home for a moment. It pulls you out of your cocoon and makes you realize quite suddenly, what it's actually all about. However beautiful and adventurous; a hike is only a hike. A mission is only a mission. The love and company of trusted family and friends is worth so much more. It's fascinating really, that we have to travel so far to be able to really feel that, deep inside of us. At home we take so much for granted and we never actually stop to really think about it.

Buns and Bears Don't Go Together

"What the hell," André suddenly says. He puts his left hand flat on the ground and slowly pushes himself up. His gaze is fixed on something straight ahead. My eyes follow the direction he's looking in. Completely out of nowhere, no more than 60 feet away from us, a big fat bear is sticking its head up out of the overgrowth. It's got a pretty good reason for coming this close to us. We have been a bit reckless.

This morning we were in Etna. One of the many adorable little western towns that are close to the trail. Today is a resupply day, and after hitchhiking a quick ride in the morning, we picked up the package we had sent to ourselves with food and new maps. There's a small breakfast / lunch diner in the town, that's famous for its delicious and super-sized Cinnamon Rolls, or Sticky Buns. These rolls are as big as a baby's head. Your mouth starts watering just looking at them. On top of the bun is a sweet, brown, sticky layer of cinnamon and it smells amazing. We bought two to eat at dinner and we're eating them right now. Normally we don't eat this close to our tent but there wasn't enough room on this steep hill to put up our tent or to cook anything. Also, the spectacular sunset view made this the perfect spot to enjoy a wonderful cinnamon roll. Without even realizing it, we haven't been careful enough and now it's here, and we didn't see it coming...

They're staring into each other's eyes; André and the bear. The first five seconds are crucial. Who is the alpha here? André stands up even further, straightens his back and with a loud voice, but not yelling, he calmly approaches the bear. It's a black bear and that means showing off your dominance is vital. The bear gets up on its back legs. Half its body is sticking out above the bushes.

André takes another step, and another and starts talking.
"Hey, bear. How are you? Is everything OK?"
"Yeah, you smelled my bun and that's why you've come, isn't it? Yeah, that was careless on our part. We should have known better."
The bear sticks its nose into the air to take in the scent. It lowers its left front paw. The eyes look alright. No aggression so far. So clumsy. We should have known better and eaten this somewhere else, where there's more open terrain. But it's too late to go back and now we're here on a mountain cliff, literally with our backs against the wall.
"But we're definitely going to eat this ourselves, and you are going to leave," André says when he's within thirty feet of the bear. This is getting very close. I can see André is slowing his pace, but he's moving closer, in a straight line towards the bear, looking it straight in the eyes.

We're not the bear's primary prey, they are much more interested in our food. So, I'm not just sitting around either. Quickly, but not rushing, I'm stuffing all the food we've taken out of the Ursack back into it. The buns too. I close it with a special knot, that the bear can't open with its claws or its teeth. If it tries to grab our food now, it can try as it may; the food won't come out. Bears are incredibly smart: If just one hiker, camper, or anyone for that matter makes a mistake by not protecting his food properly, a bear will find it and eat it, and learn that it can find food around people. The next hiker it comes across will have a serious problem. Especially if he's hiking alone.
The bear is looking around, unsure what to do. Meanwhile, André has entered into the bear's comfort zone. Is it leaving or attacking? That's the thought going through my mind as I wait for the bear to make its next move. Black bears usually tend to cut their losses and leave, but they are still wild animals, that each have their own personality. We've come across very cheeky young bears before. They had just left their mother and wanted to try their luck, like adolescents. This bear seems more mature.

André changes his direction, going towards the bear at a slight angle now instead of the straight line. After a few steps he blocks the bear's line of attack from me, the camp, and the food. With a confident voice he slowly steps towards the bear again. It's getting nervous now and gets back down on four feet. To André's right is open terrain; enough room to make an escape. The bear is still looking around, but when André suddenly starts clapping his hands loudly, it shoots away and runs towards the open space. It always amazes us how fast they can run, even though they look so bulky and tough. It runs towards the woods, exactly to the spot where the PCT-trail comes out of the trees. It takes the trail and runs into the forest. That's the last we ever saw of it.

We know there are a few other hikers that are not far behind us, like Fire Cracker. We talked to her earlier this afternoon in Etna, during lunch. She found someone there who had emigrated from Denmark, so she can speak Danish as much as she wants now. It's made her feel less homesick and we're happy for her. She also told us that she was planning to leave a few hours after us. If that's true, she'll be in the middle of a bear adventure of her own right about now.

Close Encounter

The smell of smoke wakes us up at night. It stings our eyes. It's been like this for the past couple of days, in a milder form, but now it's sharp and extremely annoying. My nose is filled with it. Lian is uneasy; ever since the lava eruption on Hawaii, where the lava rushed right by us and melted the soles of our shoes, she's not been a fan of fire or anything to do with burning. She's become extremely alert at even the slightest trace of fire. Consequently, she's the first to wake up. "We have to check out how close it is. I think it's close, it's making me cough." It's still dark outside. We get out of the tent, hoping to see a hint of a red glow somewhere. We look around, we even go up the ridge, but we don't see any clues as to where the fire is. The smoke hasn't been this thick so far, and we're starting to worry. "I can't see anything," I say. The middle of the night is not my strongest time of the day and I really just want to go back to bed.

Because of the smoke, we haven't been sleeping in the valleys for days anyway. Carbon monoxide is heavier than air, so it sinks to the ground, and we heard that someone had been found dead in his tent recently due to carbon monoxide poisoning. On top of a hill, just below the ridge, with a nice breeze seemed to be the perfect place to spend the night, so I think we'll be OK. "Let's wait until morning, we'll be able to see better," I say, a bit sleepy and naive. Fortunately, Lian stays alert. "No, we're packing up and moving out. The dark makes it easier to see if anything's burning or smoldering. If the smoke gets too thick, we can always turn back," she says sternly. "Alright then..." I know that Lian is usually the more sensible of us both, so I concede, like a little boy obeying his mother. We pack up our stuff.

Not long after that we see the plumes of smoke rising at first light. Helicopters are flying in and out. Carrying a large cable underneath, with an enormous red bag of water. This fire can't be more than two miles away from us. It doesn't look very big, but these things tend to spread faster than you'd think, so we pick up the pace.

Not much later we arrive at a small lake. We only planned to take a short break here, but the loud noise from the helicopter blades catches our attention. Over the hill, just above the treetops, we see the big red water bag coming right at us. The helicopter soaring high above it. "The fire can't have reached this far already, can it?" I say, with a bit of a sore throat. We stand up, climb up the hill and see nothing. The smoke in the air stings in our eyes and breathing is no fun at all. "Can you see anything?" She looks around. "No, I can't, there's nothing in our immediate surroundings." We turn on our cell phone, hoping to be able to communicate with somebody, anybody, but as usual: no signal. What do we do next? We have a PLB with us, a Personal Locator Beacon. It's an emergency transmitter. We can use it to send a mayday signal with our exact location to Search and Rescue via satellite. But we don't want to use it unless it's an absolute emergency, and it's not that bad yet. Plus, there's a helicopter quite close to us.

The helicopter comes down and lowers the water bag. The cable loosens and the bag disappears under water. Very slowly, the cable gets tighter again and when the water bag is filled up, the helicopter leaves before we get a chance to talk to the pilot. The whole thing didn't even take a minute and in that time, we walked into a clearing, where he'd be able to see us clearly. Or we hope he's seen us anyway. We made a conscious decision not to wave, because he might think we're in trouble, which we aren't yet, hopefully.

The uncertainty is killing us. There's a fire nearby, no more than half an hour away from us, according to the plumes of smoke we saw this morning. Do we hike on, or not? We discuss it and decide to stay here for now. One of the most important things in rescue missions, is that they need to know where you are. This is where they get water, and the lake is quite high up, so it's not in a valley. The hilltop has no overgrowth and is primarily rocky. If the fire reaches us, we can probably escape that way. If we keep going, we don't know what kind of terrain and vegetation we'll run into. The map indicates a quite densely overgrown area with a huge forest that seems to go on for days. Would they ever be able to find us in there?

The suspense rises, as helicopters follow each other to the lake to pick up water. We've put on our red raincoats and we're on the shore of the lake now, in a clearing. We think they know we're here by now. After about two hours we see that one of the helicopters is letting down the water bag and cable on the other side of the lake instead of in the water. We stand up right away. This is our chance! We get our backpacks and make our way over there. The helicopter lands on a level spot. The pilot, dressed in orange, gets out, but the blades keep turning. Are we being evacuated? We quicken our pace and within a minute we've reached him.

"Hi, how are you? Is the fire close?" Lian asks. The pilot nods. "Yeah, it's pretty close; about two and a half miles," he answers. "Should we go with you?" He looks at us inquisitively and you can tell that he's thinking about it. "No, I don't think that's necessary. We've got it under control for the most part. Maybe about another hour, and the worst will be over. But, just to be sure, which way are you going?" We show him the map and the route we plan to take. We also show him that there aren't any escape routes for the next two days. Just forest and wilderness, no side roads.

His finger rests on the map. He follows the line and says, "I think you'll be OK. The wind will be blowing in the opposite direction for the next few days, so away from you. If it does pick up and come your way again, you'd be long gone before it got to you." We're so happy! We tell him that we're carrying an emergency transmitter and we give him our names. He'll pass that on to his headquarters, including the route we intend to take. He also tells us that he'd seen us earlier and had already passed it on to headquarters. He only landed because he'd gotten tired and wanted a bite to eat before getting back to work. With our minds put at ease we say goodbye and wish him good luck. He turns off the helicopter blades and we walk back towards the trail. Away from all that fire and smoke.

The Pancake Challenge

It's a hot, sticky morning when we walk slowly into Seiad Valley. A mornings when you feel like you can't move. It's almost 90 degrees and the day has barely begun. Forest fires are ravaging the area, so the air in this place is thick with greasy, fiery smoke. Breathing is slow and hard. We cross a bridge under which we spot a beaver and enter the very small town.

There's a strange vibe around here and it's not just the smoke. We're about to enter a small shop to buy some things when a rusty old pick-up truck pulls up next to us. In the driver's seat is a man with a very long beard, like those guys from the old rock band 'ZZ Top'. He's just sitting there, staring at us, in his dungarees with one loose button. Next to him, in the passenger seat, is a double-barrel shotgun. He gets out of the truck without saying a word and walks up to the shop. We're glad to see him leave the shotgun behind. He even cracked the window. This is not something we're used to seeing when we go to the supermarket at home in Belgium.

"Are you sure you want to go inside?" Lian asks me. After a moment of doubt, we decide to follow him in. A friendly lady helps us at the counter. It turns out he's a regular customer who lives a bit further down the road. As for the gun... "Oh well, this place attracts a lot of free-spirited folk. People who don't really fit in with the rest of society. They live here and about in trailers or in small houses, sometimes legally, sometimes not." I look at her vacant expression. "Is it customary for people to have their shotgun in the car?" I ask. "It's a matter of not asking too many questions," she answers, after which she passionately starts ranting like a real small-town country girl. She tells us that Seiad Valley is a part of Jefferson State; a part of California that's trying to become independent. "We're not about to let them communist bastards rule over us! We need our own state and we're fighting hard for it." We listen patiently to her plea. We never knew something like this was going on here. We pay for our stuff and go outside, after which we go straight into the diner. We're starving and they have air conditioning!

The vibe is pleasant and there's a greasy smell in the air. There are at least ten other hikers here, chatting away at tables and enjoying their hamburgers. Behind the counter is a big lady, who looks very busy at the grill. Above her are all kinds of little jars with herbs and bottles of Tabasco. Her red-checkered apron is dingy, which doesn't surprise me, as she's flinging chunks of butter on the grill like there's no tomorrow. On top of the butter she pours a thick layer of batter.

If there's anything this town is famous for, it's the 'Pancake Challenge'. It's a legend among PCT-hikers. They've all been looking forward to it for days and everyone keeps asking each other the same question: "Are you going to try?" We can see exactly what this lady is doing, and what a huge tower of pancakes this is turning out to be. Each one is at least as big, and as thick, as a medium pizza. When she's finished, a waitress takes the enormous pile to a table next to ours. She puts it down in front of a massive guy, who is so tall and bearded, he looks like he could have come straight out of a Viking movie. Gentle Giant is his nickname and he's up for the challenge! He has two hours to eat about fifteen pancakes. If he succeeds, he doesn't have to pay for his meal. "Do you have some maple syrup and some butter, please?" he asks the waitress. I guess he didn't see how much butter is already in there... The tension is rising. Everyone around him is laughing and cheering him on. "Are you really going to eat all that?" I ask, doubtfully. He smiles and says, "Why not!" but after the third pancake, signs of resistance are starting to show. How on Earth is he supposed to finish all that? He's starting to feel sick from all the binging and after he stuffs down a few more pieces, he decides to share the rest with his friends. Everyone applauds him for trying and we all thank him for our share of the pancake. It's almost one o'clock by now and the diner is closing. We go back outside, into the heat.

Like busty Greek goddesses they're lying there, Chef and Thunder Bunny, resting on the bench and on the table. Their mighty strong, toned legs pulled up a bit, their curves pointing proudly into the sky. They are in the shade, processing their food and bested by the heat. After about half an hour a strange man approaches them. He's sitting on something that looks a bit like a chopper motorcycle. Only, there's no engine. Even stranger: there are no pedals, no gas handles, and no gas tank. As he comes closer, we see that it's an adult balance bike. He's trying to impress the two ladies. "Weird bike," one of them says. "Yeah, I bought it because I wasn't allowed to ride a motorcycle anymore. It's nice, isn't it? Looks just like a real chopper!" He seems to think he's pretty cool and doesn't really notice that, despite all his tall tales, he doesn't stand a chance. At some point he starts to see the signs and kicks it up a notch. He starts making bizarre karate-like movements - shirtless - while his belly vaguely wiggles along. We look at this spectacle for a little while and then walk away laughing.
By now the temperature has gone up to 116 Fahrenheit and the thick smog is making it extremely hard to breathe. It's too hot to continue. We decide to cool off in a shallow creek. The water slowly streams around our feet. Unfortunately, it's too shallow to get all the way in. We eat some blackberries that grow on the riverbanks.

"Where is all this smoke coming from? It only seems to be getting worse," Lian says. "The map says there's a Ranger Station down the road. Why don't we walk down there and find out what's going on," I reply and that's what we did. When we get there, the deputy sheriff stares at us with a smile that's missing a few teeth. Brown goo is squiggling over his teeth. He's chewing tobacco. I didn't know people still did that. He spits some of it out to the side, like that's a very normal thing to do, and starts talking. "What can I do for you?" I ask him why the smoke is so thick around here and if we should be worried about anything. "We're surrounded by four very large fires and quite a few smaller ones too. But there's no need to worry about that. They're very far away, but since we're in a lower section out here, the smoke is coming towards us from all corners."

Lian asks him about the conditions on the trail and if we're OK to keep hiking. "No problem! When you climb out of this valley, you'll see that there's a lot less smoke there." Feeling somewhat reassured we return to the creek. It's still way too hot to hike. We put our feet back into the water and doze off.

At the end of the day, it's still 104 degrees, but we don't think we should hang around here any longer. The heat, the stickiness, the smog, the strange people... No, it was an interesting place to visit, but it's time for us to move on. Around five o'clock we make an attempt to leave. Our t-shirts stick to our backs. We drink as much as we can to keep hydrated, but because of that our water supply seems to be evaporating as we speak. The first climb is a tough one, and we have to rest regularly. Our bodies are having a hard time keeping cool. Eventually we find a good spot up in the mountains. There's still smog here, but it's a lot less than down in the valley.

Mind Games

'The blues' or 'I'm feeling blue': both are expressions of a melancholy, sad, even depressed feeling. A lot of people on the trail are experiencing this. It's called the 'California Blues'. After conquering the desert and crossing the Sierra Nevada mountains, we're now entering an area that has less impressive impulses. Huge forests, nothing but trees, day in, day out. The blues set in just after you pass the halfway point. It's the realization that you have to hike the same distance AGAIN, that really affects your mental state. With not much variety, you start to retreat into your mind and your mind starts to play tricks on you. Every hiker that's still on the trail now knows at least five or six people that have quit. An estimated 60% of all the people that were granted a PCT-permit have stopped by this point. We were told that on average, only 20% of all hikers make it to the finish line, so we will be saying goodbye to even more people before we get there.

It all starts with your own physical limitations, like a wall you have to conquer. All long-distance hikers know the problem; your body won't go any further, even though your mind wants to. You're constantly hungry and you're not getting enough nutrients. Even though you eat like a bear; you can't get rid of the gnawing, empty feeling inside. Your body is telling you, "Enough is enough, I can't go any further." We too have been through this a number of times. You just can't go on. You're done. After the physical depletion has set in, the mental dip kicks in. The fatigue, the immensely long distance you still have to go and being completely overwhelmed by everything you've experienced, all contribute to the games that your mind will try to play on you now. Everything that's ever bothered you, or that you've ever had to go through, gets all the room it needs to surface right now.

How you handle this, is crucial. Mind Games. Any professional athlete will tell you that trying to perform when you're feeling down, isn't going to get you a gold medal. The mind needs to be happy, strong, but above all calm and balanced.

Everyone has their own way to get through this uneventful part of the trail. Some hikers leave the trail and visit the towns to find some distraction. Others hike like crazy and walk up to thirty or forty miles a day. Only to end up at some town completely exhausted and stuffing themselves with food. Some hikers skip large pieces of this section of the trail and will come up with all kinds of excuses to explain why they couldn't walk that part. They'll say it's too hard, too hot, too high, too boring, etc. Others use what they call Vitamin W or 'Smoking Weed'. They smoke a whole lot of pot just to take the edge off.

Other hikers listen to music or audio books. We recently came across someone who had listened to thirteen books since the start. There are even people that go home for a few days. However, if you stay in your comfort zone too long - like a comfy bed, soft pillows, taking showers whenever you want to, gaming, watching TV, hanging around and doing nothing, having dinner with friends, etc. - you never know if you'll even want to go back to the trail. It's very tempting to just stay there. Some people do decide to just stay home and there's nothing wrong with that. It's their adventure. They can end it however they want to.

We have a hard time too, sometimes. All the trees are starting to look the same and we've seen pretty much every plant and creature there is to see by now. We try to stay positive, even though we sometimes find ourselves in deep places in our mind. There are still a few unresolved traumas there and they apparently want to say something right now. By talking about it, they all get a new place in our minds and slowly they start to disappear from our system.

The endless forest, an area of about 500 miles, hasn't got much variety to it. Still, we experience many things. We can still marvel at all the amazing tiny details. Every day, we keep ourselves busy by trying to spot a new kind of bird or butterfly in the beautiful, blue California sky. We also try to look at the ground more consciously and find all kinds of pretty things. Like the Cobra Lily, a carnivorous pitcher plant. Sometimes we find a view that shatters the monotony, such as the Trinity Alps. Beautiful peaks that remind us mostly of the area on the border of Austria and Germany. Marble Mountain is an absolute winner too. A bright white mountain made up entirely of solid marble.

We didn't suffer from the blues this time, we think. Sometimes we do have a bad and depressing day, but we have each other to pull us through it. If we don't have any physical issues, we will make it to Canada. Or will we? There are still massive forest fires in Washington State, at the final section of the trail. Large parts of the PCT are still closed off. So how are we going to get to Canada? Fortunately, we're still several weeks away from that but at times the uncertainty flares up. Why would we walk all that way if we won't be able to get to the end?
Hmmm...maybe we secretly are suffering from mind games.

Part Four
Volcanoes

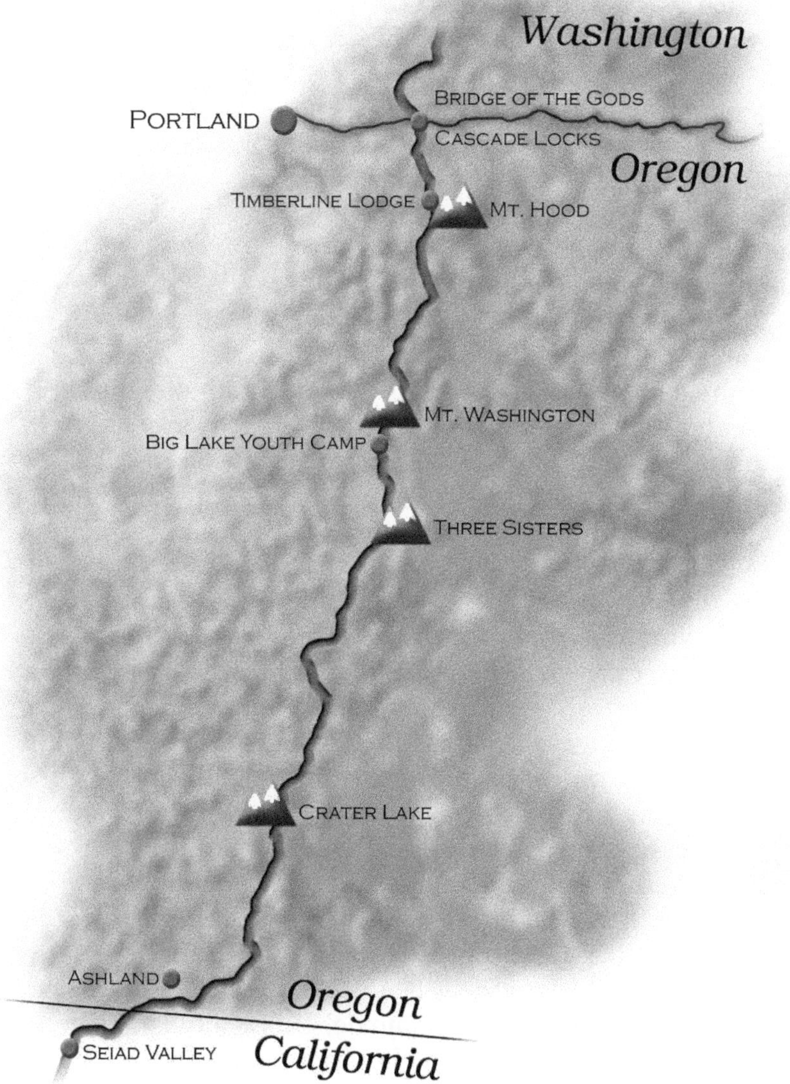
Washington
Bridge of the Gods
Portland
Cascade Locks
Oregon
Timberline Lodge
Mt. Hood
Mt. Washington
Big Lake Youth Camp
Three Sisters
Crater Lake
Ashland
Oregon
Seiad Valley
California

Shooting Stars

White lines soar through the night sky and reflect in the pitch-black water below us. It's one o'clock at night and we're on the ridge of a volcanic crater, with vertical slopes going straight down into the lake next to us. Above us the yearly Perseid meteor shower fills the sky with beautiful shooting stars while we look out over the enormous lake that fills this crater. An amazing romantic night on the ridge of Crater Lake.

Unfortunately, this is not how it happened at all. This was the romantic plan we had made for today. But everything turns out to be much more intense. What ends up happening isn't anything like what we had imagined. We get through it, eventually, but one bad decision could have been fatal here. Let's go back in time a few hours.

"Woooooow!" I blurt out before I even realize it. Lian is walking next to me. She doesn't say anything, but she is clearly as stunned as I am by what we see. We stop chatting and slow our pace. From out of nowhere the immense volcano crater suddenly appears in front of us. "Wow...This is amazing!" I say, not knowing where to look first. After Lassen National Park this is the second biggest highlight of the trail for me. I've dreamed of seeing this place for as long as I can remember. It's so much more beautiful than I thought it would be, and much more impressive than seeing it in the documentaries. The large volcano is filled with crystal-clear meltwater. The water is so still, and it has a magnificent blue color. I feel tears welling up immediately. "This view is epic...," I softly mutter. Lian nods. "I feel like we're in a movie. This is almost too good to be true. So beautiful," she says. Suddenly our busy, chatty mood has given way to bashful humility. A moment of admiration and silence. The overwhelming forces of nature have taken control of us yet again...

We walk up, right to the edge of the crater and stop at a look-out point along the trail. It's a semicircle made of pink granite rock. From here we can see the slopes below us going straight down. Lian points to her right. "It's so deep. Look at that boat. It's tiny." My eyes follow her outstretched arm. I see a white tourist boat making a tiny white line in the water. Teeny tiny waves are forming next to it. It's too far away to see how many people are on board, but judging by the large variety of colors, it's probably a lot. "That boat must be quite large to be carrying all those people. It looks so small. This lake is massive!" I answer. That little boat gives us a nice sense of perspective. I follow it for a little while, and then my eyes go back to scanning the slopes. Some of these slopes are bare, while others are completely overgrown with pine trees. To my left is Wizard Island; A small, green island in the middle of this clear blue open water. This volcano is one of the highlights of our trip. We calmly walk along the ridge of the crater, taking all the time we need to enjoy every inch of it.

A couple of hours ago, down at the campsite, we ran into 'Rob Steady'. He's a funny hiker we've been running into every now and then since the desert. He's walked with us to the top of the volcano, to a restaurant at the lodge on the crater's ridge. The terrace is already full, but we manage to get a nice table by the window. Soft lamb chops, baked salmon with shrimp scampi... The food is exquisite and we're in good company. After dinner we go out onto the crater's ridge again. The sun is low on the horizon and colors are dancing all around us. It's absolutely breathtaking. All we need now, are shooting stars.
"Look at that, on the other side of the lake," I say, and point to the huge clouds of ground fog in the distance. They roll over the edge of the crater and then they stop, floating just above the water. Lian is completely astonished, she stops and says, "It's like a fairy-tale. It looks like it might fill up the entire crater. Beautiful, isn't it? Look at those wisps of fog slowly sliding down over the edge." Our trail is going

in that exact direction. We come closer and closer, and after a while the whole crater is filled with fog. Slowly it bounces up and down. Sometimes small tufts shoot up. "It looks like a huge wizard's cauldron, with all kinds of fumes coming out of it," I say, as I picture a giant wizard in my mind, stirring his brew in the crater with a giant ladle. Lian's right, it's like a fairy-tale movie.

Not much later, when we're completely surrounded by thin fog, Rob Steady asks, "My eyes are itchy and teary. Do you feel that too?" I nod and say, "Yes, for about half an hour, and it seems to be getting worse." Lian rubs her eyes and at the same time says, "Me, too. I thought it was just me. I also feel a bit short of breath, I think." Rob shakes his head a bit, as if to say no. He looks around and continues, "It smells a bit off too. Like a burnt, smokey kind of scent blended in with the fog." I had noticed that as well, and before I can answer, Lian does it for me. "I don't think this is fog at all. I think we're walking straight into a cloud of smoke." I think she's right, but I don't want to admit it yet. I answer, "The trail ends up at a road in about half an hour. Maybe visibility will be better there? Let's go on and see what happens." We don't agree on what to do. Lian wants to turn back and Rob doesn't know what he wants to do. We compromise. We go on for another fifteen minutes and then we reevaluate.

Well, we haven't even gotten ten minutes further and our eyes are tearing up more and more. Breathing is starting to get difficult as well. Not only is visibility getting lower and lower, we're feeling worse, with every minute that goes by. "This is just not funny anymore!" I say, feeling the sharp, burnt sent enter my nostrils. Rob Steady pulls a handkerchief over his nose and mouth, which makes him look like a cowboy. "Guys, this is a big fat forest fire!" He says from behind the handkerchief. Lian grabs the map from the side pocket of my pants. She looks at it and points to her left. "That's where we need to go. If we follow the slope, we'll end up at the road. We can determine what to do from there." As she says that, huge clouds of smoke roll in and quickly surround us. This is no romantic fog on a pretty lake. And we can forget about seeing the shooting stars tonight.

Frustrated, we decide to walk back down from the crater's edge. We find the road quite quickly and the discussion starts up again. "Well, do we go right or left now? I can't see where the fire is. Can you?" Rob Steady says. No, we can't. Whichever way we go; we've got a 50% chance of walking straight into a fire. We decide to turn back to the lodge and the campsite. At least there will be people there.

After about ten minutes, we see yellow lights shining through the smoke. We're a bit far away from them, so we quicken our pace. A large fire truck emerges in front of us. A man in a red suit and a helmet is standing right next to it. We call out to him. He turns around and comes towards us. "What the hell are you doing here!!" He looks tense. "We've cut off all the roads. You're not supposed to be here!" He talks loudly and looks angry. We explain the situation to him and his facial expression changes. The anger disappears. "You really can't stay here. We're evacuating the town down the road. The fire is still about six miles out, but with this wind it's just not smart to be out here. If you had gone any further tonight, you would have walked right into it. You really can't sleep in a tent out here now. It's way too dangerous with all this smoke." We can tell that he's thinking about what to do next. "I'll take you down." That surprises us. It's more than we could have expected, and we're very happy. He signals us to get in the truck and he moves the roadblock to the side so he can drive through it. Before we know it, we're back at the campsite where we set out this morning. We thank him heartily. He gives us a friendly smile, gets back behind the wheel, and leaves to go back to where we found him.

Phew... We sigh a deep sigh of relief and look around. It's very busy. A lot of people are stranded here and there isn't much room. We find a small place to pitch our tent right next to the toilet building. Here we are, trying to sleep, right across from a building with bright lights. So we finally get to see lights in the night after all. Even though they're not the ones we'd hoped for...

The next day is amazing. The wind has changed direction and has blown all the smoke away. What's left is a clear blue sky. We start our climb again and see the beautiful blue lake. Not a trace of smoke anywhere. It's almost like it was all a surreal dream of something that never took place. We move north at a rapid pace. Evidently, the fire is still blazing, but the fire brigade tells us that the PCT trail is still open, for now...

We're in a hurry because we want to get past it quickly. Today we hike on discipline. Ninety minutes hiking, fifteen minutes break, etc., etc. We also take a half-hour lunch break. Along the way we see a mushroom cloud in the distance. Luckily, it's nowhere near us. At the end of the day, we have covered thirty miles. The next day we hike another marathon and it's a good thing we did. Two days later this fire turned into an inferno and half the park was destroyed. All the hikers that were a day or more behind us, weren't able to go on. They were stuck and were forced to hitchhike for days to go around it.

Green Islands in a Black Sea

"I don't understand any of this," I say to André. I'm staring at the map and wondering what those purple areas are supposed to be. "It's not in the legend. What do you think it is?" I look at him. "I don't know. It's quite a large area. I'll try and find it in the GPS app." He scrolls up and down a bit on the phone. "It's purple on here as well, and it doesn't say what that means. Weird. It's not a forest and it's not sand. I have no idea." He puts the phone away. "I'm sure we'll find out when we get there."
It doesn't take us long to find out what it is: rough, black lava. Large areas are completely covered in it. Our red-brown trail winds through big black blocks of it. "This is so different from the lava fields in Iceland, where everything is barren. Nothing grows there. Here, there are small green islands scattered around all over the place," André says. He's standing still on the trail and points to the islands in front of us with his hiking pole. They do look like islands. They're overgrown with bright green moss, shrubs, and dark green pine trees. "It's just like small oases, floating in a big black sea," I say. André moves his pole across the horizon and points to something else. "Do you see that strip there? I think a forest used to be there before the eruption." Burnt pine trees stick up out from the lava like big white-grey poles. He could be right… it looks like something that might even become a petrified forest one day. I look at my shoes. The lava is so sharp, it's already made holes in them. Even though the trail is clean, the texture and structure of the area makes it hard to hike at times. Sometimes we have to find our way through large blocks of lava or even climb over them, which is definitely not good for my shoes. This is my fourth pair so far on this trip. I hope they make it until Cascade Locks in Washington State, because I bought new shoes online, and had them shipped over there.

We've been on the trail for 120 days now, and we're close to The Three Sisters. It's a formation of three pointy volcanoes in a row. The sun is scorching this pitch-black, crumbly landscape. "Is it just me, or is it really hot? I'm sweating like a pig" I say. My armpits are sticky and underneath my bra, it's soaking wet. "It's so hot! Even under the umbrella." André is hiking in front of me. His head turns and he answers, "Maybe this is similar to the kind of radiation we felt at the beginning of our trip. When I collapsed from heat exhaustion, remember? Strong infrared radiation." Yes, that must be it. I see a few more purple areas on the map. "Shall we start out early again tomorrow? Then we'll get through most of our daily mileage before it gets too hot?" It wasn't really a question. In fact, it was a statement, and I know what his answer will be before he tells me: "Sure, no problem, that's fine." Today's experience teaches us that it's better to hike across the lava fields early in the morning, because the hot afternoon and evening might kill you.

Bzzz Bzzzzz We've only just sat down for lunch and the first stinging insects are swarming around us already; Yellow Jackets. We've seen lots of them lately. They look a bit like ordinary wasps, but they're much more aggressive. I'm allergic to wasps, so I'm feeling quite uneasy. "Ooouuuuch. You stupid, horrible creature!" André just got stung in his arm. "Wow, that hurts!" He shows me. That's a mean sting. It's his second one. The last one was five days ago, and his arm is still red and swollen from it. I pack my things. "Let's get out of here!" I say, and before we know it, we're a few miles further down the road.

In Oregon, the PCT passes through an area with lots of volcanoes. We're hiking among them, and each one is even more spectacular than the last. We're close to Mount Washington and we decide to take a small detour to Big Lake Youth Camp. It's a Christian youth camp and we heard it's a place we can go, to get a hot meal. There are hardly any towns along the PCT here in Oregon, so this Youth Camp will be a welcome change after so many days of eating dried food. We also heard that we can take a shower there!

After an hour's walk we come across a group of horseback riders. They're moving slowly on the same trail as us. We can't pass them, unfortunately, but the camp isn't far now, so we stay behind them. At some point we see a large wooden gate appearing in front of us. Under the horizontal beam at the top of it is a big white sign. 'Welcome to Big Lake Youth Camp' it says. We're here. We walk past the gate and not much further we see the first pyramid-shaped houses. In front of us, a large clearing opens up. This is a really big camp.

"Good afternoon." A very polite young man comes to help us. I wouldn't estimate him to be any older than eighteen. "Hi, I'm Lian, and this is André. We're hiking the PCT and we heard that we might be able to have a shower here, and maybe a bite to eat too." I look at his blond hair. I haven't seen a parting that straight in a long time. "That's right, ma'am. There, in the middle of the square, are the showers. We're all eating together tonight at seven. If you like, you're welcome to join us." Good, what we heard about this place was true. "Do we pay in advance or afterwards?" He looks surprised. "Ma'am, we see this as a way of being good Samaritans. You've been on the road for a long time. The best thing we could offer you, is a hot meal but if you insist on paying; there's a donation box at the entrance of the mess hall. If you wish, you can put something in there, so that we can continue to do the Lord's work." Wow, these are nice people! "Do you hear that?" I say to André. He's looking at postcards a bit further on and looks up. "Huh? What did you say?" He walks up to me. "This young man says, we can join them for dinner for free. They're like Trail Angels in their own way." Or is it the other way around and are Trail Angels more like them? That thought just crosses my mind. "OH, that's nice of them." André puts his

189

hand out and thanks the young man for his kind gesture. "We also have washing machines, but at the moment they're busy washing our own towels and sheets. We would be happy to wash your clothes for you in the morning."
This camp employee doesn't cease to amaze us. Cool folks around here. Still, I don't really feel comfortable taking advantage of things. Even though our clothes really do need washing, I can do it myself later on, in a lake. "That is so sweet of you, but we're leaving first thing tomorrow morning. You're very generous. Thank you for offering."

It's eight p.m. and it's lovely outside. After the wonderful meal we just had, I've decided to get two ice-creams. When I come back, I see André sitting on a bench. He's in a lively conversation with a man, and they look like they're having a lot of fun. I give André the ice-cream and sit down next to him. "Lian, this is John. John, this is my wife, Lian." I shake his hand. "Would you like an ice-cream too?" I ask. "No, thank you kindly. I've just had a nice dinner." I nod in agreement. "Yes, it was very good. Your staff have done a good job cooking. All vegetarian and very tasteful. Thank you so much!" John isn't a hiker, he's a 22-year-old young man who's here with his family. They've been coming here for years. "That's very kind of you to say. Thank you," he says with a nice, soft smile. "Lian, get this. We couldn't stop laughing just now." I stay quiet and wait patiently. I was curious to know what that was all about.
"We've just had the most hilarious misunderstanding: He said, "I'm going to serve." and I thought he said, "I'm going to surf." So, I asked where he was going to surf, Hawaii or something. Then he replied, "No, I'm not going to that mission post. I'm going to help the poor and homeless near San Francisco."" They start laughing again. "It didn't start to ring a bell with either of us and it went on like that for a while. Hilarious. I was picturing him on a surfboard doing cool stuff in the waves. He was talking about serving mankind!" We laugh about it together. We keep talking until it's late in the evening. He finally accepts my offer to buy him a soda, which felt good for both of us.

Grey Chameleons

Like a small, miniature tornado the wind blows the dust from the trail up into the air. It lasts for about ten seconds and then it all disintegrates. It's very fine volcanic dust, that looks a bit like grey flour and it's everywhere. Even with our long pants, it finds a way to get all the way up our legs into our butt cracks. Which, consequently, feels quite sore now. It feels like having sandpaper rubbing against our butt cheeks. Although I've never tried that, I suspect the feeling is quite similar. It's definitely not making it very comfortable to walk. We look grey and dusty. Like an urn has been emptied over our heads. Or like cowboys, that have been driving dusty cattle around for weeks.

I'm constantly sneezing and picking dry chunks from my nose. "How long do you think we have to climb to get to Timberline Lodge?" André sinks into the dust as deeply as I do. "Another hour. Why?" I take another step and sink back half a step again. "I'm tired and I've kind of had it with this loose sand. We're not getting anywhere. I want to take a shower." He looks up towards the top of Mount Hood, the volcano we've been climbing for the last three hours. The lodge is on its flank, exactly on the tree line. "Yeah, I could use a nice bath, too. A bit further. It's not far now."

We stand in front of the entrance, exhausted. All around us are very expensive cars. We sit down on the big round steps in front of the entrance, while people in nice suits and gowns enter the building. We might as well be chameleons. They walk right past us, like we're invisible. We can't really blame them. We're grey from top to bottom and we're camouflaged against the grey granite stairs. My hair looks like hay and I wonder how many times I'll have to wash it to get it to look anything like normal again. "What

do you think? Can we go inside looking like this?" André says. He pats the sleeve of his shirt with his right hand. An enormous cloud of dust comes off. "I...want...to...take...a... shower..." Slowly, one by one, the words come out of my mouth. I get up, walk up the steps and open the large wooden door.
"Woooooow, look at this!" Like in a cartoon, André's mouth falls open. From the outside, the lodge looks big and bland; on the inside it's astonishing. In front of us is a large open round room. In the middle of it is a large supporting pillar, made of natural stone masonry, with various open fireplaces in it. The pillar keeps the entire construction upright. It's built in a minimalistic way and is constructed beautifully. Real artisans must have been at work here. From the roof, thick beams drop down diagonally. They rest on huge wooden supports that are as thick as tree trunks. Around the pillar there are nice, soft sofas with small wooden tables between them. I start grinning.
"Wow! That looks cozy! That's where I want to sit later on!" I can picture it already. Washed clean and chilling in a chair with a beer in my hand. All I have to do is fix my hair and then I can enjoy myself!! Yes!! I would actually like to plop down right away, but let's get a room first.

André looks around in the meantime. He's enjoying every minute of this. "Wow, there's no way I could make that! Look at the precision. Such quality craftsmanship!" He's looking at a huge carving of a cougar that's hanging on the wall. At home, he sometimes makes wooden carvings as a hobby. He almost always makes landscapes with animals. This is right up his alley. "This guy's put in a lot of work to create this. It's in a league of its own." There are more pretty wood carvings hanging in this building. He might just go and wander around later on while I have a few beers.

We're at the reception. "Hi, do you have a room available?" An older lady looks at her screen and answers, "Yes, sure. For how many people and how many nights?" She looks friendly and doesn't mention our dusty appearance at all. "Well, one night. Two beds if it's possible. I'd like a big wide bed all to myself," I say with a smile. "OH yes, and a bath please." She clicks on her computer mouse for a bit. "We have various prices ranging from 175 to 375 dollars a night. Let's take a look. Yes. We have a suite available at 375 dollars." She looks up at us, like it's the most ordinary thing in the world. "We could eat for two weeks for that kind of money," André says to me in Dutch. "Uhm...do you have anything cheaper? A small room with a shower, maybe?" She shakes her head, "No, I'm sorry. We don't have anything cheaper. The standard rooms at 175 are all booked." We lock eyes. We're in doubt. I've been looking forward to this so much, but it's a lot of money for one night. I sigh, and we walk away, disappointed. I guess we'll just have to put up the tent tonight.

I wander around the halls for a while and suddenly discover that they have a sauna. One at the men's room and one at the ladies' room. There's also a shower. Wow. I have got to tell André. I walk up to him and whisper it into his ear. He looks at me and smiles. I go to my backpack and get out some things. Quietly I walk up there with my shampoo and my bandana. I quickly get in the shower and close the door. I undress and carefully open the faucet. A beautiful, wide spray of water comes down. I get in and close my eyes. This is wonderful. I can feel all the nice warm water streaming down my back. This is amazing. I'm so happy I found this. Officially, the sauna is only for hotel guests, but technically, we're staying here too. We're camping out among the trees, in the designated area for PCT hikers. We might not officially be hotel guests, but unofficially maybe we kind of are. I didn't ask. Better let sleeping dogs lie...

"Aaaaahhhhh. That does the trick. Mmmmmmm." I'm nice and comfy on the pillows in front of the fireplace, having a cold beer. My hair is untangled, and I actually smell like a girl again. I smile just thinking about my illegal shower. OH well; sometimes rules are meant to be bent... As expected, André is off exploring the grounds. He's upstairs on the balcony somewhere looking at carvings. I have a moment to myself. Just a moment of solitary bliss. Being together is fun, but this is nice too. Later we'll have a pizza here and do absolutely nothing. Just hang out. And when we're tired and satisfied, we'll crawl back into our warm down sleeping bag.

Deep Dark Thoughts

The next morning, we pack up our tent and return to the lodge to have a wonderful breakfast. André looks at the beautiful things around him. It's quite chic here. I take a bite of my fried egg and look at a mosaic made of tiny stones, shaped like a bear that's fishing for salmon. Every detail is thought out.
"When I was wandering around yesterday, I found out that the building is from the 1930s. Apparently, the architects and masons of that period didn't have much work during the recession, so the government had this built to keep them busy. This lodge is said to be a very famous and iconic building," André says. That explains all the beautiful craftsmanship. "And, Oh yes, the movie 'The Shining' was partially filmed here. You know, the thriller by Stanley Kubrick and Stephen King." That's surprising. I sit up a bit more. "Seriously?!" I look around right away to see if I recognize anything, but I don't. The movie is quite old. "Now that we're talking about depression... Have you noticed the sad, dark vibe in this place?" André nods. "Yes, yesterday people were much more cheerful. This morning they all seem quite grumpy."

"Have you heard? The trail around Mount Adams is closed off! We can't go any further!" It's Bear Lee. He's suddenly appeared at our breakfast table. "What? What do you mean?" André looks serious. "Well, there's a fire and they say we can only go as far as Cascade Locks. No further." Cascade Locks? That's right next to Washington State. Does this mean we can't go through Washington at all? My mind is working overtime suddenly. "Who are 'they'? André asks. "Well... the other hikers. Toy Story said it first and then it spread like wildfire. Everyone started checking it out on their smartphones. There's no alternative route. Two days from now is the end. This sucks!!" We stare at him in shock. Only two more days? Nooooooo, this cannot be happening. We can't stop now. We have to get to Canada! We have to go on. This can't be. Not with only four weeks to go. It's only 500 miles to the end! We lock eyes, silently. A sadness comes over us. Maybe it's this building. The Shining, the big depression... No matter how beautiful all the wood carvings and the paintings are; the depression is still alive here after a century. We don't even feel like having breakfast anymore. We stop eating and go and talk to the other hikers. It's not a happy occasion. "So you're quitting in two days as well?" I ask Big Foot. "Yes, I am. What's the point? Why even bother going on at all? We can't get to Canada anyway." He's not the only one. Many are dropping out, with heavy hearts. It's contagious. Everyone around us is in doubt. Us too. We've gotten quiet and dim. This can't be how it ends, can it? What do we do now? We don't know. We pick up our backpacks and leave.

We walk through beautiful landscapes for two days, but it doesn't really sink in. We get grumpy with each other and most of the time our minds are turned inwards. We're enjoying this, but not deeply, not really. Even the famous Tunnel Falls - a waterfall that has a tunnel behind it, so you can walk through it - doesn't really impress us. Deep, negative thoughts have taken over our minds. Like a big loss. A grieving process and we're right in the middle of it. All these months, we've been through so much and now this. I start crying. This is awful. André puts his arm around me and together we hike the last few miles to Cascade Locks. We meet many more hikers there. Many have mixed feelings and seeing them doesn't cheer us up at all.

We pick up our resupply packages, and guess what? There are lots of presents and surprises there! Our people back home have no idea how much this means to us! There are some beautiful letters full of support and chocolate from home. André gets emotional reading a very big postcard from Candy and Jan, our family members who live in England. The Big Ben in London is on it. There's a banner on the tower that says: "ANDRÉ & LIAN, GOOD LUCK GUYS." I stand next to him and give him a big hug. This is hard for him. Our friends and family can't even imagine how much these sweet little things boost our morale and push us to go on. We unpack even more presents and suddenly I see André's got that sharp look in his eyes again. Very different from the past few days, when his eyes looked dim and empty. Now his bright blue eyes are fixed and sharp again. He sits upright and takes a deep breath. "To hell with all this negativity!" I can feel his energy beaming out, like it's oozing from his pores. It's a regenerative power, I'm feeling it too. It's crazy how your mood can flip in an instant, and there's so much strength you can draw from that. We look into each other's eyes, full of energy. It's time to conquer our fears again. These fires aren't going to stop us! We WILL find a way around them! Canada, here we come!!!

We decide to step out of the trail scene for a while. There's too much negativity and there's nothing we can do here. We book a hotel room in the nearby town of Portland and reach out to our good friend Shutterbug. We met him back in the desert and he quit a while ago. He's coming to get us. We enjoy a nice lunch together and not much later he drops us off at the hotel. We fall down onto the bed. Exhausted from it all, André turns on the TV and it turns on at a news station. One fire after the other is shown, complete with all the drama of people that have lost everything. I don't even realize it at first, but suddenly there is a deep wail, like a wolf's cry, a cry I've only ever heard from André when we've lost someone we love. He's in a fetal position and the tears are streaming down his face. This is just too much for him.

After a good night's sleep, we feel a lot better. We're going into town to do some homework and to get our thoughts straight. The vibe here is completely different from the trail and it's really lifting our spirits. We talk to local Trail Angels, National Park Rangers and a few hikers that are from this region. And... We have a plan! We may not be able to finish the PCT, but we can still try to get from Mexico to Canada on foot.

I take a sip of my cappuccino on a sunny terrace. Next to our cups is a large map of Washington State, open on the table. "Look, that's Olympic National Park. It's supposed to be a beautiful area for hiking." My finger moves to a green colored area. "I've heard of the Hoh River Trail and the Coastal Trails before. They seem awesome." André bends over forward to see the map better. "That big volcano, Mount St. Helens, should be there somewhere," he says. I have heard of that. It erupted very violently a while back but not too long ago. Our fingers move over the map and we line up hiking trails one after the other. When we finish, we've made a zigzag pattern all the way from Cascade Locks to Canada. I see André's face light up. "We're going to make it, aren't we?" I'm very happy as well. "Yes, we can make it to Canada! Let's do this!"

Bridge of the Gods

The next morning, I wake up in the hotel. Lian is still sound asleep. I get my phone, open Facebook, and click on the PCT group. This is where everyone keeps each other posted. I scroll through the funny and not-so-funny stories and suddenly I see something that grabs my attention. My eyes open wide. "What the heck!" I jump up and scroll down further. "You have to read this!" My voice woke her up already. "What is it?" She rubs her eyes with her little fists. "You aren't going to believe this!" I hand her my phone and she starts reading. I can see her expression changing as she reads. Suddenly, she's wide awake. "OH wow! What is this?!" The enormous fire in the north is still there, but a detour has been created around Mount Adams. We both start cheering loudly. The neighbors must be pretty annoyed with the noise we're making, but we don't care. We're happy and we're letting everybody know it. This is really, really good news. We can go further on the PCT. At least until Skykomish!!!

We rush to get on our way because who knows how long this opportunity will last. We finish our shopping and make resupply packages for the last part of the trail. Shutterbug gives us a lift back, which is so nice of him! And before we know it, we're back in Cascade Locks and as coincidence would have it, we arrive there exactly at the same time of the yearly PCT-days.
There are all kinds of stands of tent and backpack manufacturers, Park Rangers, associations and many more. Behind the fair is a large open field on a small island. It's full of hiker tents. We walk through them and see a lot of familiar faces. It's pleasant and fun. A very different vibe from when we were here two days ago.

"How did you get here? I thought you were two weeks or so behind us?" I say. I give Spontaneous, a hiker from Korea, a friendly pat on the shoulder. "I'm fine. Very good in fact." We lock eyes. I point to his belly. "You've lost weight since we last saw each other. Where was it again, Sierra City, right? You changed your beard too, I see." He laughs. "Yeah, I see some changes in you as well. You're fitter." Korean politeness is different from Dutch politeness I notice. More refined. Next to him is an older man. Spontaneous turns his head towards him, says something in Korean and then introduces him to us in English. He turns out to be someone from the company that sponsors him. We shake hands. "I didn't know you had a sponsor?" He nods. "Yeah, my tent and some other stuff is from them. Nice, isn't it?" I smile. "That is very nice! How is He-Man? I don't see him." His head drops a bit, his eyes look at the ground. "He's not doing so well. His feet are very sore. He's in a lot of pain and he has some injuries. We are falling more and more behind. We're taking it slowly, so he has a chance to make it too. We think we're going to succeed but if we arrive in the northern mountains too late, we might have to plough through snow again." So that's why they fell so far behind. He-Man is his Korean hiking buddy. He runs marathons and practices mountain climbing. I feel sorry for them. He-Man is an excellent hiker. It's too bad it had to go this way, but it's nice to see them sticking together. Good camaraderie. Start together, finish together. "How did you get here?" His head comes back up. "Well, we planned to come here in advance. Our brand has a stand here. The sponsors picked us up from the trail and tomorrow, they will take us back."

It seems a lot of people are here that we haven't seen in a long time. The PCT-days attract a lot of hikers, wherever they are on the trail. It's like a party of brotherhood, camaraderie and sharing stories. A moment in time to get that final push to get through the last section of the trail. But it's also a moment to say goodbye. I can see that

Shutterbug is having a hard time with that. We walk over to the fair together and hang out for a while. "I've been off the PCT for two months now, but I still can't let it go, you know." He stares straight ahead. "I still have this strong connection to the trail, even though I had to quit." There's a silence. "I keep in touch with everyone, and I'm trying to be a Trail Angel now, but after this weekend, I'll probably never see many of these people I care about ever again. In a few weeks this will all be over." He talks about it like it's a beautiful dream that you wake up from in the morning. The sort of dream that makes you feel amazing, but then slowly fades out of your mind, until you don't remember it at all. Like it's being sucked into the black hole of reality, only to leave a deep emptiness behind.

The black hole. Many people fall into it. Now that the end of the trail is in sight, the time has come to let go. But that's a hard thing to do. How could it not be, after all that you've been through. Here, you are understood. After this, you'll be all alone in another reality where ego, status and greed get the upper hand most of the time. Who would want to go back to that after all these warm, beautiful experiences? Fortunately, we have many loving people surrounding us at home. We have something wonderful to look forward to, but I understand Shutterbug completely. Letting go of this intense experience, and the connection to all these people is very hard. Some people get depressed or can't stop chasing that feeling for the rest of their lives. For us, it'll be a while before that dark moment arrives. We're still in the cocoon. Though after today, that cocoon is starting to show a few cracks here and there.

We're saying goodbye to a lot of people. They're quitting. For some, the emotional roller coaster of the past few days was the final straw. Others suffer from injuries or homesickness. Some see the PCT-days as a good time to drop out.

We're going on. We are now part of the last 20% that have remained. Out of 2000 hikers who started this adventure, there are less than 400 left. We say goodbye to the last of our friends and with mixed feelings, we leave the area. After less than a mile we're back on the trail. We look back at the PCT-days fair. In the distance we see the flag flapping in the wind and people hustling about and having fun. I take a deep breath, turn around, look forward and take a step.

And there she is. Like an iron lady over the mighty Columbia River: The Bridge of the Gods. A historical bridge that links the states of Oregon and Washington. For all the hikers that are still on the trail, this is an important moment.

Hand in hand we stand at the beginning of the bridge and look into each other's eyes. The powerful Columbia River is rushing underneath us. With tears in our eyes we step onto the bridge, step by step. It's an emotional moment. After more than 2100 miles of hiking, this is the final phase of the trail: crossing through Washington State with its northern Cascade mountains. The dessert of the journey that's going to be wildly tough. A spectacular 500-mile-long mountainous area.

Halfway across the bridge, on the border between Oregon and Washington, we stop. We look at each other in slight disbelief. This is actually going to happen! Another four weeks, give or take.

We walk to the end of the bridge, wipe the tears from our eyes and step into Washington.

"Canada, here we come!!"

Part Five
Fall

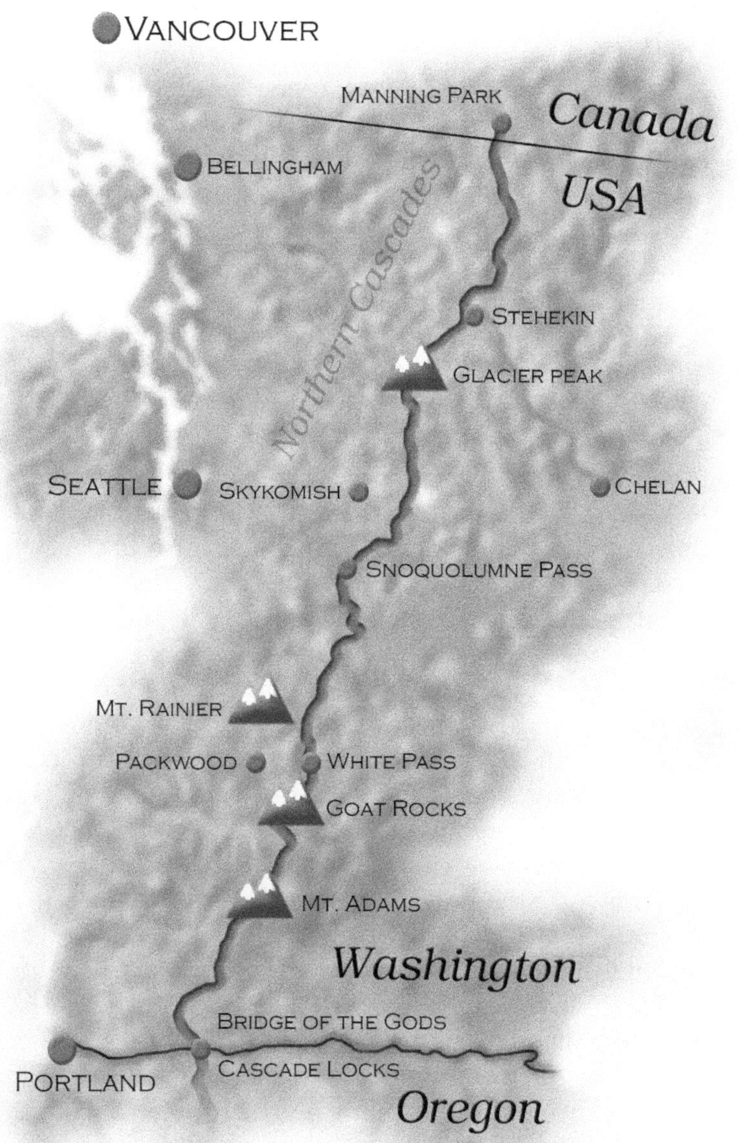
Vancouver
Manning Park
Canada
USA
Bellingham
Northern Cascades
Stehekin
Glacier peak
Seattle
Skykomish
Chelan
Snoquolumne Pass
Mt. Rainier
Packwood
White Pass
Goat Rocks
Mt. Adams
Washington
Bridge of the Gods
Portland
Cascade Locks
Oregon

Eeeeh, Crrrack, Whooshhhh, BOOM!

"What was that!" I'm upright in bed, eyes wide open. It's eleven o'clock in the evening and we're suddenly scared awake when a giant tree decides to drop dead right next to us. André quickly wiggles out of his sleeping bag, opens up the tent, puts on his shoes and walks outside naked. "That was close!" I hear him say. I quickly join him outside and together we look at the enormous tree. It's a cedar, which is basically a giant coniferous tree that's hundreds of years old. It's at least ten feet thick, 160 feet tall, and covered in moss. Now that it's on the ground like this, we are dumbfounded, for this way we are able to fully grasp the magnitude of this species of tree. André steps forward and climbs on top of it. "Another 60 feet to the left and it would have crushed us," he calls out. "Look at those branches; this thing is huge!" He turns back around, amazed at what's just happened. We are in a forest that's full of giant trees like this. It makes you feel small, like a little mouse looking up from under a mushroom, marveling at the immense trees going straight up into the seemingly endless sky. "Brrr... it's too cold outside. I'm going back in." I kick off my shoes and crawl back into my warm sleeping bag. I fall asleep thinking to myself: 'We're so lucky. This could have gone horribly wrong.'

The tree isn't the only thing in this forest that's fallen to the ground. "Where did you find that?" André asks me curiously the next morning, when I show him a beautifully yellow-colored leaf. "A few feet back. Look, the leaves are starting to change color." It's the time of year. Everywhere around us, the forest is starting to turn yellow, red, and orange. The first mushrooms are carefully showing their heads above ground. Even the air smells different. A bit stuffier. It's not full-on fall yet, but it won't be long now. The state of Washington is famous for its beautiful rain forests, and we're right in the middle of one. And they're called rain forests for a reason. Whether it was a coincidence or not; we had barely set foot off the Bridge of the Gods when the rain started coming down in buckets. We are soaked. We've had nothing but rain for the past few days. Even our Gore-Tex clothing and shoes are having trouble keeping the water out. It's so wet now, that our clothes can't even air out the sweat anymore. Everything we have is moist and sticky. The fabric rubs against the skin in our armpits, under my breasts and in our butt cracks. Even the sleeping bags are damp now, which makes them less warm because they don't insulate as well. Fortunately, it's not very cold yet. I hope the rain stops soon, so we can dry out our gear.

André suddenly turns around, wearing a huge, grey-green mustache. "Hahahaha!" It makes me laugh. He's picked some moss from a branch and stuck it under his nose. We're trying to keep it light here. What other option do we have? It's time to take a break. It's raining cats and dogs when we sit down. I take off my shoes and then my socks. "Look at this. They're all white and wrinkled. It won't be long until I get blisters, will it?" I wring out my socks, and they give off a musty autumn scent. Everything looks like it's starting to rot now. "I don't know, sweetie," André says, "Under normal circumstances, we would put on dry socks and let the wet ones dry on top of our backpacks. But it's no use doing that in the rain. Try to dry your feet a bit in the wind." Did he really just say that? "Uuuuhm... In case you haven't noticed... it's raining?!" He opens up the umbrella. We haven't been able to use it much lately because of the wind, but it'll work here. I get underneath it and use my towel to dry my feet. They dry quickly. "Every little bit counts," I say softly to myself. However, when I put my sticky, wet socks back on after our break, my feet are still white and wrinkly. I hope I don't get blisters.

Now that the leaves have started to fall, it means that we have to keep up the pace. We can't afford to slow down. This journey has three major parts, and for each of them the weather is vital. We had to start in the desert in springtime, because of the heat. But we couldn't start too soon, because we wouldn't have been able to pass through the Sierra Nevada mountains if there was still too much snow. Now we can't slow down because, if we go north too late, there will be too much snowfall on the highest peaks. It would be extremely difficult to reach Canada because the trail would be invisible. We would be up to our waists in snow and have no idea where to go. I don't think we'd get over it if we couldn't make it to Canada after all this hard work. So, we are sticking to our daily goal of at least 28 miles. This gives us a comfortable margin of error, just in case. Then there's nothing else we can do but pray that winter won't come early this year and surprise us with three feet of snow.

Two Brawlers on a Mountain

"Can we please talk about something else now?" I say to André. He's frustrated and needs to let off some steam. "Well, no! I've been looking forward to the Goat Rock Mountains for weeks, and now I can't see a thing!!!" he yells. I don't like it anymore than he does, but does he really have to throw a temper tantrum over it? This is the third time this has happened on this trip: We are having a fight...

Today started out dry and mostly clear with a few clouds here and there. We thought it would be a lovely day. André was in a bit of a rush to get here on time. When we started climbing the mountain, the clouds were high enough, but as we got higher, the clouds came down lower and lower. Now we're on Knife's Edge. A sharp mountain ridge with steep slopes on both sides going down deep into the valley. According to the pictures we've seen and the stories we've heard, this is supposed to be one of the most amazing views of the entire trail. Standing on a beautiful mountain ridge looking out far into the distance, with an exceptional view of the amazing white volcano: Mount Rainier, with its peak towering out above all its surroundings. We're finally here, but we can't see a thing. Just as we reach the top, a grey fog closes in around us. Now the first hail and snow are starting to fall.

"No, we have to wait!!! Maybe the sky will clear and we can still see the view!" he says angrily. He stops. "Yeah, right. It's slippery as hell out here on these slates. Have you seen how far down it is?" I answer, slipping forward with every step I take. André is still standing still in the very same spot. I yell back at him, "Are you coming or not? If you're not, I'll see you down in the valley! Can't you see that the snow is falling harder and harder? You know it's not safe here anymore!" He looks around. There's nothing but fog in front of us, but a bit further below us it seems to be clearing up a bit. Way down below us, a large patch of snow appears through the thick clouds. It looks a bit like a small glacier that's covered in snow. My foot slips on one of the slates, I turn to my left, catch my fall with my pole and stare straight down the cliff into the abyss. That was close. This side of the steep mountain ridge doesn't look very friendly either. It shoots straight down for at least 1000 feet with big grey rocks and debris at the bottom. I don't care about what he wants anymore and say, "I'm going to hike down now, and I would appreciate it if you came with me!" He saw how I almost fell and secures his poles firmly in the snow as he walks up to me.

Like brawlers we're standing there, opposite each other, neither of us wanting to give in. It seems stupid in hindsight. This is not the right place to be losing our heads. He's still not talking. His angry eyes are squinted, fixed on me. "Sometimes you can get so focused. It's horrible. You always have to be the big military man, not scared of anything, but I don't like it here at all. It's slippery as hell! I don't feel safe and I want to go down!" His expression doesn't change. He's breathing in his own, particular way, in deeply, out slowly. Trying to calm himself down.

It's not the first time we've been in situations like this. Sure, I've been in difficult circumstances before with groups. As a leader I've had to make very tough decisions, but he's got much more extreme experiences to draw from than I have. Sometimes I think he only wakes up and enjoys himself when things get dangerous. He even seems happier; it makes him smile. I get scared much more easily. Healthy tension turns into disruptive stress at moments like these. I don't like it. I prefer staying in my comfort zone. I like a bit of thrill, but I'd rather steer clear of big risks. Sometimes I really wish I could be more like him. Just turn off all my emotions and act intuitively when circumstances get extreme. It doesn't matter if he's eye to eye with a bear or standing in front of an inferno; he doesn't flinch. Those things scare me to death, but not him. He just evaluates the situation for what it is, not letting fear cloud his judgment. His emotional discharge always comes after the fact. In the heat of the moment, he's completely calm and absolutely fearless. This can be quite useful at times, because it has taken us places I would never have gotten to on my own. But now, in this moment, I don't feel safe and I want to leave. He wants to stay, so we are completely opposed on this.

"Fine, piss off then. You know how much this means to me. Why can't we just wait a few minutes? I've been looking forward to this for weeks and now I can't see a thing! Sure, the slates are slippery, but there's plenty of room on both sides of the trail." I stay quiet. When he gets started, it's better to let him get it all off his chest. "The trail is wide enough. It's not like we're on top of the Matterhorn! You're getting all carried away, once again, in your own stupid thoughts in your stupid mind! You're completely stressed out over nothing. We can wait. We might get lucky." His eagle eyes glare right through me. He stops talking. "Finished?!" I say, in a mean voice. He takes a deep breath again. He holds it for a few seconds and then slowly releases it from his mouth. "No!!" He doesn't say anything else. "You, you... oh, get lost! I'm going, whether you like it or not!" I turn around dramatically and start hiking. Fast. Maybe a little too fast. My feet keep slipping and these cliffs aren't getting any smaller. My head is buzzing with thoughts. I don't even care anymore. I'm not looking back. I want to leave. Away from the fog, away from the cliffs, away from the slippery slates and away from him.

We need some space. We've been living in each other's pockets 24/7 for almost five months now. Apparently all the frustrations, disappointments, irritations, and tension of the last few months need to get out now. André is usually a very happy, quiet, sweet man, but sometimes we can really get into each other's faces.

Not much later, I hear rocks moving behind me. I turn around and see him following me. I'm glad. Half an hour later he's calmed down, he's accepted the disappointment and he's in a much better mood. We're hiking together again, side by side. "We might be able to see that volcano from somewhere else on the trail sometime soon," he says. "Yeah, I think we might. We'll be pretty close to it for the next few days. So, if we're lucky, we just might see it." There's a silence, but not a cold one. The eagle eyes are gone, and I've calmed down as well. "I'm sorry about earlier. I wasn't really angry with you, just frustrated. I don't know why we got so mean with each other all of a sudden. I don't like it when that happens. I don't want us to fight," he says. It starts snowing even harder. Behind us, the trail is slowly turning white. He looks back. "You were kind of right; we shouldn't stay up there in these conditions." I look him in the eye, I've already forgiven him completely. "You're not usually like that, I know that, sweetie. I wasn't very nice to you back there either." He puts his arm around me and I give him a kiss. It seems like it was just time to get it all out.

A few days later we are in luck. In a clear-blue sky we see the white tip of Mount Rainier towering high above the landscape. It's an amazing sight to see, and we both enjoy it intensely. The fight we had a few days back, was already long forgotten.

Rainbow Wedding

It's about two more weeks until we reach the Canadian border and we're not going to make it in time. I turn my head towards Lian and say, "We have to think of an alternative." My hiking poles are pushing me forward, and one mile after the other slides by beneath my feet. But it doesn't matter how fast we walk; we are definitely not going to make it in time. A frown appears on her face. "What do you mean?" She has no idea what I'm talking about. My thoughts are somewhere else completely; back in the Netherlands.

A squirrel looks at me indifferently. It moves back and forth a bit, then runs up high into a tree. Home is close for him. For us, home is 5600 miles away. My thoughts have been going there more and more in the past couple of days. It's strange. Like something in my mind knows that we're counting down now. Like a cool-down phase, that's quietly preparing us to go back to another world.

"I don't think we'll be back in time for Madelief and Yvette. No matter how hard we try." Her expression changes. She knows what I'm talking about now, and nods. "Yes. I've been thinking the same thing. We have to change our plans." We've known Madelief since she was a child. She is like a daughter to us and we wanted nothing more than to be there for her wedding. We'd talked to them about it at home. With our hiking schedule, we couldn't be certain that we'd be back in the Netherlands for it. If they'd gotten married two weeks later, it might have been possible, but they couldn't change the date. So only one solution remained: we had to hike more miles per day. For the past month, we've been crunching out an extra three miles every day. We had secretly hoped we might reach the border in time to catch the first flight home and go to the wedding.

There was so much rain this past week, which actually made it easier to do more miles because it was mostly cold and boring. It's not like there was anything else to do. But no matter how fast we go, and no matter how many extra miles we manage to hike, we can't catch up. There's a limit to how much a person can do. "They get married in three days," I say. Lian nods.

During our next break, we look at the map. "I think we can make it to this town." I point my finger at Packwood, a small town, about a twenty-minute-drive from where the trail crosses a road. "Let's focus on that." Back at home, we conjured up a plan B. This might be the right place to put that in motion. "It looks big enough, and there are a number of lodges and a hotel. I think there's a good chance they'll have a good internet connection," Lian says. Even though Packwood is nowhere near our route, this might just be the only place around here that has reliable Wi-Fi.

So that's what we did. We kept on hiking, disciplined as ever. Precisely two hours of hiking, followed by a fifteen-minute break. And it's working. Six miles from White Pass, a mountain pass near Packwood, we get a phone signal. We even get a weak internet connection. I quickly search online for hotels and lodges in Packwood and start making calls. The phone rings. Ring... Ring... Ring... I'm impatient, even with all this peace and quiet around me. "Good afternoon. This is Packwood Lodge. How can I help you?" His voice is strong, but kind. "Yes, good day. This is André speaking. Do you have a room available? And do you have Wi-Fi? I mean a good, stable, reliable Wi-Fi?" After a short pause, he answers, "Yes, we have a few rooms available and all our rooms have Wi-Fi. The signal is stronger in the lobby. What do you need the Wi-Fi for?" Good, that's good news. "Well, we're hiking the Pacific Crest Trail and we need Wi-Fi in order to attend the wedding of our niece Madelief in the Netherlands tomorrow morning at five o'clock. It'll be two p.m. there, and they've set up a live stream on Skype especially for us, so that we can be present at the ceremony." He lets this sink in, and then answers, "Wow, that's so beautiful! I can help you with that. You know what? I'll let you use our private Wi-Fi. It's the one that we use to connect our register to. The connection is highly stable and none of the other guests are on it. Where are you now?" That is amazing news! A big smile appears on my face. Lian is trying to follow the conversation next to me and my reaction makes her curious. She puts her ear next to the phone. "We're about two hours away from White Pass, on foot," I say. "OK, I'll come and get you there. The weather is horrible. This way you won't have to stand in the rain for hours, trying to catch a ride." Lian and I lock eyes. This fills our hearts with joy. All the built-up tension from the past couple of days, all the doubt whether we were going to make it or not, it all comes out now. And with a shaky voice I say, "Wow. That's very kind of you. I don't know how to thank you! This is amazing!" He chuckles. "Absolutely, no problem. This sounds like such a wonderful story; I'd be happy to take some time off to help you out." We thank him again and set off down the trail enthusiastically.

Before we know it, we're on the pass. He told us about a gas station close by. And while the rain is streaming down endlessly, we wait there excitedly, under a small shelter. After about fifteen minutes a luxurious white car stops in front of us. The window rolls down. A friendly looking man looks back at us from behind the wheel. "André and Lian?" That must be him! We nod. "Yes, that's us." He pushes a button. The trunk opens. "Good, get in." We load the backpacks in the trunk, take off our wet rain gear and put it with the packs. I get in the front seat and Lian gets in the back. He's very interested and wants to know everything. After about twenty minutes we arrive at his lodge. We get our backpacks and follow him inside. We notice that he's grinning as he gets behind the counter.

"I'm going to give you the best room I have available, no extra charge," he starts. Lian and I are dumbfounded. "And guess what: your breakfast tomorrow morning is on the house." His smile widens. Completely flabbergasted we stare back at him. Unable to speak. No words come up, only warm feelings of pure happiness. "There's another surprise waiting for you in your room!" For some reason I can barely hold back the tears of joy and with a lump in my throat, the only thing I can muster up is a soft "Thank you." Our body language is clearly saying it all for us, because he's grinning ear to ear now. He puts the Wi-Fi password into our phone and then he leads us to our room. He wishes us good luck and we thank him again. We step inside into an enormous room. Two huge beds and more than enough room for us to dance around. On the beds are clean towels, folded like swans. Between the beds is a small nightstand. On top of it; a pretty green bottle of champagne with a big bow on it. What an amazing guy!

4:00 a.m.
The alarm goes off.
We take a shower, check the Wi-Fi connection and the phone battery.

4:15 a.m.
We're on the bed, dressed up, waiting impatiently.
It's about to start.
I open Skype.

4:30 a.m.
"I'm trying it now," I say to Lian.
On the screen in front of me is a photo. It's the smiling face of Rozemarijn, her sister. I click on the photo and after a short ringing sound we see movement on the screen.
It's working! We have video!

"Hey Rose!" The smiling face waves at us. Her dreadlocks are bouncing all over the screen. "Hey, hi. It's so good to see you again! How are you!" This is so great. Behind her we can clearly see that everyone's busy, bustling about. I feel like we've been transported into another world entirely. "Yeah, we're fine. We're on schedule and we feel strong. So, with a little bit of luck, we're going to make it." I haven't even finished my sentence when Lian takes over enthusiastically. "Your dress is beautiful! And your hair looks great!" Rose smiles and says, "Yeah, it does, doesn't it?!" She moves the phone around to show us what she's wearing. It's a fun, green dress with a denim jacket. Suddenly her face is back on camera. "Come, I'll take you with me." The camera bounces around a bit and we pass under a pretty arch made of blue balloons. We stop at a white party tent. There she is, our sweetheart, next to the love of her life. Rose taps her on the shoulder. Madelief turns around. She looks into the camera and greets us with a fantastic smile. "I'm so happy you're here!!!!!" We instantly get emotional and a single tear of joy rolls down Lian's cheek. Madelief looks beautiful. Her dress is like a rainbow. The colors all flow into each other. From dark red at her ankles, to light blue around her neck. Over that, she's wearing a small cyan-colored jacket. "We want to hug you!!" Lian says, moving her face towards the camera. Yvette turns around too and waves at us joyfully. "Hi, Yvette!!" She's smiling ear-to-ear and she's joining in. "Group hug!!!" she shouts. We all come in close to the camera and pretend to hold each other. Yvette looks beautiful too with her amazing, dark-purple dress. Our hearts fill with love as we watch the screen. This is spectacular! They both put an earphone in their ear, and we catch up a bit.

"Let's go, it's starting," Rozemarijn says. The camera bounces around again and then it stops perfectly. She's put it on a tripod in the front. We have front row seats! The ceremony starts and we are there, up close, for all of it.

This is so much fun. Nothing about these wonderful ladies is traditional. They follow their own path, in their own spectacular way. And even though they aren't our own children; we are so proud of them.

"Come!" Rose says at some point. The camera starts hobbling about and we get a grand tour. We see many familiar faces along the way. Some people wave, and some stop and talk to us. We also stop to talk to Lian's dad. She tells him how our journey is going. It's easy to see how proud he is. We talk to a few more people and end up at a beautiful wedding cake. Rose holds the camera close so we can watch the cake being cut. They even offer us a piece of cake in front of the camera as a joke. What a beautiful day!

What the people over there probably don't realize, is that our emotional reaction is extremely strong at this moment, like the moment we had with Thea and René. This is a highly intense experience, which we feel in every fiber of our being. After days and days of walking around in the rain, with nothing to keep us busy but the doubt if we'd make it in time, now there's an explosion of love, family, and friends that we've missed for so long. It's hitting us harder than we could ever describe.

After a little over an hour it's time for us to go. We say goodbye, the screen turns off and we lay back onto the bed, enjoying the feeling of our hearts and minds filled with so much love.

We go down to have breakfast an hour later. We arrive in the lobby. There's nobody there yet so we look outside. We see the lodge owner standing in the garden. He's hand in hand with another man. His son is on the other side. At that very moment we realize that this man understood us better than we could have ever imagined.

Heroes

"Are you CookieMonster and Morning Star?" Surprised, we answer, "Uhm, yes. Have we met?"
"No, we haven't, but I was talking to an Australian hiker named Wallaby yesterday. He said he missed you guys and asked if I had seen you around. He was wondering if you were ahead of him or behind him."

This is quite exceptional. We keep meeting people we don't know, but who seem to know a lot about us. Most of the time, these meetings are followed by: "Can we offer you something to drink, or eat? Here, have an apple or a Coke." Or: "How are you?" After which they listen to everything we have to say. They're all so friendly and interested in our stories. It's quite amazing. We're among the last few hikers that are heading towards the finish line and we're slowly realizing that this is a big deal, even for people who don't hike. Like the other day, when we ran into a couple of weekend-hikers:

"Where are you headed?"
"To Canada."
"Oh, are you hiking the Pacific Crest Trail?"
"Yes."
"Where did you start?"
"At the Mexican border."
"Wow, how long have you been on the trail?"
When they hear that we've been hiking for five months, their jaws drop. They're so amazed that they don't know what to say.

Another example is something that happened a while back at a small restaurant by the water. We were eating ice-cream there with a few other PCT-hikers and a lady just came and sat next to us for no reason. She couldn't stop staring at us, watching us eat, and listening to what we were saying like we were monkeys at the zoo. We must admit, we didn't smell very good that day, but I don't think that was the reason. She followed our conversation and figured out that we were hiking the PCT. She carefully watched every move we made and asked a question every now and then. Then she'd wait in suspense to hear the answer. She looked like a star-struck teenager the whole time, like she was thinking: "These people are the real deal!" It's really weird, and it's taken us a while to get used to it.

Americans have an extraordinary attitude towards heroes, like veterans and fire-fighters. However, I think it also has something to do with 'The American Dream.' Having ambition, striving for success, and then achieving it. They're rooting for us. There's no jealousy or envy; only support, admiration, and pride. It's a feeling that's rooted deeply in American culture, and it's very much present on this trail. We've come across 'Trail Magic' many times already. It might just be a simple granola bar, or it could be a spontaneous barbecue right in the middle of the trail. We've even seen people carry their grill, hamburgers, buns and drinks all the way up a mountain in order to cheer us on, give us food, drinks and support us in undertaking this enormous venture. It's an amazing, and a very emotional feeling. This is why Americans are such a special people. It's nice to experience what it's like to be treated like some kind of Hollywood star or professional athlete. We get the feeling that many people here really see us that way, especially in this final phase of the trail.
We Europeans, but also our Korean, Australian, and New-Zealand friends have a more down-to-earth view of what it means to be a hero. For us, this journey means we stay in the moment, we focus on today. Our morning, afternoon, and evening rituals, hiking long distances, climbing, and enjoying everything we see and just being together. Of course, we also take good care of our health.

To many Americans, that's not just what it's about. We met a nice man, who gives PCT-hikers rides wherever they need to go. He told us that in his mind, we are symbolic of the old pioneers of the Wild West. They came from far away in Europe and landed on the eastern shores. They didn't know anything about this new country, but even so they traveled through the entire continent on foot or by horse, carrying all their belongings on their backs to go west. To the promised land. On their journey they had to face and overcome many dangers. The Gold Rush pioneers are another example of this. Men that left their lives behind, took the few things they owned and walked through heat, snow, and ice to reach their goal, their dream. For many Americans, there's something heroic about our journey. They are proud of what we're doing and they want to be a part of it in their very own way. It's a wonderful thing, and we will cherish those moments and keep them in our hearts forever.

Unfortunately, some PCT hikers go too far in their newfound stardom. They act like they have a 'right' to all the attention, food, a place to stay, rides into town, etc. and they actually get angry if they don't get what they want. A young hiker told us passionately about the word 'Yogi-ing'. It means something like: 'Trying to get Trail Angels and other people to do things for you, like giving you food, or manipulate them to get what you want.' We couldn't believe we were hearing this, but they really do believe that they have the right to do this. "That's what they're there for, isn't it?" We've heard them say. It makes us sick to our stomachs.

While we've been on the trail, we've seen a lot of exploitation. We saw a hiker dramatically trying to persuade a Trail Angel to take him to town because he's run out of food. The Trail Angel felt sorry for him and gave him a ride. When they came back, she was completely disillusioned. He returned with nothing but a case of beer. We've also heard stories about hikers that stay with Trail Angels for the night, and get a meal there, but don't put anything in the donation box. Or sometimes even take money out of it. We also heard from a Trail Angel that he received an angry letter once, because he didn't put new cans of water out in the desert.

These rude hikers with bad attitudes have ruined some good memories for us, and for the Trail Angels. We even met an American hiker who quit the PCT because he couldn't bear to be around 'these kinds of people' anymore. He could not relate to many of his own countrymen anymore. His integrity and his appreciation for the Trail Angels was compromised by the large amount of abuse he saw going on. Finally, he couldn't stand it and left. "I have to get away from all this disrespectful behavior," he told us.

It's especially frequent in younger American hikers, and it's spreading like a virus. They get pulled in by peer pressure and this is how they're taught to behave. They think it's normal and it's such a shame. In the thirty years that we've been hiking in the United States, this is the first time we ever experienced this kind of disrespect on a trail. We don't condone, or appreciate this attitude at all. We cannot understand why anyone that's hiking long-distance would suddenly believe they are some kind of Marvel super-hero or a Hollywood superstar.

Fortunately, only a handful of people are like this. Maybe it's the mood or spirit of the current time we live in. Everything seems to be about self-promotion these days. YouTube, Facebook, Instagram, Twitter, heads of states.... Everything's focused on giving more power to the ego. We hope this Zeitgeist will change, sooner rather than later. That would be nice.

Like Walking Inside a Painting

A tiny gust of wind blows a beautiful bright-orange leaf from a tree branch. It slowly flutters down and lands on the water, where it makes a pretty circle of ripples. And it's not alone. Everywhere on the surface of this babbling brook, colored leaves are floating around like tiny boats. They're maple leaves, shaped like a small child's hand. Maples are only found in the north, so it's a clear sign that we're getting closer to Canada. The larches are also losing their needles and in the morning light the whole scene looks like a fairy-tale. Like golden rain floating down into the forest from the sky.

We had hoped that we might get to see a bit of what they call 'Indian Summer' but we never in our wildest dreams imagined it to be this spectacular. It's all around us, no matter where we look. The leaves on the berry bushes, the moss, the maples: all in different shades of red and orange. In between them are the bright yellow to deep-ocher-colored aspens, larches, and other plants and trees. We're in the Northern Cascade Mountains and this place is like paradise in the fall.

"I feel like I'm walking in a Japanese garden," I say softly. My hands gently touch the yellow leaves of the bushes along the trail. Small drops of water lie on the leaves like crystals. Glistening in the sunlight. "Yeah, it's like walking inside a beautiful painting," Lian says. She's right. This could just as easily be a romantic autumn painting by Claude Monet. A beautiful piece of art, in which your mind could wander off for days. And right now, we feel like we're part of that painting.

Some time later I'm looking out across a lake. Shades of red, purple, and yellow color its banks. There are a few dark-green pine trees here and there, sticking their heads up proudly into the sky. There's no wind and there aren't any ripples in the water. Under water, a trout spots an insect landing on the surface. It shoots out of the water like an arrow. I can see it jumping out of the lake. It makes a wonky pirouette and then dives back in. The whole thing only takes about two seconds, with nothing but a tiny ripple in the water to testify to what has happened here. I look to the side. A bit further down the trail, Lian is on the ground, crawling through the bushes with her backpack on; she's looking for berries.

It's hilarious. She's on her hands and knees, crawling forward slowly like a puppy. It almost looks like she's wagging her tail. She's faced down, like she's on to something. "Oooh! Look at this! I've found berry paradise!" Her face pops out from the bushes. I see her eyes twinkling under the rim of her sun hat. "I'm coming!" I answer. I put away the camera and walk up to her. "There are so many of them!" I say, as I crouch down to pick some berries. Together we crawl over the ground for at least half an hour. Stuffing ourselves with mouthfuls of berries at a time. They're delicious. We can't get enough of them. I don't think we're going to get very far today. The berries are just too good. We set out to walk long distances every day. Today we won't be reaching our goal and we don't even care. This is wonderful. The fall season is at its peak right now and there are thousands of berries just waiting to be eaten.

"Is this one edible?" Lian asks. In her hand is a large green leaf. On top of it, is a raspberry-like berry. "I don't know what this is. The leaf is completely different. It looks safe, but you never know. I'll look it up." I search through the plant guide on our phone, but I can't find it anywhere. "This guide classifies flowers, not leaves or berries. I think it's better if we don't risk it." We leave them alone, and there are more than enough other berries we can eat here anyway! Small wild strawberries, raspberries, and the delicious huckleberries. We don't have huckleberries in Europe. They look a lot like blueberries, but they have a dark-purple-black color. They're super-sweet and they are everywhere. We won't be leaving anytime soon!

Geisha Girl

We're still on the ground looking for berries when I notice someone walking in our direction. "Hey GG!" I call out smiling. Lian looks up from behind a large bush and starts waving. GG holds her hand up over her eyes and squints a little to avoid the bright sunlight. She doesn't recognize us until she comes closer, and then she smiles too. Geisha Girl isn't much older than we are. We've been running into each other every other week or so since the start of the trail. She's 56 years old and recently retired from her job as a State Trooper.

"How are you! I haven't seen you guys in ages! Still on the trail too, I see. Great! We're almost there, aren't we?!" We nod. "It looks like it. We think we'll be in Canada in another twelve, maybe thirteen days!" She laughs. "I'm hiking my legs off. I want to reach the finish in eight days!" That surprises us. Lian asks, "What's the rush? Why don't you take your time? It's so beautiful here. Are there snowstorms coming? We haven't had a signal in days, so we don't know anything." To which I immediately add, "Do you know anything about the Blankenship Fire? Is the forest fire still blocking the trail? Or is it open temporarily? Should we rush to get through it? Is that why you're in such a hurry?"

The last update we'd had on the fire was at the Bridge of the Gods, and the trail up north was still closed then. We still don't know if we'll be able to reach Canada. It's an uncertainty that's always in the back of our minds. As far as we know, the trail is still closed from Skykomish. We are heading steadily towards the end of the trail, without knowing if it's even possible to reach it.

"No, I know as much as you do. I don't know if the trail's open or closed. I guess I'll find out when I get there. I'm in a hurry because my husband's booked a lovely holiday on a whim, so we can finally have some quality time together. We're going to Hawaii!!" I look at Lian for a second and then turn back to GG. There's an answer we didn't expect. "I'm really looking forward to it! There's only one problem: he should have booked it for a later date. He thought I would be back by then. Oh well, if I don't make it, I'll just have to leave the trail a bit early. I'll finish it another time." She sounds sad and excited at the same time. To get so far and then quit right before the end. I would be devastated. I wouldn't go to Hawaii if it were up to me, but that's easy for us to say. We're together. GG and her husband haven't seen each other for months. What a dilemma.

We talk for another ten minutes or so, exchanging the latest trail gossip. She tells us about all the people that have quit. There are so many. For some of them, there was just too much tension. Couples that started this journey together, have now split up and are hiking solo, or one of the two has just quit altogether. Even after years of marriage, these six months is when you really get to know each other. It can even cause you to break up. Now that's food for thought. Lian and I are lucky, we met on a trek somewhere out in the middle of nowhere. We know what it's like to go back to basic and sleep in a tent together without all the luxuries we have at home. Don't get me wrong: we have our differences like any other couple. We just have a lot of experience dealing with situations like this, and for many people who aren't used to it, it can be a very confronting ordeal. Out here, there's no escape from each other. No 'Man Cave' or friends to pour your heart out to. Sometimes you get overwhelmed by frustration or sadness. On the trail, there's no running away from those emotions. You're stuck in the moment together, and you'll have to work it out together, right here and now, one way or another. Some people come out here and discover that their true calling in life is something completely different from the life they've been living together. The trail is a place where you truly get to know yourself, and your partner.

Geisha Girl is getting ready to leave us. "Hey GG, before you go. Do you know what this plant is? Are the berries edible?" She looks at the raspberry-like plant. "Oh, sure. It's delicious. They're called Thimble Berries. They have a lovely taste; very soft and sweet." She picks a berry and rubs it softly between her thumb and index finger. The berry falls apart into tiny balls. Lian and I pick a few berries and put them in our mouths. "They're good. Berry caviar!" Lian mumbles with a mouth full of berries. GG laughs with us. Then she throws on her backpack, adjusts her hip belt and shoulder straps and starts walking. We say goodbye to our good friend for the last time. We will never see her again. That's how it is in our lives. Wonderful people come and wonderful people go. Take in the precious moments and let them go again.

"Shall we pitch the tent here? It's nice here, like a painter's palette. We'll make up for the lost miles tomorrow." Lian laughs. "Sure, until we run into berry bushes again, right?" I smile. There's a slight drizzle now, so I put up the tent in two minutes. We brought our tarp from the bounce box because we expected to get a lot of rainy days. It's a super-light-weight nylon cloth of about nine square feet with metal rings on the corners. We put our hiking poles in the rings and use guy lines to pull it tight and secure it to the ground. Now we have a large shelter, where we can sit and relax, and stay nice and dry while we cook. Lian places her sit mat on the ground under the tarp and sits down. She takes the camping stove and the pan from her backpack, lays everything out in front of her and starts cooking. In the meantime, I put all our gear in the tent.

"Mmmm... That's actually not bad," I say while Lian frantically stirs the food. She looks up. "What do you mean?" I stick my finger in the pan and attempt to have a taste. She slaps my hand immediately. "No, you'll have to wait." I laugh and taste the tiny bit that's still on my finger. We're having mashed potatoes tonight with dehydrated apples, cinnamon, and some other herbs. It looks like thick wallpaper glue with lumps. I lick my finger. "This is actually quite good, but I wasn't talking about the food, I was thinking about GG. A few weeks in Hawaii at the end of this journey. Why didn't we think of that? It sounds amazing. A few weeks in a resort with white-sand beaches and clear blue water. Just to get our strength back. That sounds wonderful. A Piña Colada in one hand, a snack in the other, standing in the water in our swim trunks. Uuuhm... Why are we still here?" I say jokingly. "I didn't think about that when we were planning this, but we don't really have that option. We only have a visa for six months. We're not allowed to stay in the USA for longer than that, and Hawaii is also part of the USA." Ah, I hadn't thought of that. But the Canary Islands sound just as good to me. On the other hand: Lian has to go back to work as soon as we get home while I have an extra month off.

I put my sit mat down on the wet ground next to her and sit down. "I hope GG gets there in time. She deserves a nice holiday. She's such a nice woman and I really hope she finds a way past the fire." Lian nods. I wonder how Lian will react if we can't go on because of the fire. Ever since the wedding, she seems different. She's eager to see her family and friends again. If we really can't go on, will she want to go home right away? I don't bring it up right now. I want to get to the border no matter what, even if it means taking a detour around the fire. We're strong, super fit, focused and disciplined. Except for our berry cravings. But sometimes the temptation is just stronger than the mind. We'll see what happens. For now, let's just have a nice dinner and enjoy ourselves.

Extreme Weight Loss

A small, funny-looking, mouse-like creature with big ears runs past us and then turns around. "PEEEEEEEEEP!!" It's an astonishing little thing. "It makes a lot of noise for such a small creature!" I say. André tightens the hip belt on his backpack. "It's a Pika. They only live in the mountains, at higher altitudes." It walks over to a small patch of flowers and bites through the stems. Somehow it manages to stuff all of it into its mouth. The flowers drag behind it and before we know it, the little pika has skittered off and disappeared into a tiny opening between the rocks. I get in closer to watch how the last flowers are pulled inside. "Maybe it's got a nest here?" I look into the small chasm, but I don't see anything. I look up and notice that there are many more of these funny-looking little creatures scattering around. "They're so cute. With their cute, little eyes and round ears, they look like they've come right out of a cartoon. It's like watching miniature a Mickey Mouse."

The Northern Cascade Mountains do not cease to amaze us. The views, the endless emptiness. And there are nowhere near as many hikers as before. It's very noticeable. We can go for days and not see anyone. Peace and quiet, we're all alone, and I love it. There are a lot of fallen trees out here, and they add a little bit of welcome diversity to the scenery. It's really starting to feel like the north now. The pine trees, the animals, the plants, and the moss are all different than before. We're coming into grizzly bear territory too, and even though we haven't seen any yet, we've become more cautious already.

The landscape is not the only thing that's changing. Hiking these immensely long distances also means we're burning lots of calories every day. And no matter how much we try to eat, it doesn't seem to do anything for André. He has lost a substantial amount of weight on this journey. He weighed 191 pounds when we started; now he only weighs 141 pounds. He's lost fifty pounds out here and I don't know what to do about it. He takes off his shirt. "How are you feeling?" I can count the ribs on him. "I feel alright. Why?" He looks at me, smiling. He's still happy about what happened earlier. We came around the bend and suddenly there was a huge deer in the middle of the trail. It was an elk. A male with enormous antlers, still covered in velvet-soft beige skin. Amazing. "Well, I'm starting to feel a bit worried about you. I think you might not be getting enough nutrition, or maybe not the right kind." I'm sitting up against a tree. It's lunch time and I'm fixing a tortilla wrap for us. I'm putting a whole bar of marzipan in it this time. No, I don't think it has anything to do with the number of calories.

We've tried everything. Sturdy oatmeal for breakfast and wraps with large steaks of salmon or ham for lunch. When we're walking, we're constantly eating snickers bars. We also go through a few bags of nuts every day. We make sure we eat a healthy dinner, and we're eating double portions now. But it doesn't really seem to do anything. He's started adding protein powder to his meals, like I do. I haven't lost much weight since I started doing that. Maybe it will stabilize his weight too. Just to be safe, we also take vitamin supplements and electrolytes but our bodies are starting to get low on all the reserves and we're really feeling it. My CookieMonster blue pants are flopping from my hips like an old rag. It's a good thing I have a belt to keep it up.

André has the same problem with his pants. I hope he'll be alright. I've known him for thirty years now, and he's never been as fit as he is now. Not even when he just left the army. We're not sure what to do and it's killing us. Should we cut down on our daily mileage? Take a few days off and binge on food in a nearby town? Well, the snow season is coming and I don't want to get stuck in deep snow this close to the end. It's only two more weeks. We'll be alright.

"Hmmmm..." I sigh. "Is something wrong?" His question pulls me back to reality. I see him holding the wrap with both hands, it's almost in his mouth. "Oh, no. I was just thinking about some things. Don't worry about it."

Black-Haired Monster

"Eeeeeeeeeew!!!" Lian suddenly yells. She jumps up in complete shock. I almost choke on my coffee. "What on earth is going on?!" I ask. She looks around anxiously. "Something just brushed against my back!" I'm baffled. "What? What did you say?" She's shaking her head quickly from left to right. "Some kind of creature with long hair brushed against my back and then ran away!" I stand up and together we scan the area. "I don't see anything."

To save weight we only brought one headlamp from Cascade Locks. We didn't think we'd need them as much for this section since we don't have to hike at night anymore. Maybe in hindsight that wasn't such a good idea; the batteries are dead and our powerpack died before that, so there's no way to charge them. With the last little bit of light we had, we tried to get to a camp spot but we didn't make it. Now we're here, on a teeny tiny little spot next to a bridge by a creek. In the middle of nowhere, in the dark, with some kind of eerie creature lurking around.

"What was that? What was that?" Lian takes a few steps forward. "Are you sure it had long hair?" I fiddle around with the headlamp a bit. A little bit of light comes out, but it's no more than a glowing nail. "Yes! It had long hair." I start walking in the direction she points to. "So not a deer or anything? Maybe a young bear?" I say. "No, I don't think so. Why would a young bear do that?" I'm already sixty feet down the trail. The light is getting weaker and weaker. "I'm just thinking out loud. A wolverine then? They have long hair. Or a wolf?" The last of the light dribbles out of the lamp. "No, I don't think so. If a wolverine pushes you in the back, you will know it. You'd be in big trouble then. They are extremely dangerous and very aggressive. I don't think that's what it was. Nor a wolf. It would have reacted differently. Anyway, I don't even think they have wolves here." I'm not so sure about that. Why wouldn't there be wolves out here? The landscape is right for them. "I think they're further up north," she says. But these days we even have wolves in the Netherlands and Belgium, nowhere near their natural habitat. I don't know. I think there could be wolves out here.

"Do they have raccoons here?" The light goes out. I can't see a thing now and carefully walk back to Lian. "I don't really know. It wouldn't surprise me if they did. Are you sure it was black?" The tip of my shoe catches on a root. I fall forward and only just manage to keep my footing. "Yes, no, well, it's dark. I couldn't see properly. It could have had white stripes on its tail, but I didn't see them," Lian says doubtfully. I'm back at the creek. We stare into the darkness but see nothing. The creature has disappeared, and we have no idea what it was. We decide to go to bed. Tomorrow will be an exciting day.

Goodbye Sweet Angels

We're trying to get to Skykomish early. Hopefully, we will find out if we can get to Canada or not when we get there. We've had a rocky night. The strange encounter with the creature kept Lian up for quite a while. She's not feeling very fit either. She's had a bad case of diarrhea for a week now. When we were in Snoqualmie Pass, she bought some Imodium-like pills for it. They didn't do her much good though. Now she can't eat anything but crackers, and to be completely honest, my stomach is pretty upset as well. Maybe it's the food. Maybe Lian's right and I should eat more. But I feel quite good at this weight and I'm hiking like a rocket. Maybe it's stress? Who knows? We can't quite put our finger on what it is.
"If we can't go on because of that fire, maybe we should just go home early," she says. Her eyes are blank and empty, like all the joy and energy has been sucked out of her. This is the exhaustion talking. I understand it completely. But still, there it is. The moment I have been fearing above anything else: quitting early and leaving the trail just before the end.
She looks at me as if she's read my mind. I don't know what to say, so I don't say anything. I look around and see the first houses of Skykomish. This is our last big stop before Canada, and this is where all the answers lie.

We haven't had a phone signal for days, and we've been trying not to worry about it. Let it go. We'll see when we get there, I told myself, but now that we're getting closer and closer to the fire, the tension is rising more and more. It's not so easy to let go. "I understand what you're thinking, but I really want to go on. We can find another way to get to Canada. I know we're not feeling well, but to quit now, so close to the end... It's the mind games again sweetheart. The border is right there. The last mile is always the longest one. Maybe we can find a doctor here, with the right kind of medicine, and we'll feel better." I'm trying to stay positive, and I really think this could end well. But doubt is growing in my mind. We're so close, but the fire, her health... Quietly we walk on and arrive at the home of the Trail Angels called the Dinsmores.

As soon as we enter their compound, we are met with happy smiles. "Hey, hello. Welcome to Hiker Haven." A woman with long blond hair shakes our hands. "Hi, my name's Andrea. You're the first ones to arrive today! We're still cleaning up, but if you like, I'll make you a cup of coffee or tea?" It wasn't really a question because she's already leading us to the living room. When we get there, we meet Jerry, who's chilling in a lounge chair, smoking a cigar. "Jerry, this is CookieMonster and Morning Star. They're from Belgium." We shake his hand. "Hi, welcome. Only 186 miles to go till the finish! Good job. Let me think. I think you're the third Belgians to come through here." I try to tell him that we're Dutch, but we've lived in Belgium for thirteen years, but it doesn't seem to stick. He's happy enough that he sort of knows where the country is. He points to two plush chairs. We take off our backpacks and sit down. It's time for some social interaction and hopefully we can get some answers to our questions.

They listen to our stories. "Wow, that doesn't sound very good. How long have you been feeling this way?" How am I feeling? "Well, it's been getting worse and worse ever since White Pass. It feels like everything inside me is upset," I say. Lian nods: "I'm worse off than him. I have diarrhea continuously and I've been eating nothing but crackers for a week now." Jerry looks at her. "I'll take you to the hospital later. They can check you out." Lian and I lock eyes. Another hospital? We don't want to go there. We haven't had very good experiences with hospitals in the US. Bad things always seem to happen. "Isn't there a doctor here we can see? I'd rather not go to a hospital," Lian says. But we quickly realize that these people are

Trail Angels to the bone. They've had hikers come through here every summer since 2003. This wasn't a request, it was more like a warm, fatherly advice to protect us from ourselves. Advice that isn't open for discussion. Andrea joins the conversation and says, "No, no, they have better tests in the hospital. It's only a half-hour-drive from here. I think it's the right thing to do if you want to finish the trail. You might not make it if you don't get yourself checked out." Lian sighs and her shoulders drop. "Maybe you're right. I actually do want to know what's wrong with me." They smile. Jerry gets up and before we know it, we're in the car with him, feeling a little overwhelmed.

We've only just left their place when I ask him the question that's been on our minds for a while now. "Jerry? Do you know the status on the Blankenship fire? Can we go through there? Is there a detour? Is it still that bad?" I'm in the back seat and he turns halfway around, his eyes still fixed on the road in front of him. "Bad? It's been awful! The Wolverine Creek fire and the Blankenship fire joined up and together they destroyed an immense area. Many people were evacuated and are now slowly returning to their homes. The entire area around Lake Chelan was closed off for a long time. It was no picnic out there." I can't even imagine what those people went through. We're just passing through, but this is their home. "Jerry, do you know if the PCT is open again?" In the rear-view mirror, I see a frown forming on his forehead. "Oh, you haven't heard. The fire brigade wanted to keep the trail closed for a lot longer, because of all the falling trees and branches. It's still quite dangerous out there but they opened it for hikers a few days ago." My eyes are wide open. "What? Really?" I can hardly believe what I'm hearing. "Yeah, the trail is open. Andrea and I, and a lot of other people convinced the fire brigade to open it, so that way we can keep an eye on it as well. We told them that once you hikers got here, you'd be so fixed on reaching the border, an official closure wouldn't have stopped you anyway. We know quite a few people who would have gone right through the roadblocks to get to Canada and finish the trail. Like their lives depended on it." All our anxiety and all our emotions seem to unload all at once when we hear this news. It's like a mix of euphoria and intense anxiety coming out from deep down inside of me. I don't really know what to think or how to feel. I feel empty inside, while at the same time all my emotions are bouncing around. "We can go! We can finish it!" I shout out. A huge load drops from my shoulders. I had been picturing all kinds of scenarios in my mind for the past few days but I didn't think we'd be getting this wonderful news in a car on the way to a hospital. "This is fantastic news!" Lian says. Jerry smiles and says, "It's been raining a lot for the past couple of weeks, and that has put out most of the fires for now. You can hike to Canada!!" Lian and I start cheering and Jerry joins in. Lian has been praying to her late mother every day lately, hoping things would work out for us. I don't believe in gods. I think it's nothing but luck that the rain has cleared our path for us. Whatever the truth is: I'm embracing it as a 'gift from heaven'.

We arrive at a hospital, again. It's the third time already. Jerry waits in the parking lot until Lian's had all the tests. He's such an amazing person. A few hours later we get the results: Salmonella poisoning. "What?" Lian looks at the doctor in shock. "Yes, salmonella. It's not a big problem; we'll fix this in no time." The doctor wipes a lock of black hair from her face. "I'm prescribing you antibiotics. You should feel much better in a couple of days." Lian is the only one that got tested, so I ask, "Can you prescribe me the same medicine? I have the same symptoms. Just a bit milder." She stops writing and looks at me. "I can't just prescribe you something without testing you. You really should get tested." Oh, no. We'll have to wait for hours again, while Jerry waits in the parking lot. There's no way we're doing that. "Madam, when you just said salmonella, I immediately knew where we got it. We were in Packwood recently and we visited a small market. There was a lot of street food. We both ate some Chinese food there. The vendor scooped it out of heated basins, that might have been open all day for all we know. Now that you mention it: we started having symptoms a day or two after that." She's still looking at me with a doubtful look in her eye. "Can you please prescribe me the same thing?" I ask, in my best Yogi voice. "Otherwise, we might infect each other again." I have no idea if that's how it works, but she starts writing again. "For this once, I'll prescribe you a wide range of antibiotics, which should also work for salmonella. I understand that you have to get going." I thank her heartily and we take our leave. It's so stupid that I didn't think of that before. I thought it would be exhaustion or a shortage of electrolytes, but salmonella?

Jerry is taking a nap in the driver's seat. We knock on the window and he signals us to get in. On the way back we tell him the good news. "See, not such a bad idea after all, was it?" He's smiling. Yes, he was absolutely right. It was a good thing he pulled us out of our cocoon. I relax in the back seat. My mind is working overtime. We can go to Canada! We're going to get better! It's making me emotional. I sit silently and let the tears run down my cheeks. She's not talking about 'going home' anymore. She's in the front seat having a lively conversation with Jerry about Stehekin, the last little town on the trail before we reach Canada. Who could have dreamed it would end this way.

Andrea and Jerry invite us to stay the night, but we decline. They've been so very kind and good to us already. We don't want to burden these last, sweet PCT Trail Angels any more than we already have. We check into a small hotel in town and buy some food for the last part of the trail. That night we eat at a local restaurant.

On the plate in front of me is a whole fried chicken, and I think to myself, "Salmonella... Should I really be eating this?"

The Home Stretch

A few days later I'm feeling a lot better already and I'm eating like a horse again. Man, I feel amazing! Even with this cloudy, sad Washington weather. Everything is right in the world. I can smell everything, I can see all the details, and I even feel like my hearing is better than it was. Which is quite strange, actually. My senses probably haven't changed at all, but somehow a renewed kind of clarity has washed over me, and I feel more perceptive than ever. It's great to feel this good again. Apparently, I hadn't felt right for weeks, without even noticing.

We've had all kinds of weather here. Typical for Washington. The terrain has been tough and steep. We climbed a whopping five miles and we descended that much as well, in just 100 miles distance, over five days.
"I don't get it. Do you?" André looks a bit hazy, like his mind was somewhere else altogether and I've pulled him out of his daydream. "Huh, what?" I point around us. "Well, I don't see anything that suggests there was a huge fire here. There's not even as much as a burnt twig anywhere. We should be passing through that area by now." He gets a bit more alert and looks around. "Yeah, you're right. I don't get it either. Maybe it stopped just over the edge of a mountain top somewhere? I don't know. Maybe we'll pass through it later on, or maybe we'll find out in Stehekin?"

It's still early in the afternoon when we arrive at a small bridge. Still no sign of any fire. The bridge marks the beginning of a road. A pick-up truck pulls up and we manage to hitch a ride. We're dropped off at the ranch. From there it's about another hour by bus to get to Stehekin. We get out of the bus and see Lake Chelan. I stop and look out over this enormous lake. On the banks are a few tiny houses and tied to the pier are a few little boats and a bright-yellow float plane. "This town is so different than what I thought it would be. Much smaller," I say. There's no wind and we hear the float plane's propeller sputter. Slowly, it comes into motion, then faster, faster, and suddenly one float lifts out of the water and a few seconds later the other one follows. It makes a turn. The sound gets louder and it's so close now, we feel like we could touch it. We can even see the people inside. "Wooooow, that is cool," André says. He's back to his old self again since we left Skykomish. The medicine worked miracles on him. He's happy again, cracking jokes all the time.

Stehekin. According to the description, there's only one road here with a few small paths going off it. There's no road connection to the rest of the country. This truly is the end of the world, and the only way to get here is on foot via the PCT, by boat or by float plane. We're taking a day off to rest here, and we're picking up our last resupply package at the local post office.

There's a message on the door of the post office. "Who has talked to this hiker or walked with him recently?" We step inside and ask what the message is about? "We're looking for people who have spoken to him. It's a sad story. He was found dead in his tent a week ago. He was at the bottom of a valley, on a side trail of the PCT." I look at André. The only thing he manages to say is, "Wow!" The post office worker continues talking, "Considering that part of the PCT was closed off in that period because of forest fires, we strongly believe that he died of carbon-monoxide poisoning. We think he went off the trail to avoid the fire, maybe the smoke or the flames had gotten too close. There was quite a lot of smoke out there. He was very low in the valley. So, we think he suffocated in his sleep at night." André looks shocked. "Oh my, wow!" He doesn't know what to say. I turn back towards the man, who's finishing his story. "It's a theory, we don't know anything for sure. He was dead in his tent, no evidence of violence or anything else. We're looking for people who were in contact with him around that time." It's a good thing we weren't here at the time. I've really had enough of all these forest fires out here in the west. "We don't know him but we can ask other hikers about him," I say, and I ask, "Do you know where the fire was? We hiked here from Skykomish, but we haven't seen any fire damage at all." He scratches his chin. "Well, the fire came all the way up to the lake, and it was huge. It was nowhere near under control and with all the smoke, they closed everything off just to be safe. This town was evacuated too. The flames were so high that, if the wind had turned, the entire PCT would have been destroyed." This is quite a shock to us. No wonder it was closed off. Brrr. I wouldn't have wanted to be here for that.

"We'd also like to pick up our package. It should be here somewhere. There's a big red smiley sticker on it," André says. "One moment, I'll have a look." It's very small here. The man looks at various boxes that are all over the place. "A smiley, you say? I'm sorry, I don't have it for you. Do you have the track and trace code?" I give him a piece of paper from the post office we sent it from. He types the code in his computer and looks at the screen. I'm having a déjà vu moment and of course, I could have predicted it. "I'm sorry, your package has been lost somewhere. I can't trace it anywhere." I take a deep breath. "Are you absolutely certain? Could you please check again? Maybe you typed a wrong number?" I say quickly. That would be a disaster, we're so close to the end and now we might not have any food... No way! He tries again and shakes his head. "No, I'm sorry. I can't find it anywhere." He shrugs. "What do we do now? We don't have any food for the final part of the trail!" I blurt out. Only three-and-a-half days to go. We can almost smell Canada and now this! This is a catastrophe. Someone taps me on the shoulder. I don't know him, but judging by his clothes, he must be a hiker. "There's a small hiker box outside. Maybe you'll find something in there? If my package is here, I can give you some of mine. I usually have too much in there."

Wow, that's cool! Maybe we'll have some food after all. Too much food; that's not a problem we know. We've eaten everything we had these past months. I thank the man and go outside right away. In front of the post office, near the harbor, is a stainless-steel box. I walk up to it. It says 'Hiker Box' in large letters. I open the door and see a variety of things. Not much food, but enough for a day! Great. We start pulling it out, like homeless people looking through a garbage bin. Nicely dressed tourists stare at us in amazement. Hmmm... With our dusty, ripped clothes we must look a lot like homeless people by now. But I don't care about that. André gets up. "There's a small tourist shop down the road. Maybe they sell food as well," he says. We take the food from the box and go to the shop. They don't have much. The kind of stuff you can get in small gas stations. We buy a lot of snacks for the trail. Chocolate bars, nuts, dried sausages, and big bags of chips. It's all great for empty carbs and fat. There, now all we have to do is find breakfast, lunch, and dinner for two-and-a-half days.

We walk a bit further towards the end of the town. There's a small campsite there. We see a lot of familiar faces. The vibe among the hikers is noticeably changing. They all know they're going to make it. There's a sense of calm and a strong sense of togetherness: together we can make it through the mountains for the last 89 miles. It's evolved into a small community of people that have become our friends, some of them will be our friends for the rest of our lives. We've been through an intense experience together, which has touched many of our hearts. This is something we all share. We only need to look at each other to know exactly, down to the smallest detail, what it's about and what this has meant for us. We share the last of our stories and say goodbye. This is the last time we see them, all but one. This is a journey of building up relationships and letting them go again. And it's the letting go part that's starting to get to me.

We reach our place to stay for the night. It's not just a place; we've treated ourselves to a wonderful cabin on the ranch tonight and guess who we run into when we get there? Thunder Bunny! "Hey, it's so good to see you again!" She's on the veranda of the cabin next to ours and turns around. "Hey, it's nice to see you again! Come and join me!" We listen to her adventures and tell her about ours, including the one at the post office. "Oh, I have way too much food. I can give you some of mine, no problem!" André frowns a bit and asks, "What do you mean, way too much?" She gets up and picks up a few boxes. "Well, I walked super fast to catch up to my group. I have two days worth of food left over and...my parents sent me a bunch of beef jerky and some other stuff. I can't eat all of that. It's way too much. I was going to put it in the hiker box later." Wow, this girl just made our lives a whole lot easier! This completely solves our problem! "Thunder Bunny, you make me so happy!!" I say, with a big smile on my face. I get up and give her a big fat hug and a kiss on the cheek.

The next morning, we get up early and start the last part of the trail. No logistics, hospitals, or anything else from here on out. Just a final hike to the finish line. I'm really looking forward to it. We go past a bakery. The wonderful scent of freshly baked bread caresses our noses. We have a lovely breakfast with coffee, that tastes amazing. We each buy a few large cinnamon rolls and now it's really time to go. I open the door and look at the mountains in front of us. Canada, I'm on my way, don't worry, we'll be together soon. The desire is strong and as I think about this, tears start to well up in my eyes.

In heaven's name, why?

The Roller Coaster

This is it: day 162, the final day of our epic adventure. It's nothing like I imagined it to be. I feel the need to cry, but the tears don't come. Lian is right next to me, but she doesn't notice. I'm sitting on my mat, staring vacantly into nothingness. This is the end; we're here! Mixed emotions wash over me. Sure, we did it, but this is all kind of surreal. It's all over now. We have to go back home. My mind is like a roller coaster. I don't want to leave, but this is really the end. Two more days and we'll be back where I don't want to be. Back in the other world. With hollow entertainment, constant distractions, white noise, people who don't really understand me, frustration, burnout... I would much rather just stay here in the wilderness. This life seems more real to me; it has animals I can relate to and true friends on the trail, who understand how I think and what I mean.

I'm on my mat and I notice that André isn't really here. He's lost in his thoughts. I still can't believe it! Next to us are the wood pillars with the PCT notice.
THE END MONUMENT!!!!!!!!!!!!!!!!!!!!!!!!!!!!!!
But it doesn't really sink in yet. We eat our lunch silently, and slowly we realize what this really means for us. Emotions are rushing through me like a roller coaster. Intense happiness, because WE MADE IT!!! is immediately replaced by sadness, because we have to stop hiking now. One emotion after the other pops up.

My thoughts go to my best friends Anton and Chrétien and to my sisters. To my brother-in-law Hans, who is more like a big brother to me. I think of all my other friends, like Thea and René, and Melissa and Nils. There are so many people I look forward to seeing again. Like all my cousins, I'd love to go out and spend some time with them. I have missed the wonderful people at home while on this journey. But I want to stay in the cocoon. I really don't want to leave! I wonder how Lian feels. She's completely silent, and it's not like her at all.

I can't wait! This is so great! I'm going to see all my family and friends again! Oh, how I long to see them. Having a nice glass of wine with my friends or my sisters, talking and having fun. I can't wait to go home and do that. I want to go and visit nice places. Take a shower whenever I want. Have a bath! Oh, how I've dreamed of a bath. How I long to just lie down and feel all the dust washing off me. I'm going back to work. I wonder what that'll be like? Will it be the same as it was? I wonder if they've missed me? I'm sure they have. They'll be so curious to hear about all my adventures.

Maybe I should go back to being a full-time wilderness guide, like I used to be. Or a National Park Ranger? I don't know how Lian will feel about that. It would be like working at sea, I'd never be home. I wouldn't see her a lot, or my family and friends. I feel torn and I don't want to think about it. What is reality anyway? Is the cocoon reality? Is home reality? Is coming here like some kind of escape or is this the life I should be living? I don't know. The truth about reality is that I really do have to go back and I really don't want to. Dark thoughts are taking over my mind. But f**k, wait a minute, maybe I've just fallen into the black hole myself! That realization makes me sit up straight at once. What we've just accomplished was amazing! Look at this: THE END MONUMENT IS RIGHT IN FRONT OF ME! I made it! Why am I so grumpy? I have an amazing life! Slowly I feel the happiness come up again as I think about the journey we've made. A careful smile even manages to appear on my face. Tears of happiness and every other emotion well up, but they still don't push through. I look at Lian. She's still a bit blank. She doesn't say anything and nibbles on a cracker.

Memories of the past six months are flowing through my mind. Does André feel the same way? From the corner of my eye I can see him smiling. Is he thinking about the nightly hikes too? The desert heat or the cutting cold at the top of the mountains? The pain, the blisters, pinching shoes, sore knees, the weight loss, the views, the sea of flowers, the beautiful lakes. From the prairie to the highest peaks, from the desert to the rain forest. We've come through it all, and we've conquered it all.

Up and down over the mountains. Like a roller coaster. A few miles up, and down again. Every day, again and again. It was beautiful. As I think back to the last days of the trail, I feel the happiness flowing through me again. The dark thoughts leave my mind like snow in the spring. It was amazing because we've had the most gorgeous weather these past few days in the Northern Cascade Mountains. Phenomenal views! Miles of hiking over high mountain ridges. Crispy ice crystals on the trail. Yellow larches glowing in the early morning light. This has been like icing on the cake of our journey. What an amazingly wonderful feeling to finish like this, hiking through this amazing landscape! The spectacular fall colors were especially beautiful. Emotions are bursting through me like fireworks. I feel the euphoria coming up and it's like I'm back on Forester Pass all over again and I suddenly remember that Lian had a great idea a few days ago. And before I know it, my mind drifts off to those exact moments.

"André, shall we make a song we can sing when we reach the end? Like we did at the halfway point, but longer. Like a march or a battle song?" I think about it for a second and say, "Yeah, why not? That sounds like fun. Do you have something in mind?" She tilts her head slightly, pauses and shakes her head. "No, do you?" I shake my head as well. "Not really, no, but we'll think of something." I look at her. The past three days since we left Stehekin are among the most beautiful and warm moments I've ever shared with her. Pure love, no tension, no arguments, only happiness. I feel like I felt in Iceland when we had just met and were falling in love. That was decades ago. When I look at her now and see her beautiful, soft smile, I go right back to that time. She's such an amazing, beautiful, kind woman.

"Hey, I know," I say after a few miles. "How about the song 'Go West' by The Pet Shop Boys?" She loves it right away. "Yeah, we only have to change the lyrics to 'Go North!" And so it started. For two days we tinkered with the lyrics and now we sing it loud and clear with all our heart for the last few miles to the monument:

Chorus:
Go North, where the Eagles fly
Go North, where the Mountains are high
Go North, where the skies are blue
Go North, this is what we had to do:

Together, we walked many miles
Together, we had very big smiles
Together, we carried a pack
Together, we laid on our back
Together, we jumped over trees
Together, we had hurting knees
Together, we climbed mountains high
Together, we thought we could fly

Chorus

Together, we got blistering hot
Together, we got soaking wet
Together, we pooped in the woods
Together, we used 10 pair of boots
Togeter, we crossed many streams
Together, we got stung by some bees
Together, we swam in the lakes
Together, we almost stepped on some snakes

Chorus

Together, we looked at the stars
Together, we ate many muesli bars
Together, we looked at the moon
Together, we saw flowers bloom
Together, we laid in the sun
Together, we had so much fun
Together, we slept in a tent
Together, we walked till the end!!!

With these final words, we walk towards the monument and now we're here!! We made it. Man, oh man, oh man, I'm so proud. With our backpacks, tent, and everything all the way from Mexico to Canada! If we count all the detours and side tracks we took, we walked 2858 miles straight, and in total we climbed roughly 100 miles. That's about eighteen times the height of Mount Everest measured from sea level! It's crazy.

In front of us are the pillars of the end monument. I point and shout, "The end of the trail!" On the ground is a young woman. She looks up from the final trail log. She notices that we're Dutch and starts laughing. "Hey, hello. Which one of you is Morning Star?" She's even saying it in Dutch! We are completely flabbergasted to hear someone speak Dutch out here in the middle of nowhere, with no buildings what-so-ever in the middle of a huge forest. "I'm Morning Star and this is CookieMonster," I say. She looks happy. "My name's Patches and I'm from the Netherlands. I've seen your names in all the trail logs and I was hoping to meet you some day. Frankly, I'd already given up hope and now, all the way at the end of the journey, I get to meet you after all. How wonderful!" We laugh. Lian and I stand at the monument and Patches takes some pictures for us. Not much later she leaves us. Lian and I put down our sit mats next to the monument and have lunch.

We have the monument all to ourselves. There aren't any distractions, and before we know it, we're lost in our thoughts...

Canada

I get up after about half an hour, pick up my sit mat and put it on the back of my backpack. It's a crazy thought; this is probably the last time I do that. I get the rest of the stuff we used for lunch from André and put everything away. We're both still lost in our thoughts. Neither of us said much during lunch. There's a large wooden sign next to the monument. It tells us that it's another seven-and-a-half miles to Manning Park, the first signs of civilization in Canada.

Slowly we're starting to come back into the real world and I playfully give Lian a little push. She smiles and pushes back. A bit further on she picks up a huge leaf. It belongs to a young maple tree. She lifts it high into the air and yells, "We're in Canada!"

We're playing a beautiful song by Matt Simons in our minds right now. It's called Catch and Release and it's become our symbol for this trail. It's our favorite song and together we sing it for the remaining miles as we walk to Manning Park.

There is a place I'm going
No one knows me
If I breath real slowly
I let it out and let it in
It can be terrifying
To be slowly dying
Also, clarifying
We end where we begin

So let it wash over me
I'm ready to lose my feet
Take me off to the place where one reveals life's mystery
Steady on down the line
Lose every sense of time
Take it all in and wake up that small part of me

Day to day I'm blind to see
And find how far to go

Everybody got their reason
Everybody got their way
We're just catching and releasing
What builds up throughout the day
It gets into your body
It flows just through your blood
We can tell each other secrets
And remember how to love

Two hours later we reach a semi-paved road. In front of us is a huge wooden building. It's the Manning Park lodge. We step inside. It looks nice, but it feels a little bit strange when we go in. There's nobody here that knows us, and no-one to share our adventure and our achievement with. It's like in the song: "There's a place I'm going, where no-one knows me." No cheering crowd, no family waiting for us. Nothing. Although... At the lodge's reception there's a small package for us. It's from the family 'Dam' in the Netherlands. "What could it be?" André asks. I take it and open it. There are two t-shirts inside. On the front is the map of the PCT and the text 'I did it!' On the back it says, 'And all I got was this lousy t-shirt.' We laugh loudly about it. They probably don't even know how true it really is.

The staff of the lodge congratulate us as well. We are invited to sit down and we each get a free drink to celebrate our happy ending. It's a nice gesture. I raise my glass of red wine and André taps it with his glass of freshly squeezed orange-juice.
"It's a strange ending, isn't it?" I say. André nods. "Yes, I can't stop thinking about it. I feel like I'm getting sucked into the black hole. I feel torn inside." I look into his eyes. I kind of saw this coming, but it's still a bit of a shock to me. I love the wilderness, but for him it's in every single fiber of his existence. "You'll be alright. We'll go on hikes at home and think of fun stuff to do." He smiles. That's a good sign.

"You know what," he says at some point. "That black hole; it reminds me of Shutterbug and all the other people we talked to at the Bridge of the Gods." I nod and don't say anything. "I wonder if he's still a Trail Angel. He's driving PCT hikers around, right? When they have to go from the trail to a town or something like that, or like when we went to Portland?" I think about it for a second and answer, "I think so. Why are you thinking about this right now?" André sits up straight and runs his hand through his hair. "Well, maybe we could do something like that, in a smaller way. I know we don't live here, but maybe we can help out people that don't have any experience. So many people are forced to quit because they have no idea how to go about a journey like this. They make rookie mistakes. It would be great if more hikers could make it to the end." It's an interesting idea. "What are you thinking about doing?" I can see his mind working. "Well, maybe we can start by launching a website with tips and advice? Aimed at beginners? In English, so that anyone in the world can read it? Or we could make instruction videos and put them on YouTube?"

I realize that his thinking is going in a whole other direction now, and I'm immediately reassured. I don't think I have to be afraid about him falling into the black hole now. We'll have some adjusting to do because we've been living in the cocoon for months, but after that, I'm sure he'll think of something wonderful to do. I lean back and decide to spend the night here. It's a beautiful lodge, with lots of pretty wood carvings. He'll have enough exploring to do, and we get to sleep in a soft, comfy bed tonight.

I book a room for the night and we head upstairs. Our bounce box is also here in the lodge. We reorganize our things and take a shower. "Let's go downstairs and celebrate!" André yells. "There may not be anyone we know, but we have each other!" He's as happy as ever and together we have a wonderful dinner and a few glasses of wine! "This is a wonderful day, isn't it?" he says, as he kisses my neck. I totally agree.

When we get back to our room, I look at my shoes. They're ruined. This is the fifth pair already. The zipper on the tent is also broken and the down of our sleeping bag has lost most of its fluffiness. Even our three pairs of undies are worn down to the last thread. They even have holes in them. These six months have taken their toll. Materially, physically, and mentally. Everything has taken quite a beating but it was worth it. It has given us so many beautiful, unforgettable moments. We would do it again in a heartbeat. What an adventure. This has been intensely amazing on so many levels.

The next morning we're outside looking at the flagpole. A great big flag is fluttering proudly in the wind. Red and white with a large maple leaf in the middle. Canada. We still can't believe it.

We really made it!

Epilogue

Our American friend Marvin picks us up early the next morning at the lodge. He lives in Bellingham, which is quite nearby for American standards, but it's still a couple of hours away. Patches clearly made it to the lodge as well, because we run into her at breakfast. Together, all three of us go to Marvin's house and spend a night there. After that, Patches goes north, back to Canada to meet up with her boyfriend who's flown in from the Netherlands. Marvin takes us to the airport in Seattle.

When we finally get home, a warm welcome is waiting for us. And even though there's nobody there, they certainly tried their best to make us feel at home again. There's a huge banner hanging over our driveway that says, "Welcome Home!" The house has been completely cleaned and there are fresh flowers on the table. They're so sweet.

A few weeks later we receive our certificates and a huge brass medal of honor from the PCTA, which is the association that oversees the complete organization of the Pacific Crest Trail. On the front of the medal, the map of the entire trail is embossed into the metal. On the back, our names are engraved. The medal, and all the amazing adventures we had, are memories that will stay with us for the rest of our lives. Without the PCTA, the many volunteers and all the Trail Angels this would not have turned out as well as it did. We wish to thank them for everything, from the bottom of our hearts.

In the meantime, we've launched our website and we get many questions from hikers all over the world. On YouTube, more than half a million people have watched our movies and a couple of thousand are now following us.

They ask us questions or get inspired by new trails or ways to get better into long distance hiking. We also regularly give lectures at different associations, from mountaineering clubs to nature conservations. In addition to that, we coach Dutch and Belgian hikers, who are preparing for the PCT or other long-distance hikes by answering all their questions. Sometimes they just drop in, strangers, but hey, they're hikers, so it's never a problem and a lot of fun. It gives us a wonderful sense of purpose to help them out. It's our way of giving back to the community, in gratitude of the wonderful experience we had hiking the trail.

A place where no one knows me. Beautiful words from the Matt Simons song. It was very true when we arrived in America and didn't know anyone on the trail, but also when we arrived in Canada at the finish. Now we're back home, and in some ways, people here don't really know us either. How could they? They cannot feel, hear, see what we have lived through, and what this has given us.

We have been talking about this for years, just the two of us, and now finally, the decision has been made: "You know what? Let's make a movie and write a book about this."

www.friendlyhiker.com

Would you like more information on our beautiful and extraordinary journey? Please visit our website. You will find lots of information on the Pacific Crest Trail, plus many of our other hikes and adventures. We hope they will entertain and inspire you.

André and Lian de Jel

Milton Keynes UK
Ingram Content Group UK Ltd.
UKHW011257140624
444235UK00021B/136